11067Ø498

Studies in Economic Transition

General Editors: **Jens Hölscher**, Senior Lecturer in Economics, University of Brighton; and **Horst Tomann**, Professor of Economics, Free University Berlin

This new series has been established in response to a growing demand for a greater understanding of the transformation of economic systems. It brings together theoretical and empirical studies on economic transition and economic development. The post-communist transition from planned to market economies is one of the main areas of applied theory because in this field the most dramatic examples of change and economic dynamics can be found. The series aims to contribute to the understanding of specific major economic changes as well as to advance the theory of economic development. The implications of economic policy will be a major point of focus.

Titles include:

Irwin Collier, Herwig Roggemann, Oliver Scholz and Horst Tomann (*editors*)
WELFARE STATES IN TRANSITION
East and West

Hella Engerer
PRIVATIZATION AND ITS LIMITS IN CENTRAL AND EASTERN EUROPE
Property Rights in Transition

Hubert Gabrisch and Rüdiger Pohl (*editors*)
EU ENLARGEMENT AND ITS MACROECONOMIC EFFECTS IN
EASTERN EUROPE
Currencies, Prices, Investment and Competitiveness

Jens Hölscher (*editor*)
FINANCIAL TURBULENCE AND CAPITAL MARKETS IN TRANSITION
COUNTRIES

Jens Hölscher and Anja Hochberg (*editors*)
EAST GERMANY'S ECONOMIC DEVELOPMENT SINCE UNIFICATION
Domestic and Global Aspects

Mihaela Kelemen and Monika Kostera (*editors*)
CRITICAL MANAGEMENT RESEARCH IN EASTERN EUROPE
Managing the Transition

Emil J. Kirchner (*editor*)
DECENTRALIZATION AND TRANSITION IN THE VISEGRAD
Poland, Hungary, the Czech Republic and Slovakia

Julie Pellegrin
THE POLITICAL ECONOMY OF COMPETITIVENESS IN AN ENLARGED EUROPE

Stanislav Polouček (*editor*)
REFORMING THE FINANCIAL SECTOR IN CENTRAL EUROPEAN COUNTRIES

Gregg S. Robins
BANKING IN TRANSITION
East Germany after Unification

Johannes Stephan
ECONOMIC TRANSITION IN HUNGARY AND EAST GERMANY
Gradualism and Shock Therapy in Catch-up Development

Hans van Zon
THE POLITICAL ECONOMY OF INDEPENDENT UKRAINE

Adalbert Winkler (*editor*)
FINANCIAL DEVELOPMENT IN EASTERN EUROPE
The First Ten Years

Studies in Economic Transition
Series Standing Order ISBN 0–333–73353–3
(*outside North America only*)

You can receive future titles in this series as they are published by placing a standing order. Please contact your bookseller or, in case of difficulty, write to us at the address below with your name and address, the title of the series and the ISBN quoted above.

Customer Services Department, Macmillan Distribution Ltd., Houndmills, Basingstoke, Hampshire RG21 6XS, England

Reforming the Financial Sector in Central European Countries

Edited by

Stanislav Poloucek
Professor of Finance
Silesian University
School of Business Administration, Karviná

Editorial matter and selection and Chapter 3 © Stanislav Polouček 2004
Remaining chapters © Palgrave Macmillan 2004

All rights reserved. No reproduction, copy or transmission of this
publication may be made without written permission.

No paragraph of this publication may be reproduced, copied or transmitted
save with written permission or in accordance with the provisions of the
Copyright, Designs and Patents Act 1988, or under the terms of any licence
permitting limited copying issued by the Copyright Licensing Agency,
90 Tottenham Court Road, London W1T 4LP.

Any person who does any unauthorised act in relation to this publication
may be liable to criminal prosecution and civil claims for damages.

The author has asserted his right to be identified as
the author of this work in accordance with the Copyright,
Designs and Patents Act 1988.

First published 2004 by
PALGRAVE MACMILLAN
Houndmills, Basingstoke, Hampshire RG21 6XS and
175 Fifth Avenue, New York, N.Y. 10010
Companies and representatives throughout the world

PALGRAVE MACMILLAN is the global academic imprint of the Palgrave
Macmillan division of St. Martin's Press, LLC and of Palgrave Macmillan Ltd.
Macmillan® is a registered trademark in the United States, United Kingdom
and other countries. Palgrave is a registered trademark in the European
Union and other countries.

ISBN 1–4039–1546–6

This book is printed on paper suitable for recycling and made from fully
managed and sustained forest sources.

A catalogue record for this book is available from the British Library.

Library of Congress Cataloging-in-Publication Data
Reforming the financial sector in Central European countries/edited by
Stanislav Polouček.
    p. cm.—(Studies in economic transition)
Includes bibliographical references and index.
ISBN 1–4039–1546–6 (cloth)
    1. Banks and banking—Europe, Central. 2. Monetary policy—Europe,
Central. 3. Foreign exchange rates—Europe, Central. I. Polouček, Stanislav,
1949– II. Series.

HG2980.7.A6R44 2003
332.1′0943–dc21   2003053569

10 9 8 7 6 5 4 3 2 1
13 12 11 10 09 08 07 06 05 04

Printed and bound in Great Britain by
Antony Rowe Ltd., Chippenham and Eastbourne

Contents

List of Tables

List of Figures

List of Abbreviations

ACC	accession countries (10 countries with an accession agreement, that is, V4, three Baltic countries, Slovenia, Bulgaria, Romania)
BCC	Banker, Charnes and Cooper (model, 1984)
BS	Balassa–Samuelson (effect)
CA	current account
CAR	capital adequacy ratio
CCR	Charnes, Cooper and Rhodes (model, 1978)
CEC	Central European countries: the Czech Republic, Poland, Slovakia, Hungary
CEE	Central and Eastern Europe
CMEA	Council for Mutual Economic Assistance
ČNB	the Czech National Bank (Česká národní banka)
ČS	Česká spořitelna (Czech Savings Bank)
ČSOB	Československá obchodní banka (Czechoslovak Trade Bank)
CZK	Czech crown
CR	credit risk
DEA	data envelopment analysis
DMU	decision making unit
ECB	European Central Bank
EMPI	exchange market pressure index
EMU	European Monetary Union
ERM II	Exchange Rate Mechanism II of EU
ERR	exchange rate risk
EU	European Union
FDI	foreign direct investment
GDP	gross domestic product
HHI	Herfindahl–Hirschman Index
IPB	Investiční a poštovní banka (Investment and Post Bank)
IRR	interest rate risk
IMF	International Monetary Fund
KB	Komerční banka (Commercial Bank)
LR	liquidity risk
MTF	Merger Task Force
NBP	the National Bank of Poland (Narodowy bank Polski)

NBS	the National Bank of Slovakia (Národná banka Slovenska)
NPF	National Property Fund
NPLs	non-performing loans
OCA	optimum currency area
PEPs	Pre-Accession Economic Programmes
PLN	Polish zloty
PPP	purchasing power parity
PTS	permanently turning-over stocks
QR	capital risk
ROA	return on assets
ROE	return on equity
SCP	structure–conduct–performance
SFA	stochastic frontier analysis
SKK	Slovak crown
SOEs	state-owned enterprises
TFA	thick frontier analysis
V4	the Visegrad countries: the Czech Republic, Poland, Slovakia, Hungary
WB	World Bank

Acknowledgements

This book is a result of a three-year research project sponsored by GAČR (the Grant Agency of the Czech Republic). The project GAČR 402/00/ 0312 'Comparison of the Banking Sectors in Transition Countries' confirmed the variety of the banking sector's development in Central European countries (CECs) as well as in developed and other transition and developing countries.

The book and the research were conducted basically at two places: at the Czech National Bank (ČNB) in Prague and at the Silesian University, School of Business Administration in Karviná. Our colleagues at the School of Business Administration, in particular Marek Dohnal, Monika Bialonczyková and Radka Zapletalová, have truly made the book possible – partly by their contribution to the arguments made, but above all because of the data gathered. Elena Mielcová and Radka Kocurková helped with statistical analysis. Marek Dohnal provided excellent editing assistance as well as Ed Farolan, who provided language editing. We appreciate work done by Zdeněk Čech of the Czech National Bank as well as materials and support of Roman Horváth from the Central European University in Budapest. And a final word of appreciation to Jens Holscher, Amanda Watkins and her colleagues at the publishers, who approved the project and helped with their experience to finalize it.

Notes on the Contributors

Jan Frait is a member of the Board of Governors of the Czech National Bank, Prague, and Professor of Economics at the Technical University of Ostrava, Faculty of Economics. Within the Bank, he is in charge of the cash management and payments system. He is a member of editorial boards of leading Czech academic journals and President of the Czech Economic Society. His research activities focus on application of balance of payments and exchange rate theories in transition economies as well as on growth theory and empirics.

Luboš Komárek is an adviser to a Czech National Bank Board member in Prague, and Assistant Professor at the University of Economics, School of National Economy, Prague. He studied at the University of Warwick (UK). His academic and research activities focus on monetary policy of central banks, inflation and exchange rate theories in transition countries.

Lumír Kulhánek is Associate Professor of Economics at the Silesian University, School of Business Administration, Karviná. He has wide teaching experience in economic and finance courses and has published articles in respected Czech and foreign economic journals as well as in proceedings from conferences. His research activities focus on monetary policy of central banks and inflation in developed and transition countries as well as matters of EMU, including membership of transition countries in EMU.

Roman Matoušek is a senior lecturer in Financial Economics at the Business School of London Metropolitan University and Visiting Lecturer in Finance at the Silesian University, School of Business Administration, Karviná. Previously, he was a banking expert in the Czech National Bank. He holds a Master's degree in Banking and Finance from CORIPE, Turin, Italy and a Ph.D. in Economics from Charles University in Prague. His research activities focus on bank supervision and regulation in transition countries, analysis of financial crises and financial markets in transition countries.

Martin Melecký is a Ph.D. student at the University of New South Wales, the School of Economics in Sydney. He participates on research projects of the Czech National Bank. His research activities focus on policies of central banks and international monetary issues.

Stanislav Polouček is a Professor of Finance and Head of the Department of Finance at Silesian University, School of Business Administration, Karviná. He has wide teaching experience of regular finance courses in the Czech Republic, Poland and Slovakia and in lectureships in other foreign universities. He is the chairman of the International Programme Committee of a yearly banking conference that takes place at the Silesian University. His research activities focus on banking sector development in developed as well as transition countries, and monetary theory and policy.

Daniel Stavárek is a Ph.D. student and Assistant Professor at Silesian University, School of Business Administration, Karviná. He has teaching experience of lectureships in foreign universities and has published articles in respected Czech and foreign economic journals and in proceedings from conferences. He has participated in several research projects. His research activities focus on international financial institutions and restructuring of financial sectors in transition countries as well as financial sector efficiency.

Introduction

Transition countries have been one of the most popular topics in economic and financial research in recent years. Although the transition period has been under way for more than ten years, much remains to be done, even in the more advanced transition countries. Furthermore, different ways of proceeding and different sequencing of transition steps attract the attention of researchers.

A well-functioning banking system contributes very significantly to the general business environment's efficiency and simultaneously influences in a positive way the whole economy. However, the reverse relation is also true in that the macroeconomic framework, along with activities of enterprises (that are banks' clients), determines the banking sector's performance and stability. From that perspective, the reformation of the banking sector was one of the crucial components of the reforms established in transition countries. After a two-tier structure of banking was established, banking systems in the Central European countries (CEC) have been thoroughly overhauled since 1989.

The approach taken towards developing a viable financial and banking sector varies among transition countries. Depending on a number of factors, this process could be described as a qualitative change towards the modern banking system in accordance with market economy principles. In these countries, much attention was paid to the issues of harmonization of banking legislation, regulation and supervision with the European Union standards in the second half of the 1990s and appropriate amendments were passed. At the same time, the restructuring of the banking sector was under way and the development of the banking systems in the Visegrad countries (V4) forced banks to seek strategic foreign partners. The banking sector's restructuring can be therefore viewed as a condition of its further development, as well as a condition of the whole economy's transformation and effective allocation of productive sources.

The book you are holding in your hands gives very deep insight into the financial sector transformation performed by people living in Central European countries and working in various ways with the financial sector. It pulls together theory and real development in these transition countries. Through original research, it covers various aspects of the financial (banking) sector transformation in selected central European countries, comparing their development as well as the financial sectors of developed countries. Rather than a compilation of separate papers, the book is a complex interconnected and homogeneous text, which gives an overview of banking sector development of the transition countries from various points of view.

Stanislav Polouček

1
The Financial and Banking Sectors in Transition Countries

Lumír Kulhánek, Stanislav Polouček and Daniel Stavárek

Ideas and scenarios for economic reforms led to the transformation of a centrally planned economy into a market economy in Central European countries (CEC). Privatization, liberalization of prices, liberalization of foreign trade, and liberalization of capital movement were among the main pillars of transformation. The fulfilment of the transformation task was impossible without substantial changes in the banking sector. This chapter gives a brief overview of the development of the financial and banking sectors in the Czech Republic, the Slovak Republic, Hungary and Poland. In the first part, the key features of the financial sectors in these transition countries are identified. Then, by applying indicators of capital market and bank development, a comparison of the financial sector's structure will be made. The third part will deal with the restructuring of the banking sector in transition economies.

1.1 Financial sectors and intermediation in transition countries

In developed as well as in transition countries, the financial sector is very important for capital allocation, financial intermediation, transformation of savings into investments, risk sharing and risk diversification. Well-developed financial markets and bank activities also improve productivity and significantly affect economic growth.[1] Therefore, the analysis of the financial sector and its role in financial intermediation has long been a favourite topic of economic research. In addition, the relation between banking intermediation and intermediation performed by financial markets is becoming increasingly noticeable. None the less, the views of economists and financial experts are not uniform on how important banks and capital markets should be.

Deregulation, globalization, and changes in the economic as well as the political and social environment have seriously influenced financial intermediation development. If we take into account progress in information technologies, we can see that the function of an intermediator can be performed with the same effectiveness by banks or by many other financial institutions. Financial markets can also effectively perform most of these intermediation functions. As there are broad positive feedback effects between financial and economic development, it is likewise essential to analyse in detail the characteristics of the financial sector in transition economies in Central Europe, and its further development. Among a great number of aspects, it is essential to draw attention to its initial level of development, for empirical literature also confirms that initial levels of financial development are good predictors of subsequent economic growth.[2]

Financial sectors and banking systems in CEC have undergone fundamental changes since the beginning of the transition process about thirteen years ago. All four countries belong to the group of transition economies which evolved from centrally planned to market economies. Under central planning, the financial system was more or less a bookkeeping mechanism for recording the decisions of the planning bureau for allocation of resources. There were no financial markets, and banking sectors were formed almost entirely by so-called monobanks. Upon transition, the following key reforms were implemented:

- monobanks were abolished and two-tier banking systems with the central bank and commercial banks were introduced;
- sectoral restrictions on specialized banks were relaxed;
- the licensing policy for most kinds of banking business was liberalized;
- privately owned banks were admitted and the privatization of the state-owned banks was initiated;
- foreign banks and joint ventures were granted access; and
- the legal framework and supervisory system were introduced and adjusted.

The banking sectors in the CEC had also been restructured, recapitalized and privatized during the 1990s, and capital markets had been established. Thus, conditions had been established in the CEC for financial intermediation and a full development of functions of the financial intermediaries.

At present, there are already financial sectors in these countries, which can be characterized by overall financial stability, and they show a positive trend in most of the sector's segments. Our observation of the financial sector stability of the CEC is confirmed not only by research carried out in the ECB (Caviglia *et al.*, 2002), but also by the reports of the Financial Sector Assessment Programmes conducted by the International Monetary Fund and the World Bank. However, financial sectors in most of the CEC are still relatively small in comparison to the economic activity, size and depth of financial sectors in developed countries. Up to now they had not been fully developed in terms of market segments or instruments. One can assume that these will eventually increase in depth and efficiency. The overview of the current state is presented in this chapter.

To assess the level of development of the financial sector in the CEC, several frequently applied measures of size and performance allow a comparison with advanced economy benchmarks. None the less, for the purposes of the international comparison of banks' activities and the operation of capital markets, economists do not use one ideal cross-country measure of how well banks operate. They have not been able to measure accurately the financial services of the banking sector for a broad cross-section of countries. Therefore, they use, along with Goldsmith (1969) or McKinnon (1973), measures of the overall size of the banking sector to proxy for financial depth. For the introductory comparison of the depth of bank intermediation we can apply, as in Rousseau and Wachtel (2000) or King and Levine (1993a, 1993b), the ratio of broad money (M2) to GDP[3] and banking assets to GDP.

As noted by King and Levine (1993a), however, the ratio of broad money to GDP as a financial depth indicator does not measure whether the liabilities are those of banks, the central bank, or other financial intermediaries; nor does this financial depth indicator measure or identify where the financial system allocates capital. Thus we also use bank assets, bank loans and bank deposits as other indicators.

For measuring stock market development, we use three indicators – one measure of stock market size, and two measures of stock market liquidity. Stock market capitalization measures the size of the stock market and equals the value of listed domestic shares on domestic exchanges divided by GDP. Although large markets do not necessarily function effectively and taxes may distort incentives to be listed on the exchange, as is accentuated by Levine and Zervos (1998), numerous observers use stock market capitalization as an indicator of stock market development. The indicator is applied in section 1.2 when comparing the structure of the financial sector and its development in particular countries, where the indicators of bank deposits, stock market capitalization and corporate bonds are used. The World Bank observes these indicators too, and applies them in its statistics of World Development Indicators.

For comparing liquidity, we use two related measures of market liquidity – the turnover ratio and the value traded. The turnover ratio equals the value of the trades of domestic shares on domestic exchanges divided by the value of listed domestic shares. It measures the volume of domestic stocks traded on domestic exchanges relative to the size of the market. A large stock market is not necessarily a liquid market – a large but inactive market will have large capitalization but a small turnover ratio. The measure of value traded equals the value of the trades of domestic shares on domestic exchanges divided by GDP. It measures trading volume as a share of national output, and should therefore positively reflect liquidity on an economy-wide basis. The value traded may be significantly different from the turnover ratio. While value traded captures trading relative to the size of the economy, turnover ratio measures trading relative to the size of the stock market. Thus a small, liquid capital market will have a high turnover ratio, but a small value traded.

The indicator M2/GDP as a common indicator of bank development (depth of bank intermediation) amounts to almost 70 per cent in the euro area (Wagner and Iakova, 2001, p. 50). In the CEC, the level of financial intermediation, measured by this indicator,[4] is considerably different (Table 1.1).

Even after more than a decade of transition and bank restructuring, this ratio in Hungary and Poland is still under 50 per cent. In Poland, the ratio of M2 to GDP had distinctively increased from 35.2 per cent in 1996 and in the year 2001 had achieved levels comparable with Hungary, at around 46 per cent. On the other hand, in Hungary, the ratio of M2 to GDP had dropped slightly in the period studied. However, Czechoslovakia entered transition with a very high ratio of M2 to GDP, and this was reflected in high ratios when it split into the Czech Republic and the Slovak Republic (74.4 per cent and 70.5 per cent in 2001, respectively).

Table 1.1   Broad money (M2) in CEC (% of GDP, 1996–2001)

	1996	1997	1998	1999	2000	2001
Czech Republic	68.8	70.1	67.6	70.9	72.1	74.4
Hungary	48.1	46.5	45.6	46.7	45.3	46.8
Poland	35.2	37.3	39.9	42.8	43.0	46.3
Slovak Republic	68.8	66.1	63.0	64.6	68.5	70.5

Source: Stability and Structure of Financial Systems in CEC5 (2002).

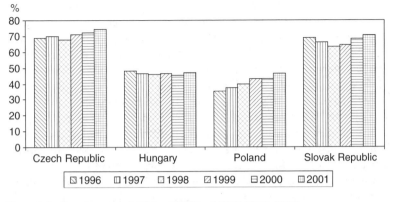

Figure 1.1   Broad money (M2) in CEC (% of GDP, 1996–2001)
Source: Authors' calculations.

As is evident from Figure 1.1 and Table 1.1, the higher ratio of broad money to GDP in the Czech Republic as against other CEC is still slightly increasing. In the Slovak Republic, the M2/GDP ratio decreased until 1998, but started increasing in 1999, and now approximates the value in the Czech Republic.

The low ratio of broad money to GDP indicates a low monetary depth of the economy in Hungary and Poland. It stems not only from the low initial level of this indicator at the beginning of the transformation but also from many other factors. In our opinion, inflation, which was relatively high and more volatile during the 1990s, played a crucial role. The high inflation expectations and those pertaining to the development of the exchange rate also influenced the M2/GDP ratio very greatly. In this connection, Wagner and Iakova (2001, p. 50) also mention many other factors: the relatively recent restructuring and consolidation of the banking sector; the large and growing share of multinational corporations in the domestic economies, with recourse to direct borrowing from abroad; the risk of lending to the consumer sector and to small and medium enterprises; the tendency of domestic firms to finance themselves from retained earnings; and the stabilization and restructuring during transition, which temporarily depressed income and savings. When observing the indicator of M2/GDP and its application in international comparisons, it is necessary to take into consideration the fact that a higher M2/GDP ratio does not have to correspond to a higher quality of financial intermediation in the relevant country.

Banking assets to GDP is another common indicator of the depth of bank intermediation and size of the banking sector. This ratio and its development are highly diversified across the CEC. In 1996 the ratio of banking assets to GDP ranged from as low as 50.9 per cent in Poland to well above 115 per cent in the Slovak Republic and in the Czech Republic (Table 1.2). In the Czech Republic this ratio reached 129 per cent at the end of 2001 while decreasing to 96.3 per cent in Slovakia. In Hungary this ratio stagnated at a level of 66 to 69.7 per cent (Figure 1.2), while in Poland it was still growing. In 2001 Poland reached a level comparable with Hungary with a ratio of 66.3 per cent.

The ratio of banking assets to GDP confirms that the levels of financial intermediation in CEC are relatively low. These banking sectors are currently still small relative to economic activity. In Poland and Hungary the ratio of banking assets to GDP amounts to about one-quarter of the corresponding level for the euro area in 2001, where the bank assets amounted to about 265 per cent of GDP in 2001 (Caviglia *et al.*, 2002, p. 18). Only the Czech Republic and, to a lesser degree, the Slovak Republic stand out as the CEC with the largest banking systems. The high ratio in these two countries is partially a consequence of an already existent significant banking system under the former centrally planned regime.[5]

Table 1.2   Banking assets in CEC (% of GDP, 1996–2001)

	1996	1997	1998	1999	2000 2001
Czech Republic	115.4	125.0	122.0	122.8	127.2	129.0
Hungary	66.0	69.7	68.8	68.6	68.2	68.3
Poland	50.9	53.3	57.7	59.2	62.8	66.3
Slovak Republic	118.2	113.2	106.6	94.4	95.5	96.3

Source: Stability and Structure of Financial Systems in CEC5 (2002).

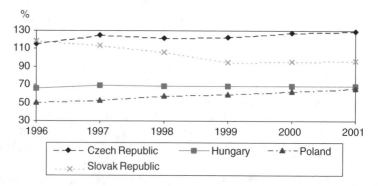

Figure 1.2   Banking assets in CEC (in % of GDP, 1996–2001)
Source: Authors' calculations.

Comparing the development of banking assets to GDP ratio in the CEC in the second half of the 1990s, we can see that the development of this indicator in the CEC corresponds to a great extent to the development of the preceding indicator – broad money (M2) to GDP. However, the higher ratio of banking assets to GDP is not evidence of a healthier banking system.

The low share of domestic credit in GDP or relatively low loans to the GDP ratio could also illustrate the limited level of banking intermediation in the CEC. Domestic credit provided by the banking sector includes all credit to various sectors on a gross basis, with the exception of credit to the central government, which is net. The banking sector includes monetary authorities and deposit money banks, as well as other banking institutions where data are available. The ratio of loans to GDP (the value of loans made by commercial banks and other banks that accept deposits to the private sector divided by GDP) has better information capability in comparison with the domestic credit to GDP ratio and other traditional financial depth indicators. The reason is that it does not take into account credits issued by the central bank and because it considers only credits granted to the private sector, not credits granted to governments.

In the Czech Republic, the country with the largest banking sector measured by the ratio of domestic credit to GDP, this indicator amounts to only about 60 per cent of GDP compared with 135 per cent of GDP in the euro area.[6] The ratio of loans to GDP as compared to the domestic credit ratio was substantially lower in the Czech Republic in 2001, and reached only 36.9 per cent. It was even lower in other CEC in comparison with the Czech Republic. This development is illustrated in Figure 1.3 and Table 1.3.

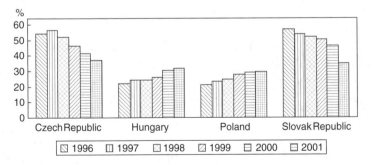

Figure 1.3   Loans in CEC (in % of GDP, 1996–2001)
Source: Authors' calculations.

Table 1.3   Loans in CEC (% of GDP, 1996–2001)

	1996	1997	1998	1999	2000	2001
Czech Republic	54.3	56.7	52.3	46.5	41.5	36.9
Hungary	22.1	24.3	24.2	26.0	30.4	31.8
Poland	21.2	23.2	24.8	27.8	29.1	29.6
Slovak Republic	56.8	53.9	52.1	50.2	46.3	34.8

Source: *Stability and Structure of Financial Systems in CEC5* (2002).

Both the Czech Republic and Slovakia had a noticeably higher level of this indicator in the first half of the 1990s, when it considerably exceeded the level in Hungary and Poland. However, the share of loans to GDP had slumped since the year 1996 in the Czech Republic and Slovakia. On the other hand, during the growth of this share in Hungary and Poland the level of indicators came noticeably together in all CEC until the year 2001, ranging from nearly 30 to 37 per cent.

There are many reasons for the low levels of bank intermediation in transition countries. All CEC experienced a sharp economic downturn upon transition, with output falling to between 10 and 25 per cent in the first few years. These stern recessions led to massive bad-debt problems in the corporate sector (Begg and Portes, 1993) and extensive reductions of its bank loans portfolio (see Anderson and Kegels, 1998, among others).

The low level of intermediation is also detected on the liabilities side. It is reflected in a low ratio of deposits to GDP. The development of this indicator in the CEC is analysed simultaneously with the analysis of the structure of the financial sector's funds in Section 1.2.

Capital markets in the CEC comprise both stock markets and markets for debt securities denominated in local currency. A complex comparison of the capital markets' development requires application of indicators of size, liquidity and volatility of capital markets. The indicator of integration with world capital markets is also often used, because application of a variety of measures provides a richer picture of the state, the structure and the development of the capital markets. In this section, we shall use only some indicators. As liquidity of equity markets in the CEC is limited, we shall focus in particular on liquidity of equity markets in these countries.

Their capital markets have had a relatively short history of development, as their establishment required enterprise restructuring, privatization[7] and the establishment of an appropriate legal and regulatory framework, including corporate governance and shareholder protection.

In terms of market capitalization, stock markets initially developed most rapidly in countries where mass privatization schemes via vouchers were initiated, most notably in the Czech Republic and Slovakia. Market infrastructure and regulation were often put in place after the establishment of a rudimentary market. In Poland and Hungary, new listings gradually entered the equity market; infrastructure and an extensive regulatory framework were mostly set up first. This approach proved to be more successful, resulting in higher liquidity and better performance of stock indices in Hungary and Poland. We shall now assess the size of equity markets and also corporate bonds markets in connection with the comparison of the total structure of the financial sector in the CEC.

Unlike the developed economies, capital markets in the CEC are little used as a source of finance. The ranking of the CEC by the total capitalization of their stock markets differs when measured in absolute or relative terms. Poland had the highest total market capitalization in absolute terms (29 billion EUR at the end of 2001, and 31.4 billion USD at the end of 2000), while Hungary clearly exhibited the highest total market capitalization in relation to GDP, with 25.9 per cent at the end of 2000 (Schardax and Reininger, 2001, p. 45). But compared with the equity markets of advanced economies, even the Hungarian equity market is still small in relation to the size of the economy. Among developed countries, only Austria is an exception in this respect, where equity market capitalization amounted to only 16 per cent of GDP (see Figure 1.7 in Section 1.2).

As stated above, the market turnover ratio measures the volume of domestic equities traded on domestic exchanges relative to the size of the market. In developed countries, a high turnover ratio is often used as an indicator of low transaction costs. For transition economies an important fact is that big stock markets are not necessarily liquid markets. This is apparent from Figure 1.4 with the stock markets in the Czech Republic and the Slovak Republic.

The market capitalization of debt securities largely emulated the absolute size of the economy at the end of 2000 (see Figure 1.5 for selected developed countries and Figure 1.6 for CEC). Similarly to stock market capitalization, debt market capitalization in CEC is much lower than in developed countries. The absolute values of bonds at the end of 2000 were USD (billions) 17.95 for Poland, 9.5 for Hungary, 7.4 and 2.5 for the Czech Republic and Slovakia, respectively. In measuring market capitalization of debt securities relative to GDP, the Hungarian market for debt securities was the largest, followed by the Czech Republic and Poland.

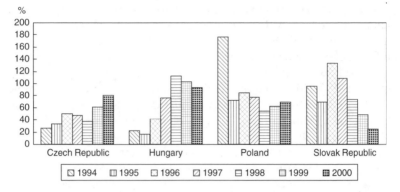

Figure 1.4   Market turnover in % of market capitalization in CEC (1994–2000)
Source: Authors' calculations based on World Bank, World Development Indicators, 2001.

Capitalization of both stock and bond markets relative to GDP was only a fraction in the advanced economies. In addition, given the relatively low levels of GDP per capita of CEC, market capitalization is low. The conclusion by Caviglia *et al.* (2002, p. 21) – that in an international context, only the capital markets of Poland and, to a lesser extent, of the Czech Republic and Hungary, played some role – can be, from that perspective, fully accepted.

1.2   Comparison of financial sector structures

The characteristics of financial systems in CEC indicate that they have developed towards bank-based systems – as in Germany or Austria – rather than the market-based systems of the UK or the USA. The analysis we carried out of the structure of the financial sector in CEC confirms this.

There are several different classifications of financial systems used in economic theory. But two basic models are often mentioned: The B-system and the M-system (Allen and Gale, 2000, pp. 1–9), and a combination of both, which is typical in most countries. This differentiation is not new. Gerschenkron (1962) had already sought to explain a perceived relation between the differences in the pattern of economic development between the UK and the continental European economies and the differences between bank-based and market-based financial systems. Since then, a large body of theoretical and empirical research has analysed how financial goals are achieved in a market-based system, and how they are achieved in a system where banks and other financial intermediaries play a major role.

The predominant standing of banks is typical of the B-system, which is based on the fact that companies obtain external resources above all from banks, particularly in such financial markets where banks and their daughter investment companies are the main investors in stocks and bonds. In such a case a financial market is only a supplement to banks granting credits, as well as banks as the main source of investments, which come from deposits of individual and household savings. The M-system is based on the market – households and individuals not only invest directly in stocks and bonds on the capital market, but they also invest more and more in securities through non-bank intermediaries (pension funds, investment funds and so on).

A basic description of a financial sector can thus be based on indicators that reflect the standing and significance of its fundamental segments: financial markets and financial intermediaries. A chosen indicator is usually expressed as a relative magnitude depending on GDP or a similar value, such as comparing different countries using size as the indicator.

An indicator related to the banking sector is usually used to indicate the role of financial intermediaries, for instance, the amount of credits granted by banks, the amount of bank deposits, or the amount of bank assets. In this section, just as in many other research papers, we will be using bank deposits related to GDP.

As an indicator of the financial markets' significance, various indicators of stock markets and bond markets are combined. For instance, the amount of corporate securities and market capitalization of the stock market, especially the amount of corporate bonds, reflects exactly how important financial markets are for intermediation. This approach is used in this analysis as well.

Thus the total sources of the financial sectors and the structure of the financial sectors will be analysed by means of an indicator made up of bank deposits, stock market capitalization and outstanding values of corporate bonds.

From the point of view of absolute size, financial sectors show substantial differences, particularly in developed countries and in transition countries. Figures 1.5 and 1.6 show the size of bank deposits, stock market capitalization and outstanding values of corporate bonds in selected developed and transition countries. It is understandable that in relation to the amount of funds in financial sectors (that is as to the total size of bank deposits, shares and bonds), large countries reached the highest values among developed countries as well as among CEC (Poland), while small countries reached the lowest values (Ireland, Greece, Austria). Since the values for the USA, Japan and the UK noticeably

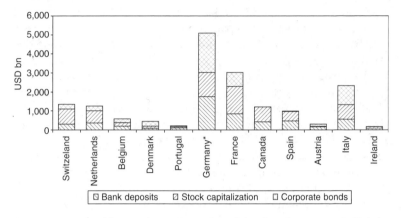

Figure 1.5   Funds of financial sectors in selected developed countries (USD bn, 2000)
* 1999

Source: Authors' calculations based on World Bank, World Development Indicators, 2001.

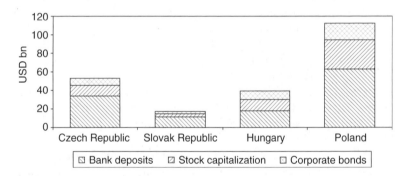

Figure 1.6   Funds of financial sectors in CEC (USD bn, 2000)
Source: Authors' calculations based on World Bank, World Development Indicators, 2001.

exceed the values not only of small European countries but also of other large developed economies (Germany, France and Italy), they are not included in Figure 1.5.

Generally, there is a relatively underdeveloped financial sector as well as a low level of financial intermediation in transition countries. A comparison of funds in financial sectors of developed countries as well as transition countries allows us to come to the clear conclusion that financial sectors in transition countries (measured by size) are far behind those of developed countries. There is a lower efficiency of financial and banking intermediation in CEC, too. Efficiency of banking intermediation is comprehensively analysed in Chapter 4, Section 4.2.

In comparing the size of financial sectors, it is essential to consider the size of the country's economy and to measure quantitatively the size of the financial sectors relative to the GDP ratio. Figures 1.7 and 1.8, which depict the size of financial sectors as a share of GDP in selected developed and transition countries respectively, confirm that the size of the financial sector is related to the level of economic development of the country.

In developed countries, the share of the financial sector's funds in GDP ranges from 130 to 400 per cent, except Switzerland (not reported

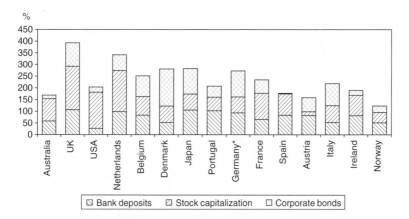

Figure 1.7 Size of financial sectors in selected developed countries (% of GDP, 2000)
* 1999

Source: Authors' calculations based on World Bank, World Development Indicators, 2001.

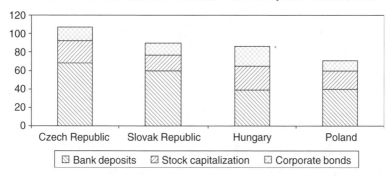

Figure 1.8 Size of financial sectors in CEC (% of GDP, 2000)
Source: Authors' calculations.

in Figure 1.7 since it exceeds 550 per cent [126 + 330 + 102 per cent]). Among transition countries only the Czech Republic has reached an indicator higher than 1.0, and there are indicators higher than 0.8 in only two other countries (Slovakia and Hungary), illustrating that all the CEC, with the exception of Poland, represent the transition countries with the largest financial sector.

Comparison of data in Figure 1.9 and in Figure 1.10 confirm that in the CEC, relatively more funds are reallocated by the banking sector than by capital markets. With the exception of Hungary, Lithuania and Estonia, the share of the banking sector in all the other countries

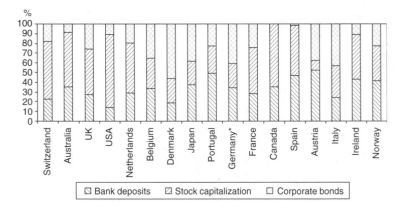

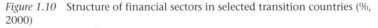

Figure 1.9   Structure of financial sectors in selected developed countries (%, 2000)
* 1999

Source: Authors' calculations.

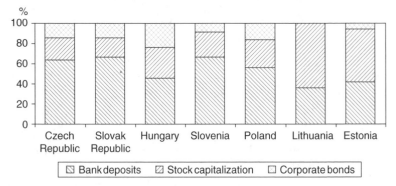

Figure 1.10   Structure of financial sectors in selected transition countries (%, 2000)

Source: Authors' calculations.

is higher than 50 per cent. In the case of the Ukraine, Moldova and Lithuania, the high share of the financial market is a result of voucher privatization. Although banking sectors in transition countries are relatively small, they dominate the financial sector because of the other segments of the financial sectors (capital markets) are even less developed. Capital markets evidently play a much more important role in developed countries. They do so even in countries where the financial system is based on the banking sector (Germany) and where financial systems are considered to be B-systems (Allen and Gale, 2000, Chs 1 and 3). The corporate bonds market is quite developed in Denmark, Italy and also in Austria. The market for corporate bonds is relatively narrow in transition countries. In the Czech Republic, the bond market is one of the most developed segments of the capital market, but corporate bonds comprise only around one quarter of it. In some transition countries, the market for corporate bonds does not exist at all – companies do not obtain funds in this market.

Financial sectors have recorded relatively important changes in some countries in recent times. Data imply that many more changes take place in developed countries (see Figure 1.11), while in transition countries, serious changes or explicit trend changes are rather the exception (Figure 1.12).

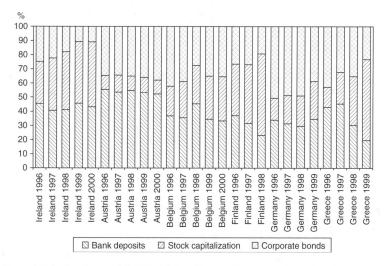

Figure 1.11 Development of the financial sector's structure in selected developed countries (%, 1996–2000)

Source: Authors' calculations.

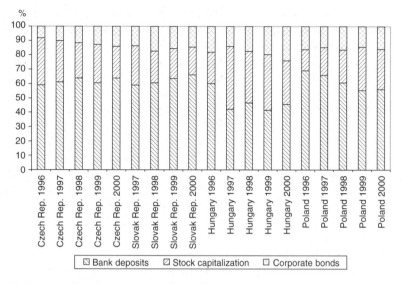

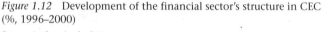

Figure 1.12   Development of the financial sector's structure in CEC (%, 1996–2000)

Source: Authors' calculations.

In developed countries, for instance in Finland and Greece, a serious change in the structure of the financial sector is apparent. In Finland, companies and households boldly invested in the capital market after the banking crisis at the beginning of the 1990s, which was followed by the loss of confidence in the sector. Securities issued in Finland grew very rapidly, especially in 1995–99. Therefore, the financial system in Finland is unambiguously the M-system (Figure 1.11). In most developed countries, the financial system stays relatively diversified, especially in comparison with the CEC, where changes in the structure of the financial sector are rather exceptional, with a lasting high share of banking intermediation. Possibly, only in the case of Poland (and Slovenia, not displayed in the figure) can we record a more permanent decrease of bank intermediation to the detriment of financial markets.

In the CEC, the structure of the financial sector is usually considered not to be well developed. In particular, a point to be criticized is the low share of financial markets in financial intermediation. The fact is that during recent years there has been a general trend towards strengthening market systems and growing financial markets to the detriment of the banking sector. But this trend has not been supported by clear conclusions or economic theory statements declaring which financial system is more effective – whether the B-system or the M-system. Is the current trend toward market-based systems desirable? (Allen and Gale, 2000, Ch. 1). The answer is not unambiguous, in particular if we take into account that countries with a higher share of the banking sector in the economy (as, for instance, Japan or Germany) reached a higher growth in their GDP, as Freixas and Rochet (1998, pp. 7–8) report. Nowadays, numerous empirical research studies point to the fact that it is irrelevant whether the financial sector of a country is bank-based or market-based in influencing long-term economic growth. Most countries are still looking for a suitable, 'tailor-made' financial system. There is a huge variety of financial systems among countries. For the time being, the only certainty is that an optimal, healthy and effective financial sector needs a well-balanced structure that must rely on both the developed banking sector and the working financial market. Countries with underdeveloped banking and financial sectors, low level of financial intermediation and illiquid financial markets may have problems with effective resource allocation, effective level of savings and investments, effective intermediation and therefore, stability of economic growth.

A comparison of transition and developed countries confirms that financial sectors in transition countries are still relatively narrow and also depend on banking intermediation. In addition, there are enormous differences in the relative size of financial sectors among transition countries, as well as in the structure of their financial sectors. In recent years (1996–2000) we have not seen any serious changes in the financial sectors of transition countries with regard to their structure.

1.3   Development and restructuring of banking sectors in the CEC

The term 'restructuring of the banking sector' can be understood from either a broader or narrower point of view. The broader definition covers radical and significant changes which affect all banks in the sector and consequently influence the whole economy. Changes in ownership structure, implementations of new forms of banking business, concentration or changes of the banks' role in the economy are the main aspects. This chapter focuses on the broader formulation of the restructuring process.[8] We will emphasize the total number of operating banks, their dispersion to specific groups according to their size, changes in ownership structure and concentration of the banking sector characterized by market shares or mergers and acquisitions.

All CEC banking sectors have gone through several disruptions and developmental periods of crucial importance, which have gradually created their new shape and structure. The establishment of two-tier banking systems based on market principles characterized the first stage. In this period, a completely new legal and institutional framework had to be established.

In the former Czechoslovakia, the two-tier banking system came into effect in January 1990. The following period (1990–93) was distinct in that the banking market opened up with the establishment of many new small banks supplied with domestic capital. The quick growth of banking institutions was caused by demand factors because of the gap between supply and demand of banking products. Gradually, this development reflected the improvement of a regulatory framework, creating new operational guidelines and principles for banks' prudential behaviour.

The significant decline in the growth of a number of banks started at the end of 1993, caused above all by a more restrictive licence policy of the Czech National Bank (ČNB). Step-by-step capital requirements as well as other requirements for granting a bank licence were in effect tightened up. This meant that there were – according to the ČNB – too many banks in the Czech Republic and the ČNB even refrained from granting licences to strong foreign banks. The recommendation of the ČNB was to obtain a share or to merge with already licensed banks. But buying mostly non-transparent banks with NPLs appeared to be very risky. That is one of the reasons why foreign investors entered the banking sector in the Czech Republic only at the end of the 1990s.

Escalation of small banks' problems that resulted in failures of many of them (Hölscher, 2000) worsened the situation of the whole banking sector. Even the largest banks could not avoid immediate problems and the crisis of credibility afflicted the entire Czech banking system (Polouček, 1999, p. 188, and ch. 5). The ČNB's Department of Banking Supervision acknowledged accountability for some problems in the banking sector during these years; on the other hand, however, the Central Bank did not accept responsibility. Table 1.4 illustrates the growth and decline in the number of banks[9] in the Czech Republic during this period.

In the period 1997–99, the Czech banking system confronted a serious crisis caused by a sluggish restructuring of companies, a slack regulation regime, growing bank debts and deep losses in the largest banks. The concentration of the banking sector is the most notable feature of this developmental stage (Chapter 3 deals with the concentration of banking

Table 1.4 Number of banks by group in the Czech Republic (1990–2001)

	1.1.90	31.12.90	31.12.91	31.12.92	31.12.93	31.12.94	31.12.95	31.12.96	31.12.97	31.12.98	31.12.99	31.12.00	31.12.01
Banks, total	5	9	24	37	52	55	55	53	50	45	42	40	38
of which:													
Large banks	5	5	6	6	5	5	5	5	5	5	5	4	3
Medium-sized banks					2	5	10	9	13	12	12	11	10
Small banks*		4	18	27	32	30	24	19	13	12	9	8	8
Foreign bank branches				3	7	8	10	9	9	10	10	10	10
Building societies				1	5	6	6	6	6	6	6	6	6
Under conservatorship				0	1	1	0	5	4	0	0	1	1
Banks without licences				0	0	1	4	6	10	18	21	23	25

* Until 1992 including foreign banks.

Source: ČNB.

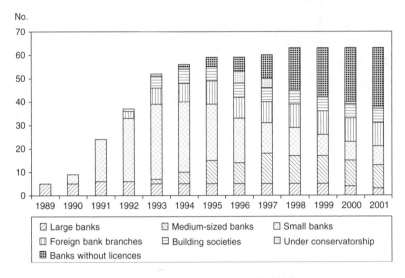

Figure 1.13   Number of banks (Czech Republic, 1989–2001)

Source: Authors' calculations.

sectors in transition countries). The main sources of concentration can be identified by the gradual decrease of the total number of small banks since 1995, the progress of medium-sized banks, privatization, mergers and acquisitions.

The development of the number of banks is portrayed in Figure 1.13 in the years 1989–2001 in the Czech Republic, confirming not only the fast-growing number of banks at the beginning of the 1990s but also the growing number of banks without licence as well as banks under conservatorship.

As outlined above, there have been shifts in the total number of active banks in the Czech Republic since 1990. The sharp decline in the number of small banks is associated with the revoking of their licences because of poor performance as well as the increase in the number of foreign banks, which gradually formed part of the group of medium-sized banks. Out of the 63 banking licences granted since 1989, a total of 23 had been terminated, 17 of them due to poor financial conditions and non-compliance with rules of prudence initiated by the ČNB's Department of Banking Supervision and also at the request of the banks themselves. Seven banking licences had been terminated because of sales and mergers, and one bank failed to start operating within the mandatory deadline. Some licences were terminated because of poor performance from 1999 until 2001, and others as a result of mergers and acquisitions.

The growth in the number of banks in the Czech Republic and in the other CEC since 1996 is illustrated in Table 1.5, and the growth in the number of commercial banks in Table 1.6 and Figure 1.14. These tables take into account a particular method of indicating the number of financial institutions of the banking sector in the CEC.[10]

It is apparent from the data in Tables 1.5 and 1.6 that both the number of regular and commercial banks has gradually decreased in the CEC. The number of entities operating as commercial banks in the Czech Republic and in the Slovak Republic declined considerably in the period studied. In Hungary, the number of commercial banks increased until 1997, afterwards it began to drop. Since cooperative banks and credit unions were categorized as banks in Poland and Hungary, there was a large decrease in numbers in these countries. To a great extent this was due to their declining assets compared to the commercial banks.[11]

As is apparent from Table 1.7, the decline in the number of commercial banks in CEC decelerated towards the end of the 1990s both

Table 1.5   Number of banks in CEC (1996–2001)

	1996	*1997*	*1998*	*1999*	*2000*	*2001*	*Index 2001/1996*
Czech Republic	53	50	45	42	40	38	71.7
Hungary	289	289	282	256	238	231	79.9
Poland	1475	1378	1272	858	754	713	48.3
Slovakia	29	29	27	25	23	21	72.4
Total CEC	1846	1746	1626	1181	1055	1003	54.3

Source: Authors' calculations based on data of national banks of CEC.

Table 1.6   Number of commercial banks in CEC (1996–2001)

	1996	*1997*	*1998*	*1999*	*2000*	*2001*	*Index 2001/1996*
Czech Republic	53	50	45	42	40	38	71.7
Hungary	42	46	45	44	43	42	100.0
Poland	81	83	83	77	74	71	87.7
Slovakia	29	29	27	25	23	21	72.4
Total CEC	205	208	200	188	180	172	83.9

Source: Authors' calculations based on data of national banks of CEC.

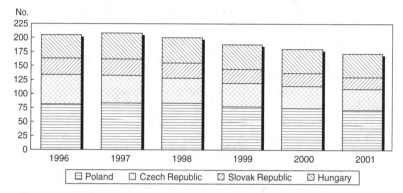

Figure 1.14 Number of commercial banks in CEC (1996–2001)
Source: Authors' calculations.

Table 1.7 Changes in numbers of commercial banks in CEC (1996–2001)

	1997		1998		1999		2000		2001	
	No.	%	No.	%	No.	%	No.	%	No.	%
Czech Republic	−3	−5.7	−5	−10.0	−3	−6.7	−2	−4.8	−2	−5.0
Hungary	4	9.5	−1	−2.2	−1	−2.2	−1	−2.3	−1	−2.3
Poland	2	2.5	0	0.0	−6	−7.2	−3	−3.9	−3	−4.1
Slovakia	0	0.0	−2	−6.9	−2	−7.4	−2	−8.0	−2	−8.7
CEC	3	1.5	−8	−3.8	−12	−6.0	−8	−4.3	−8	−4.4

Source: Authors' calculations.

absolutely and relatively – measured as a percentage of the entire number of commercial banks. This fact resulted in increasing concentration in the banking sector of the CEC (see Chapter 3) and is manifested in the increasing average volume of assets per commercial bank.

The declining number and the development of assets of commercial banks (Figure 1.15) brought about changes in bank grading according to size and logically led to the growth of the average volume of assets per one bank in each of the CEC.

The Czech Republic showed the highest average size of assets of one active bank (Table 1.8 and Figure 1.16). Since 1996, the indicator rose by 47.2 per cent.

The most dynamic development was manifested in Poland, where the average size of assets of one active bank increased twofold and came close to approximately 80 per cent of the Czech level in the same period.

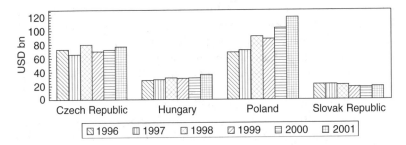

Figure 1.15   Assets of commercial banks in CEC (USD bn, 1996–2001)
Source: Authors' calculations.

Table 1.8   Average assets per commercial bank in CEC (USD mn, 1996–2001)

	1996	1997	1998	1999	2000	2001	Index 2001/1996
Czech Republic	1 373.1	1 309.7	1 773.2	1 663.8	1 800.8	2 021.1	147.2
Hungary	635.9	603.8	665.9	663.0	688.9	812.2	127.7
Poland	807.0	823.0	1 055.5	1 092.7	1 345.1	1 610.7	199.6
Slovakia	774.7	770.2	798.9	728.5	777.1	915.0	118.1
CEC	913.7	884.1	1 094.7	1 071.3	1 217.0	1 421.4	155.6

Source: Authors' calculations.

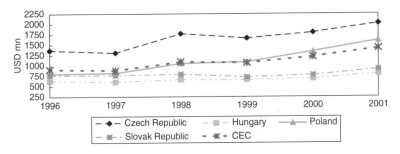

Figure 1.16   Average assets per commercial bank in CEC (USD mn, 1996–2001)
Source: Authors' calculations.

The Polish banking sector differs somewhat from its Czech counterpart, not only because the Polish economy is noticeably larger, but also because there are more banks in its banking system. As data and further analysis confirm, it has a considerably lower concentration in its banking sector (see Chapter 3). In the Slovak Republic and Hungary, the indicator is much lower. Both countries demonstrate that the average volume of assets per commercial bank is lower than the CEC average. The dynamics in the development of the above mentioned countries is also lower than that of the Czech Republic and Poland.

From the banking sector's point of view of the share of the different bank groups in total assets, there was, above all, an increasing share of medium-sized banks and a rapidly decreasing share of small banks. Concurrently, the share of foreign bank branches increased and the share of large banks decreased. The positive influence of foreign banks on the banking sector in all CEC is evident (see Chapter 4). Since the beginning of the 1990s, foreign banks have been bringing in new products, services, know-how and management procedures of a higher quality, not to mention invested capital. In the Czech Republic, foreign banks also started an expansion in the retail banking market only a few years ago, which corresponds to shifts in the banking sector's market shares. Above all, the share of large banks decreased. Detail segmentation is shown in Table 1.9.

Privatization was the crucial factor affecting the ownership structure during the transformation process. Foreign strategic investors (foreign banks) became the new owners of the largest Czech banks which were formerly state-owned. This hugely strengthened representation of foreign capital to the detriment of state claims. The rate of increase in capital in Czech-owned as well as foreign-owned banks, along with failures of small banks supplied only with Czech capital, also determined the ownership structure of the Czech banking sector.

Linking all the developments mentioned above, the growing number of investors from European Union countries was accompanied by an

Table 1.9   Share of bank groups in the banking sector's total assets in the Czech Republic (%, 1994–2001)

	1994	1995	1996	1997	1998	1999	2000	2001
Large banks	73.7	70.0	68.1	66.6	66.2	65.0	61.9	58.6
Medium-sized banks	9.1	14.7	12.6	16.4	16.9	17.4	19.6	21.4
Small banks	12.3	8.2	6.9	3.1	3.2	1.7	2.0	2.3
Foreign bank branches	4.0	6.0	6.4	7.8	9.5	11.4	11.1	12.0
Building societies	0.6	1.1	2.0	3.0	4.2	4.5	4.8	5.7
Banks under conservatorship	0.3	0.0	4.0	3.1	0.0	0.0	0.6	0.0
Total	100.0	100.0	100.0	100.0	100.0	100.0	100.0	100.0

Source: ČNB.

Table 1.10   Ownership structure of the Czech banking sector (%, 1994–2001)

	1994	1995	1996	1997	1998	1999	2000	2001
State, municipalities	29.1	31.5	31.0	20.3	25.1	27.0	23.6	4.3
Czech private	48.3	45.7	44.9	50.2	36.2	24.7	21.9	25.7
USA	1.3	2.8	4.3	3.1	4.6	7.5	7.7	6.3
EU countries	13.1	13.3	15.1	22.1	28.6	37.3	43.5	58.1
Other foreign	8.2	6.7	4.7	4.3	5.5	3.5	3.3	5.6
Total	100.0	100.0	100.0	100.0	100.0	100.0	100.0	100.0

Source: ČNB.

almost symmetrical decrease in Czech capital shares in the banking sector. This was quite a prominent development tendency. In spite of the continuing process of privatization, the share of the state and municipalities' ownership has remained, since 1997, almost at the same level. The implementation of privatization and the decrease of the government share in the banking sector also required the participation of the state in the pre-privatization capital increases of large banks. State shares plummeted dramatically after the privatization of Komerční banka in 2001. Tables 1.10 and 1.11 give detailed information.

A significant role of foreign capital in the Czech banking sector is also apparent in relation to the amount of capital. More than 50 per cent of capital under the control of foreign-owned banks as of 31 December 2000, and after the privatization of Komerční banka in 2001, the share rose even higher to 70 per cent.

The privatization of the Hungarian banking sector, which took place in the wake of the bank restructuring programmes between 1993 and 1994, was completed by the second half of the 1990s. Privatization was carried out in the form of open tenders, and one of the new responsibilities undertaken by the new owners was to reinforce further bank capital. As a result, today's foreign strategic owners hold some two-thirds of the Hungarian banking sector. The year 2001 witnessed only minor changes in the ownership structure of the banking system. Foreign ownership decreased by 3.6 percentage points to 63 per cent at the year end, whereas the share of state ownership through domestic equity holdings rose at the expense of credit institutions, enterprises and individuals.

In Poland, in December 2001, there were 71 commercial banks. The ownership structure had perceptibly changed in the course of the 1990s as a consequence of privatization of state-owned banks. In 1993, the state still owned, directly or indirectly, 29 banks, representing 80 per cent of the assets and 77 per cent of the capital of the banking sector in

Table 1.11 Ownership structure of the three largest banks in the Czech Republic before and after privatization (%)

31. 12. 1997		ČSOB 31. 12. 1999		30. 6. 2002	
ČNB	26.5	KBC Bank NV	82.3	KBC Bank NV	81.5
Ministry of Finance	19.6	EBRD	7.5	EBRD	7.5
NPF	19.6	IFC	4.4	IFC	4.4
Others from the Czech Republic	8.5	Shareholders from the Czech Republic	4.5	Others	6.6
NBS	24.1	Shareholders from the Slovak Republic	1.4		
Others from the Slovak Republic	1.7				
Total	100.0	Total	100.0	Total	100.0
30. 6. 1999		**ČS 31. 12. 2000**		**30. 6. 2002**	
NPF	52.1	Erste Bank	52.6	Erste Bank	52.4
Česká pojišt'ovna	9.2	Česká pojišt'ovna	8.6	AVS	32.6
Municipalities	7.4	Municipalities	7.4	Municipalities	7.4
EBRD	5.9	EBRD	5.9	Česká pojišt'ovna	5.0
Others	25.4	Others – foreign	21.5	Others	3.0
		Others – domestic	4.0		
Total	100.0	Total	100.0	Total	100.0
30. 6. 1999		**KB 31. 12. 2001**		**30. 6. 2002**	
NPF	49.0	NPF	60.0	Société Générale	60.0
The Bank of NY	18.0	The Bank of NY	6.7	The Bank of NY	7.4
RIF	3.0	Chase Nominees	2.0	Others	32.6
Česká pojišt'ovna	3.0	Chase Ireland L.	1.6		
PIAS fund	2.0	Others	29.8		
Bank Austria	2.0				
Others	23.0				
Total	100.0	Total	100.0	Total	100.0

Source: Annual reports of ČSOB, ČS and KB.

Poland. On the other hand there were only seven banks controlled by the state at the end of the year 2001, representing 23.1 per cent and 12.5 per cent, respectively, of banking assets and total capital. Foreign strategic investors had acquired most of the capital in the largest Polish banks. Aside from commercial banks, cooperative banks are an important element of the banking sector, however small, in asset terms. The privatization agenda has not been completed, however, with the largest retail bank PEKAO still government-owned. The government holds shares directly in three banks: two banks in the top 11 with respect to asset size, and one minor bank. As a result of previous government efforts, investors are diversified in respect of country of origin. The shares of different countries are fairly equal, with a slight domination of American and German banks (22 and 20 per cent of foreign capital, respectively). The variety of investors should protect the Polish market from excessive exposure to the country's problems. The important feature of the presence of foreign capital in Poland is the legal status of banks. Contrary to the situation in the Czech Republic, all the 45 foreign-owned banks except one are subsidiaries. This leads to capital being invested within the country and renders the banks subject to supervision by a Polish agency, thus giving some degree of reassurance in case of financial distress.

In the Slovak Republic, towards the end of 2001, state ownership, on the basis of registered capital, accounted for 36.7 per cent of the banking sector. The residual share is in private ownership, and foreign investors account for 60.6 per cent. As a consequence of privatization in the first half of the year 2002, the share in foreign capital increased to 82.8 per cent. From a territorial point of view, foreign capital includes capital from Luxembourg, Austria, the Czech Republic, Holland, Italy, the UK, the USA, and to a lesser extent also from Germany and France.

1.4 Conclusion

Today's banking sector in transition countries, its structure and its development, have been notably influenced by the first years of transformation. Apparently, the development of the CEC banks is proceeding very quickly and their financial force and know-how are currently at an incomparably higher level than several years ago. Data from the EBRD *Transition Report* (cf. EBRD *Transition Report*, November 1999 and November 2001) confirm a noticeable progress, but also serious differences among transition countries. CEC are without any doubt among the best performers. Now the banking sectors of these countries have aligned themselves closely with the standards of smaller developed countries according to the number and structure of banking institutions and to the number of banking locations. Nevertheless, it is necessary to take into account that in most CEC, even the strongest and soundest banks are in international terms banks, and are not too unsound. Domestic banks still have to take many steps to approach the level of banks in most advanced countries. At the same time the analysis presented confirms that the Czech Republic, Slovakia, Poland and Hungary have much in common (starting with their transition from centrally planned economies to market economies), but also many differences in their financial and banking sector development.

Notes

1. See Levine (1997) for a literature review on the importance of financial development for economic growth. Recent relevant studies also include Beck *et al.* (2000a); for the Czech Republic see Kulhánek (2002), among others.
2. For example, Beck *et al.* (2000b) find that measures of the initial level of financial depth and stock market liquidity have independent causal effects on the subsequent rates of GDP growth and economic efficiency improvements.
3. To measure a bank's development Rousseau and Wachtel (2000) use M3/GDP. King and Levine (1993a, 1993b) use the total liquid liabilities of financial intermediaries (M3) divided by GDP and show that the bank's development helps explain economic growth in a sample of more than 80 countries.
4. For the Czech Republic: M2 = currency in circulation + CZK demand deposits + CZK time deposits + deposits bills of exchange and other bonds (01/98–12/00 incl. certificates of deposit) + foreign currency deposits. Hungary: M2 = sight and time (including savings) deposits in HUF and all foreign currencies. Poland: M2 = domestic money supply (cash in circulation excluding cash in foreign currencies and deposits of households and the corporate sector in domestic currency) + foreign currency deposits of households and the corporate sector. Slovak Republic: M2 = currency outside banks + demand deposits and saving deposits without statutory notice held by domestic non-banks (residents + non-residents, in SKK) exclude deposits of central and local government + time deposits and savings deposits at statutory notice including deposit certificates + deposits in foreign currencies held by residents with domestic banks exclude deposits of central and local government.
5. Caviglia *et al.* (2002) came to a similar conclusion. If another, much higher figure is given in statistics for the Czech Republic (Wagner and Iakova, 2001, Table 1), then the high ratio in the Czech Republic reflects, in part, incomplete consolidation of the aggregate balance sheets, with double-counting of interbank credits.
6. Own calculation for end of 2000 based on World Development Indicators, Series: Domestic credit provided by banking sector (per cent of GDP) (FS.AST.DOMS.GD.ZS) and ECB (2002b).
7. There is more about privatization in the banking sectors of CEC in Section 1.3 and Chapter 4, Section 4.3.
8. The narrower definition of the banking sector's restructuring is considered as specific changes of one individual bank or group of banks with similar characteristics. They mainly relate to the restructuring of credit portfolios and covering losses from non-performing loans by provisions and reserves.
9. The Department of Banking Supervision of the ČNB stated in its reports a division of banks into large and small banks, foreign banks, foreign banks

branches and specialized banks until 1999. Since 2000, the ČNB has also stated, besides large banks and small banks, a separate group of medium-sized banks. The cohesive criterion for banks' division into groups is the size of total balance. The group of large banks includes banks with total balance higher than CZK 100 billion, among medium-sized banks are ranked banks with total balance between CZK 15 and 100 billion.

10. In the Czech Republic, financial institutions ('banks') are entirely represented by institutions of 'commercial banks'. Pursuant to the Act on Banks, commercial banks in the Czech Republic have the only legal status of joint-stock companies. The Act on Banks does not provide for the establishment of cooperative banks. Credit unions are not part of the banking sector. In the Slovak Republic, 'banks' are identical as to content with 'banks' in the Czech Republic. 'Commercial banks', on the other hand, do not include branches of foreign banks. In Hungary, both commercial banks and specialized credit institutions, and 'cooperative banks' are classed as financial institutions ('banks'). Credit unions are not mentioned. In Poland, the components of the financial system are classified into 'banks' and 'credit unions'; both 'commercial banks' and 'cooperative banks' are classed as 'banks'.

11. In Hungary, assets of 255 cooperative banks amounted to USD 1,462 million, 1996, and assets of 42 commercial banks and specialized institutions to USD 26,708 million, that is 5.16 per cent as against 94.84 per cent. In Poland, in 1996, assets of 81 commercial banks, 1,394 cooperative banks and 168 credit unions amounted to USD 65,365.9 million, USD 3,171.7 million and USD 76.3 million, respectively. In 2001, they amounted to USD 114,357.3 million, USD 5,395.7 million and USD 445.8 million, respectively.

References

Allen, F. and Gale, D. *Comparing Financial Systems* (Cambridge, MA and London: The MIT Press, 2000).

Anderson, R. and Kegels, Ch. *Transition Banking – The Financial Development of Central and Eastern Europe* (Oxford: The Clarendon Press, 1998).

Beck, T., Levine, R. and Loayza, N. 'Finance and the Sources of Growth', *Journal of Financial Economics*, LVIII, 1–2 (2000a), 261–300.

Beck, T., Levine, R. and Loayza, N. 'Financial Intermediation and Growth: Causality and Causes', *Journal of Monetary Economics*, XLVI, 1 (2000b), 31–77.

Begg, D. and Portes, R. 'Enterprise debt and economic transformation: financial restructuring in central and Eastern Europe', in Mayer, C. and Vives, X. (eds), *Capital Markets and Financial Intermediation* (London: Cambridge University Press, 1993).

Caviglia, G., Krause, G. and Thimann, Ch. 'Key features of the financial sectors in EU accession countries', in *Financial Sectors in EU Accession Countries* (Frankfurt: ECB, 2002).

European Central Bank (2002a). *Financial Sectors in EU Accession Countries* (Frankfurt: ECB, 2002, http://www.ecb.int/pub/pdf/financialsectorseuaccession.pdf).

European Central Bank (2002b). *Monthly Bulletin*, 7 (2002b).

Freixas, X. and Rochet, J.Ch. *Microeconomics of Banking* (Cambridge, MA and London, UK: MIT Press, 1998).

Gerschenkron, A. *Economic backwardness in Historical Perspective – A Book of Essays* (Cambridge, MA: Harvard University Press, 1962).

Goldsmith, R.W. *Financial Structure and Development* (New Haven, CT: Yale University Press, 1969).

Hölscher, J. (ed.), *Financial Turbulence and Capital Markets in Transition Countries* (London: Macmillan, 2000).

King, R.G. and Levine, R. 'Finance and Growth: Schumpeter Might Be Right', *Quarterly Journal of Economics*, 108, 3 (1993a), 717–38.

King, R.G. and Levine, R. 'Finance, Entrepreneurship, and Growth', *Journal of Monetary Economics*, 32, 3 (1993b), 513–42.

Kulhánek, L. 'Financial Markets and the Gross Domestic Product in the Czech Republic and in the EU Countries', in *Transition Countries Joining the European Union* (Karviná, Canakkale: Silesian University, Canakkale Onsekiz Mart University 2002).

Levine, R. 'Financial Development and Economic Growth: Views and Agenda', *Journal of Economic Literature*, 35 (1997), 688–726.

Levine, R. and Zevros, S. 'Stock Markets, Banks, and Economic Growth', *American Economic Review*, 88, 3 (1998), 537–58.

McKinnon, R.I. *Money and Capital in Economic Development* (Washington, DC: Brookings Institution, 1973).

Polouček, S. *České bankovnictví na přelomu tisíciletí* (Ostrava: Ethics, 1999).

Rousseau, P.L. and Wachtel, P. 'Financial Intermediation and Economic Performance: Historical Evidence from Five Industrial Countries', *Journal of Money, Credit, and Banking*, 30, 4 (1998), 657–78.

Rousseau, P.L. and Wachtel, P. 'Equity Markets and Growth: Cross Country Evidence on Timing and Outcomes, 1980–1995', *Journal of Business and Finance*, 24 (2000), 1933–57.

Schardax, F. and Reininger, T. 'The Financial Sector in Five Central and Eastern European Countries: An Overview', *Focus on Transition*, 1 (2001), 30–64.

Stability and Structure of Financial Systems in CEC5. Background document for the CEC5 Governors' meeting (Warsaw: NBP, 2002).

Wagner, N. and Iakova, D. 'Financial Sector Evolution in the Central European Economies: Challenges in Supporting Macroeconomic Stability and Sustainable Growth' (*IMF Working Paper*, 141, 2001).

International Financial Statistics. International Monetary Fund, *Statistical Yearbook*, 2000.

Central banks' web pages, Commercial banks' web pages.

2
The Czech Banking Sector in the 1990s: Regulation and Supervision

Roman Matoušek

The fundamental changes of the banking sector reform that involved breaking up the monobank system into a two-tier banking system occurred in an institutional and legislative environment tailored to the prevailing economy. There was not only an underdeveloped institutional framework, but also a legislative framework covering bankruptcy law, corporate law, laws protecting creditors as well as debtors, accounting standards, reliable auditor firms and so on. Therefore, it was subsequently recognized that the resolution in the first stage of transition was insufficient, and repeated rescue operations were needed.

The approach taken towards developing a viable financial sector varies among transition countries and has been dependent on a number of factors. The most important factors have been the start-up conditions, the macroeconomic setting and development, the pace of other reforms – including institutional and legal – and, last but not least, the political consensus in support of market-based institutions.

Looking at the development of banking sectors across CEC, some differences are noteworthy. Hungary, for example, had already initiated banking reforms in the early 1980s and this was accompanied by legal and enterprise reforms. The other aspect that had an impact on the future development of banking systems was whether transition countries followed the so-called 'rehabilitation', or the 'new entry' approach. The rehabilitation approach is based on recapitalization and consolidation of state banks, including limited privatization and new entry (Hungary, Poland and, to some extent, the Czech Republic). The second approach – new entry – applied mostly in the countries of the former Soviet Union and was based on the relatively liberal entry of new banks, including rapid privatization.

Macroeconomic conditions and development and the microeconomic restructuring process have become fundamental factors for the development, stability and soundness of the banking system. All CEC were exposed to both domestic and external shocks that could not be accommodated by the existing economic system. Such shocks, including price liberalization, currency devaluation, privatization, industrial conversion, foreign trade liberalization, and the collapse of the former trade organization the Council for Mutual Economic Assistance (CMEA), significantly affected the transition economies, particularly their banking sectors. At the beginning of the 1990s, these shocks resulted in a deep decline in output and, consequently, in a further deterioration of the financial position of state-owned enterprises (SOEs).

Macroeconomic destabilization, above all, through high inflation induced by a monetary overhang, had a direct impact on the burden of non-performing loans (NPLs). An environment of relatively low inflation, such as in the Czech Republic, helped to avoid a credit crunch in the early 1990s, and caused the erosion of household savings in the first phase of the transformation by wiping out most of the value of existing debt and savings in domestic currency. On the other hand, unexpected high inflation reduced the burden for debtors by eroding their loans through negative real interest rates. An analysis comparing the advantages and disadvantages of high inflation for banks' solvency is inconclusive (see Claessens, 1996).

At the outset of banking reforms, the CEC had a unique opportunity to build a two-tier banking system almost from scratch. Nevertheless, several questions arose regarding the expansion and openness of the banking system in transition economies. It was recognized that the way banking systems were set up would have direct implications on the extent of rescue operations by governments and central banks.

In the Czech Republic, five state-owned commercial banks were created at the beginning of 1990. All five banks were highly specialized. Since these banks had in the first stage of transition only a few branches across the Czech Republic, except the Česká spořitelna (Savings Bank), there was a lack of financial services in the regions outside Prague. A similar strategy was adopted in Hungary, where four banks had an oligopolistic position within the Hungarian market as a whole. These banks were created from the commercial banking departments of the monobank.

Transition countries have been undergoing a complex process of liberalization similar to, but more radical than, those in EU countries in the 1970s and 1980s. The authorities set the basic regulatory and supervisory framework, new operational guidelines and principles for the banks' prudent behaviour. However, regulatory and supervisory capacity was severely limited and banks lacked, among other things, basic credit skills. This was reflected later, in a further destabilization in the banking sector.

2.1 The role and place of banking regulation and supervision

The behaviour of the banking sector, that is, the behaviour of individual banks, their stability, efficiency and transparency, is an important measure of the maturity of the regulator and the regulator's ability to create an environment supporting the goals mentioned above. Regulation of the banking sector should be understood in its broad macroeconomic and microeconomic sense. Provided that the banking sector is understood as a subsystem of the economic system, then banks, which are elements of this subsystem allocating resources, affect the system and are an integral part of the whole. This means that the macroeconomic environment influences the financial sector and, in turn, this sector influences the economy as a whole. Understanding the banking sector in this way leads to the question: to what extent can regulatory norms change or influence the behaviour of the regulated entities?

Banking supervision policy cannot succeed without adequate monetary policy, and vice versa. Measures that lead to reduction of risk and, in turn, an increase in the prudent behaviour of banks influence monetary policy. The banking sector is, therefore, an integral part of the monetary transmission mechanism. On the other hand, the central bank influences the banking sector through its monetary instruments.

Banking regulation applies a wide variety of indicators to the prudent behaviour of banks, for example, liquidity, capital adequacy and loan classification, as well as creation of adequate revisions and restrictions on credit involvement. For example, a change (rise) in the capital adequacy of banks can lead to stagnation of asset growth, or a decline in growth, which, as a result, restricts the flow of money into the economy even in the presence of expanding monetary policy. Banks can also negatively affect the structure of their portfolios. In a period of recession, stricter demands for the creation of provisions and reserves could lead to unwanted credit restriction and a rise in interest rates. In relation to the need to create additional provisions and reserves, banks should increase the level of disposable resources, which results primarily in a rise in interest rate margins. In other words, banks increase the spread between interest rates for loans and deposits. In extreme cases, this leads to financial disintermediation and to limiting the effectiveness of monetary policy. The worsening structure of bank portfolios also affects the allocation of rare resources when there is a reduction in new lending. A similar negative effect can be caused by the development of a systematic crisis inside the banking sector or within key banks.

In regard to the role of bank regulation in the CEC, the issues faced by policy-makers at the beginning of banking reforms were: what could and should be the pace of reforms to liberalize and restructure the financial and banking system (enhancing their functional efficiency)? How can the objective of functional efficiency be reconciled with that of stability and soundness? What degree of intervention in the banking system is admissible?

A regulatory body must first decide what the main objectives of banking supervision are. The principal objective of regulation might be seen as the mitigation of the potential instability of the banking system – in the limitation of systemic risk. The growth in the number of commercial banks, their shares within a market, the complexity of applied technology, and new products contribute to the increase in hostility in the environment in this sector; thus, competition pressures and inexorably rising costs jeopardize a bank's success (see Lastra, 1996).

In order to make banking regulation and supervision efficient, the regulator has to state clearly the objectives of, and accountability for, its activities. The failure of several small-sized commercial banks in the Czech Republic demonstrates the importance of this principle (Matoušek and Taci, 2000). The ČNB, as the banking supervisory body, faced criticism of its accountability for the current situation of banking in the Czech Republic. Further criticisms have been that interventions and rescue activities have come too late and had an uncertain impact at best.

This situation could have been prevented by the ČNB if it had set a clear and transparent policy for the banking system. Certainly, there are those who have argued that in the framework of the Czech National Bank Act, the role and accountability of the ČNB is clearly defined, whether or not the goals of banking supervision are clear and transparent. One can agree with the statement that the ČNB is responsible for the stability of the banking system. However, this definition is too general. If the banking supervisory body (ČNB) had declared its main aims, it would not be blamed for the problems that some banks faced in the early stages of transition.[1] Therefore, in order to avoid a repetition of this situation, the regulator must make clear its policy goals for the banking sector. In other words, the priorities of regulation should be clearly stated, such as the stability and soundness of the banking system, and the protection of retail clients. These priorities could be listed as follows:

- preventing failures and systemic externalities of the banking system. This measure can be achieved, for example, via financial support. This is, of course, accompanied by significant costs but in many cases is less expensive than the costs incurred by a series of systemic failures within the sector;
- meeting the objectives of optimal resource allocation. This means, above all, applying a licensing policy which will eliminate 'capture banks'. These banks are characterized by providing credits to their shareholders, with little, if any, regard for the creditworthiness of such lending;
- providing instruments of control and conducting monetary policy. If the regulatory body is a part of the central bank, the monetary policy department can better set their policy targets, since the stability of banks is essential for a sound and efficient monetary policy;
- protecting depositors by setting prudent rules and deposit insurance schemes.

2.2 Banking regulation and supervision – legislative framework

The legislative framework of the ČNB has undergone substantial changes since 1990, when a two-tier banking system was introduced. The ČNB has gradually amended the legislative framework for commercial banking activities in order to meet EU regulatory standards (EU Directives) as well as the recommendations of the Basel Committee on Banking Supervision. The focus has been on incorporating EU Directives into Czech banking law.

The principal task of the ČNB has been the implementation of the White Paper (Stage I and Stage II) for the associated countries. The ČNB has adopted into Czech banking law the First Banking Directive (77/780/EEC), the Own Funds Directive (89/299/EEC), Directive 89/647/EEC, regarding solvency ratios, Directive 89/646/EEC, regarding the provision of banking services, and Directive 94/19/EEC, on deposit guarantee schemes. The measures of Stage II have been implemented as well, including Directive 86/635/EEC on consolidated accounts, Directive 92/30/EEC on a consolidated supervision, and Directive 93/6/EEC, on capital adequacy.

In order to meet the EU Directives, the ČNB revised the Banking Act of 1992 in two stages. The 'small amendment' (Banking Act No. 16/1998) was approved by Parliament in January 1998, and the 'large amendment' (Banking Act No. 165/1998) took effect in September 1998. The deteriorating situation in the Czech banking sector catalysed these changes. The failures and irregularities among small and medium-sized banks revealed the absence of internal effective controls. At the same time, the former Banking Act did not enable the ČNB to deal effectively with problem banks. Although the amendments go hand in hand with the EU Directives, there are still shortcomings in the Czech legislative framework (see Matoušek, 2002).

The 'small amendment' addressed the following problems: the interconnection of banks with the corporate sector, the separation of investment and commercial banking; and the increase in the amount of coverage provided in the Czech deposit insurance scheme.

The fulfilment of these new rules and obligations for banks has been implemented on a step-by-step basis rather than all at once. The rules dealing with ownership participation have been phased in over three years, and changes regarding participation in statutory and supervisory boards over six months.

A fundamental change included within this amendment was the separation of commercial and investment banking. However, the Czech banking system was deliberately built up as a universal one, resembling the German banking model. Therefore, such a radical change after eight years raised a significant question regarding the optimal banking system. Undoubtedly, the German banking model has contributed to the so-called 'closed triangle' between commercial banks, investment funds and firms in the Czech Republic. The suggested changes or restrictions have had a direct impact on the business strategy of these banks, although opponents argued that only a few banks do not already meet these limits.

The 'second amendment' involved further substantial changes in the legislative framework for commercial banks. The revision of the Banking Act, above all, enhanced general confidence in the banking sector.

As elsewhere, the introduced rules of prudential regulation followed both EU standards and the recommendations of the Basel Committee on Banking Supervision. However, in their targeting and in setting the time profile, the ČNB had to allow for certain constraining factors, in particular, the legacy of the past financial and industrial structure. Consequently, a stepwise approach was adopted for the most part.

Table 2.1 Comparison of the Czech legal system with EU banking directives

Area of regulation	EU Directives	Czech Republic
Access to market	Directive 77/780/EEC (First Banking Directive)	Harmonized
Provision of banking services	Directive 89/646/EEC (Second Banking Directive)	Principal rules for providing are harmonized
Pursuit of business	Directive 89/299/EEC on own funds	Remaining discrepancies are of a technical nature
Minimum capital	EUR 5 mn (USD 6 mn)	CZK 500 mn (EUR ca. 16 mn)
CAR	> 8% risk-adjusted and Directive 93/6/EEC on capital adequacy market risk	Only > 8% risk-adjusted
Investments in non-financial firms	< 15% core capital in one firm; < 60% core capital in aggregate	< 15% core capital in one firm; < 60% core capital in aggregate
Large exposure	< 25% core capital	< 25% core capital
Connected exposure	< 20% core capital	< 20% core capital
Aggregate large exposure	< 800% core capital	< 230% core capital
Deposit insurance	< EUR 20,000	EUR 25,000
Bank supervision	Directive 92/30/EEC on consolidated supervision	Adopted
Licensing	Open	Open
Loan loss provisions	Tax-deductible	Total annual tax-deductible provisions may not exceed 2% of the average level of credits during the tax period

Sources: World Bank, Czech National Bank.

In addition to the Banking Act, which provides the essential legislative framework governing the activities of commercial banks, the ČNB issued various 'provisions'. The provisions are an integral part of the Banking Act. The advantage of these provisions is that they react flexibly according to the situation within the Czech banking sector. In contrast, the Hungarian Banking Act includes all 'provisions' in the Act itself, and therefore any amendment requires the approval of Parliament. This may hamper prompt reaction to new circumstances within the sector. In the Czech case, it would be a misunderstanding to assume that these provisions have been misused by the ČNB. Nevertheless, there has been some discussion among lawyers of their legitimacy.

A main bottleneck in banking development in transition economies has been the extent of problem loans. However, the identification of the extent is not straightforward (Lindgren *et al.*, 1998). In the discussion of transition economies, the term 'bad loans' has often been used with two different meanings, which causes some confusion. In a wider sense it comprises all types of classified credits, for which the Czech banking statistics used the term 'risk credits' and later on 'classified credits'. In a narrow interpretation it is confined to the worst sub-category of problem loans, that is, to NPLs. The second qualification refers to the

Table 2.2   Loan classification in the Czech Republic

	Delay in servicing	Required total provisions (%)	Annual tax-deductible provisions/reserves* (%)
Standard	Up to 30 days	0	1
Watch	31 to 90 days	5	1
Substandard	91 to 180 days	20	5
Doubtful	181 to 360 days	50	10
Loss	More than 360 days	100	20

* Total annual tax-deductible provisions may not exceed 2% of the average level of credits during the tax period.

Source: Czech National Bank.

amendments in classification that have been implemented several times in the course of the transition, the most recent one becoming effective in the second half of 1994. As a result, the identification of problem loans (classified credits) as well as their division into individual sub-categories has been changing. The third constraining factor is related to the available data themselves. Their quality and coverage have also undergone considerable changes. While at the start of transition only big banks were scrutinized by external auditors, over time, all banking institutions have become subject to auditing procedures and to increasingly more in-depth and more sophisticated supervision both on-site and off-site.

Table 2.2 shows the classification in the Czech case. The issue of NPLs is discussed in more detail in Chapter 1 and above all in Chapter 4.

2.3   Entry into and exit from the banking sector

At the beginning of the banking reforms in the Czech Republic, it was widely accepted that the more banks operating within the financial market, the better, as it was assumed that this would result in the system as a whole being more competitive and efficient.[2]

The Czech Republic (among other countries) had a unique opportunity to start building a banking system almost from scratch. At the beginning of 1990, there were a few large commercial banks carved out from the former Czechoslovak State Bank – Komerční Banka (Czech Republic) and Všeobecná Úvěrová Banka (Slovak Republic). In addition, Česká Spořitelna (Savings Bank), Živnostenská Banka, Československá Obchodní Banka (Czechoslovak Trade Bank) and Investiční Banka (Investment Bank), all of which existed as specialized financial institutions in the old system, started operating as commercial banks in 1990. However, it does not appear that the composition of commercial banks has been optimal.

The rapid growth of new commercial banks in the period 1991–92 brought a certain degree of competition into the financial market, but later the financial position of these banks was considerably impaired. This development was almost identical for most of the former communist countries undergoing transformation of domestic banking sectors. But considering the current situation within the segment of the biggest commercial banks, several shortcomings can be seen in the applied measures.

For example, in Poland, several regional banks were established instead of one or two large banks. The advantage of such a policy is, at least for the first stage of development, to avoid creating 'capture banks' (see below). This approach to decentralization also led to all major regions in the country being covered by the banking sector, and made monitoring of the allocation of credits easier, through better knowledge of debtors and regional conditions.

Developing a banking sector requires two policies to be carried out simultaneously: liberalization of the sector and the prudentially regulated entry of new banks. The licensing policy applied by the ČNB that evolved from a lax to tough one was inappropriate, as evident from the licensing policy applied by the ČNB and the Ministry of Finance. At the outset of banking reforms the minimum amount of capital was CZK 50 million. This amount was later increased by the ČNB to CZK 300 million. Since 1994 the capital has been CZK 500 million. A relatively low required limit on the bank capital, in the early stage, has undeniably helped the growth of so-called 'capture banks' or 'zero banks'.

Experience has shown that when establishing a banking system, one should adopt thorough criteria for granting banking licences for domestic banks or banks which do not have a sufficiently long track record. On the other hand, when a number of highly regarded foreign commercial banks have applied for banking licences, the ČNB overruled their applications or suggested that they acquire banks that were already operating on the market (and usually in financial distress). One must take into account the remarkable deregulation process, which has been strengthened by the criteria of the Second Banking Directive in EU countries. Finally, foreign banks do not necessarily increase the competitiveness of the banking sector, but they can provide stability within the financial system, unlike 'zero banks'. Furthermore, the biggest commercial banks play a crucial role in the Czech financial market, extending their activities over the entire Czech Republic. As a result of these activities, a number of small-sized banks, including 'zero banks', are finding themselves in difficulty. It is far more difficult for small banks to find a place in the market. One of the possible ways to remedy this situation is for these banks to become niche players, focusing their attention on special activities and banking services which are not (or only marginally) performed by larger banks. This hypothesis is empirically verified in Chapter 4, Section 4.2 by the analysis of banking efficiency. A minor comfort, though hardly a practical consolation for the bank regulation authority, is the fact that some EU countries have also struggled with a similar phenomenon.

The IMF has listed the key factors in assessing the viability of small and medium-sized commercial banks that have faced financial difficulties. These factors are as follows:

1. The integrity and probity of shareholders, directors, and/or officers of the bank.
2. The actual objectives pursued by the major shareholders of the proposed bank relative to its safety and soundness.
3. The qualifications, experience, and judgement of all or some of the directors, members of the supervisory board, and other high-ranking officials of the proposed bank relative to the nature, size and sophistication of the proposed business.
4. The presence of a financial buffer to absorb losses that may surface as the bank's business is conducted, which is dependent on the nature and scale of the proposed bank relative to the nature and scale of the proposed business and the risk attached to the same.
5. The quality of corporate governance and the distribution and segregation of duties and responsibilities within the bank.
6. The quality of the policies, management system, internal controls and procedures in the bank, in particular with regard to risk management, pricing, provisioning and internal audit.

If a bank fails to comply with the regulatory requirements, the authority responsible for regulation and supervision must make a decision about the future of that institution. The outcome of this decision is constrained above all by the legislative framework – the range of supervisory instruments. Broadly speaking, there are a number of measures that can be employed. If normal prudential regulations fail to prevent banks from imprudent behaviour, remedial measures are required to avoid the further financial deterioration of the bank in question. By remedial measures we mean the effort of the bank management and the regulatory body to improve a given situation. However, in many cases there is no consensus between management and the regulator about which measures to take in order to restore financial stability. In this situation there must be a legal framework and available instruments enabling a regulator to impose mandatory measures. And finally, when all else fails, the regulator should revoke the banking licence.[3]

Banking Act No. 21/1992, banking regulation and supervision, had a limited array of instruments to cope with banks in financial difficulty. These legislative limitations were recognized during the turbulence in the Czech banking sector in 1995–96. For this reason, the Banking Act was revised and the legal instruments available to authorities were strengthened and widened. At the same time, the range of operating instruments for forced administration on a bank was limited, and the new Banking Act also redefined criteria for the suspension of banking licences.[4]

2.4 Deposit insurance scheme

If banking markets were complete and information between all agents were symmetric, there would be no need to protect their users. In this case, intervention by the authorities, as discussed in the course of this chapter (law, regulations, supervisors), would be unnecessary. However, the real financial world (and not exclusively the financial one) is far from perfect and its users must be protected (Diamond and Dybvig, 1983).

The existence of asymmetric information is far more perceptible in a retail market than in a wholesale market. One can argue that its moderation can be carried out via a fuller disclosure by banks, which would undoubtedly lead to a reduction in costs and in the extent of banking regulation.[5] But this may incur unreasonable costs for small depositors. Nevertheless, by no means it is argued that the information disclosure within the Czech banking system has been sufficient. Annual reports issued by the Czech commercial banks did not provide relevant information as far as their financial position is concerned, particularly small and medium-sized banks. Regarding retail customers, there are a number of legitimate questions as to whether protection should be provided. The reasons for protection are based on the absence of repeat orders, which does not enable learning by experience; the suppliers and demanders are less equal in a retail market than in a wholesale one; individuals are limited to monitoring the behaviour of the supplier of financial contracts.

The need for banking protection appears reasonable. However, it is also closely linked to a moral hazard problem because any protection, for clients or bankers, is likely to lead to riskier decisions being taken. A further negative consequence of protection is that it incurs costs. Therefore, an optimal scheme of deposit protection must be established, one that is neither too generous in its protection (mitigating the moral hazard problem) nor too limited, and one that favours the stability of the banking sector. Broadly speaking, generous protection discourages the prudent behaviour of bankers and depositors, although only partial compensation can have a negative impact as well. It follows that the best solution would be to set up a fairly priced deposit insurance scheme. But such a scheme is very difficult to establish and therefore most countries have deposit schemes based on fixed rates.

In regard to deposit insurance, several different types of framework can be discussed. The main distinguishing feature is whether the insurance scheme works on a legal basis or as an informal arrangement. Further classifications are whether these schemes work on a voluntary basis or through compulsory membership, and whether the schemes are administered officially or privately.

For example, in France, Austria, the Netherlands, Italy and Switzerland, deposit insurance is compulsory and operates on an *ad hoc* levy. The system does not require annual contributions from member banks, but the realized losses of declining banks are divided *ex post* among participants. Norway, Germany, Spain, Belgium and Finland have a deposit insurance system that is financed through periodic premium payments. The representatives of the banks themselves manage these funds. Japan, Canada and the USA apply a deposit insurance system based on collecting periodic insurance premia from banks through a deposit insurance corporation managed by the government.

According to the Deposit Insurance Directive, the minimum level of deposit insurance for all EU countries is EUR 20,000. The task of this deposit insurance scheme is not only to protect deposits but also to discourage runs on banks. In addition, the home member country protects branch depositors, but branches have the option of joining the host country scheme.

In the Czech Republic a question linked to depositor protection was raised after the first failure of the banks. The amount of compensation available was well below the EU average. The Deposit Insurance Fund was set up in the Czech Republic to ensure compensation to depositors. Compensation amounted to 80 per cent of an account; however, the maximum amount of any compensation was CZK 100,000 per depositor per bank. The contribution paid by the bank amounted to 0.5 per cent of the volume of insured deposits. Recently the compensation increased to 90 per cent of an account but not more than EUR 25,000. A further significant change was that this compensation scheme includes all accounts and not only household savings accounts. However, this deposit scheme does not cover accounts in foreign currencies, only CZK-denominated accounts.

However, even though a deposit insurance fund exists in the Czech Republic, it must be said that depositors were compensated only once through the above-mentioned schemes. In the other cases, retail deposits were compensated not through the fund but rather through support of the authorities. The compensation was CZK 4 million per depositor. These measures could not only be understood as an effort to avoid social tension before parliamentary elections in 1996, but also as an attempt to mitigate potential runs on small and medium-sized commercial banks. However, due to their discretionary (rather than rule-based) nature, these measures can cause a considerable moral hazard problem. Both clients and managers of commercial banks may assume that they can depend on repeat orders of such rescue activities from the authorities in the future, and take greater risks as a result.

2.5 The institutional framework of supervision and regulation

Banking supervision and regulation has a two-edged target: macro-economic and microeconomic. Therefore, it raises the problem of what the optimal institutional settlement of banking supervision should be, taking into account its complexity. There are three main possibilities for an institutional framework entrusting banking supervision: the central bank, a separate government agency, or the Ministry of Finance.

Before examining these possibilities in the Czech Republic, a basic survey of the institutional frameworks of bank supervisory bodies in an overwhelming number of member countries of the IMF is offered. Table 2.3 provides us with a view of banking supervision arrangements across the European member countries of the IMF. The UK, Finland, France, Greece, Italy, Ireland, Luxembourg, the Netherlands, Portugal and Spain have included supervision authorities in central banks, whereas in Austria, Belgium, Denmark, Germany,[6] Norway, Sweden and Switzerland, bank supervision is carried out by a separate government agency. It is worth noting that the Maastricht Treaty does not presume to include banking supervision within the European Central Bank.

Table 2.3   Banking supervision arrangements

Country	Central bank	Ministry of Finance	Other agency
Albania	X		
Austria		X	
Belgium			X
Czech Republic	X		
Denmark			X
Finland	X		
France	X		
Germany			X
Greece	X		
Hungary			X
Ireland	X		
Italy	X		
Luxembourg	X		
Netherlands	X		
Norway		X	
Poland	X		
Portugal	X		
Romania	X		
Slovak Republic	X		
Spain	X		
Sweden			X
Switzerland			X
(UK)	X		

Source: Tuya and Zamalloa (1994).

As for the situation in Central and Eastern European countries, the institutional framework is as follows: in Hungary, banking supervision is being performed by a separate supervisory agency, whereas in Poland, the Czech Republic and Romania banking supervision is carried out by the central banks; in Bulgaria banking supervision is done by the central bank up to now, although an appropriate settlement is currently being sought.

In order to answer the question regarding the adequate institutional framework of banking supervision, we should recall our discussion regarding the reasons for having banking supervision. The basic difference between the policy of the central bank and bank supervision lies in their targets. The key task of banking supervision is to ensure that the banking system displays the elements of efficiency, stability and credibility, whereas with monetary policy, the primary target is to ensure the stability of the currency. The question might thus be: are these apparently opposite targets achievable by one institution – the central bank?

As far as the institutional framework is concerned, a potential problem is that of a conflict of interest. A classic example of this arises when the central bank wants to operate a tough monetary policy in order to ease inflation pressures. This undeniably entails an interest rate increase, which increases the probability of a growth in loan defaults for banks. Conversely, banking supervision decisions also have a direct impact on monetary policy. For instance, the limitations of bank risks could cause the reduction of new loans, which might have a negative effect on investment.

By no means do we provide an exhaustive list of all the distinctive features of potential conflicts of interest between monetary policy and the supervisor. But what we want to do is find out if banking supervision arrangements are sustainable in respect of the above-described objectives. Nevertheless, we do believe that the inclusion of banking supervision by the central bank has a number of advantages. First of all, it is quite clear that if banking supervision were encompassed by the central bank, negotiations and coordination regarding targets between monetary policy and bank supervision policy would be easier. At the same time, it is required, or it should be required, that bank supervision is independent of political pressures. Therefore, if the ČNB presents a high degree of independence, then it is beneficial to place banking supervision with the central bank.

A further factor which might largely influence bank supervision activities is adequate resources. In addition, assigning bank supervision to the central bank guarantees that it will receive information about other banks' house activities. However, the opposite argument is based on the fact that any information regarding the banking sector and individual banks must be strictly confidential. If banking supervision is carried out by the central bank, leakage of relevant information is presumably more likely. Apart from this, as a strong argument for those supporting the separation of banking supervision from the central bank, there is the question of central bank credibility.

Taking another option, that of bank supervision being a role included within the Ministry of Finance, a potential peril could be that the Ministry would put pressure on a banking supervisory authority to soften its requirements on banks with respect to a negative budget impact. A similar situation has existed up to now in the Czech Republic. The Ministry of Finance has an adverse position, for example, in the case of commercial banks that are able to increase and therefore improve their reserves via a tax deduction.

The third alternative approach is to establish a state-independent agency, as is the case in Hungary. Although the results of this type of institutional framework have not displayed any weaknesses up to now, the independence of such an institution can be threatened by state bureaucracy. Such a decision on placing banking supervision in the hands of an independent agency might be quite ambiguous.

From the past we can trace the fact that whenever there are banking questions and disputes among economists and policy-makers, then policies regarding the appropriate framework of banking supervision are established. For example, the crisis in Finland at the beginning of the 1990s led to the re-establishment of banking supervision. Storms within UK banking in 1995 (Barings collapse) led to discussions about the necessity of replacing banking supervision from the Bank of England. However, we argue that establishing banking supervision has its pros and cons. Thus, these discussions among policy-makers have only one topic: concern for public welfare.

On the other hand, though, we admit that if banking supervision does not work at all, then necessary steps must be taken. The banking situation in the Czech Republic is very complicated. It is obvious that a market banking system cannot be set up in the course of only five or six years. We therefore assert that the current banking supervision that has been set up is appropriate, on condition that the objectives and strategies be made absolutely clear.

2.6   Conclusion

The banking supervision policy carried out in the Czech Republic and other CEC has taken into account a range of specific phenomena. The key distinctive factor of banking supervision and regulation in these economies was until recently the absence of a market-oriented banking system. This meant that banking supervisors actually had to establish 'the rules of the game' and ensure 'a level playing field' for all participants in a given financial market. In the Czech Republic, this period in banking supervision could be labelled as a 'learning-by-doing' process.

The ČNB has amended the legislative framework regarding commercial banks, with the primary goal of implementing the EU Directives. The present situation in CEC is more than gradually converging to standard economies and remarkable progress has been made in creating a legislative framework for the prudential operation of commercial banks since the beginning of the 1990s.

The restructuring and consolidation process of banks in the Czech Republic has seemingly come to an end, as has the transformation process. The banking system has stabilized and is not suffering from any external or internal shocks as it did at the beginning of its reformation. A legislative and institutional environment has been cultivated, regulator and prudential rules have been systematically introduced and applied, privatization is ending, and corporate governance has been gradually improved. The Czech banking system, however, is not at the end of its transition period, nor out of the transition path. The final stage is yet to come.

Notes

1. The credibility of the ČNB declined when a number of small and medium-sized banks faced bankruptcy.
2. The argument widely used by the private sector was based on the false idea that foreign banks could strengthen competitive pressures within the banking sector. There has been no evidence in EU countries that foreign banks have substantially influenced competitive pressures on domestic banks.
3. It is suggested that in many cases early regulatory intervention and closure when serious undercapitalization appears, that is, closure before technical insolvency, can help reduce the contagion effects of the collapse of an individual bank (Lastra, 1996).
4. The ČNB can remove a banking licence when bank capital falls below one-third of the required rate. The time period for removal of a banking licence in the case of a bank that does not take deposits or start operations was reduced from 18 months to 12 months.
5. The issue of fuller disclosure is an important topic in New Zealand, where no protection of depositors exists.
6. In Germany, however, the Federal Banking Supervisory Office mainly provides licences. Off-site supervision is carried out by the Deutsche Bundesbank.

References

Claessens, S. *Banking Reform in Transition-Countries* (Washington, DC: World Development Report, World Bank, 1996).

Diamond, W.D. and Dybrig, P. 'Bank Runs, Deposit Insurance, and Liquidity', *Journal of Political Economy*, 93, 3 (1983), 401–19.

Lastra, M.R. *Central Banking and Banking Regulation* (London: London School of Economics, Financial market Group, 1996).

Lindgren, C.J. *et al. Bank Soundness and Macroeconomic Policy* (Washington, DC: International Monetary Fund, 1998).

Matoušek, R. 'Banking sector restructuring and debt consolidation in the Czech Republic', in Dickinson, D. and Mullineux, A. (eds) *Financial and Monetary Integration in the New Europe: Convergence between the EU and Central and Eastern Europe* (Aldershot, UK: Edward Elgar, 2002).

Matoušek, R. and Taci, A. 'The Assessment of the Costs and Benefits of the Small and Medium Commercial Banks within the Czech Banking Sector', in Hölscher, J. (ed.) *Financial Turbulence and Capital Markets in Transition Countries* (London: Macmillan, 2000).

Tuya, J. and Zamalloa, I. 'Issues on Placing Banking Supervision in the Central Bank', in Balino, J.T. and Cottarelli, C. (eds) *Frameworks for Monetary Stability* (Washington, DC: IMF Institute, 1994).

3
Concentration of Banking Sectors

Stanislav Polouček

After the Second World War, with the increase in government intervention, and therefore the restricted role of market forces in the restoration of equilibrium, much greater attention was given to problems of market structure, concentration and competition. Concentration is a vital factor because it is closely connected with market equilibrium; it also directly affects companies' efficiency and their position in the market.

The goal of this chapter is to evaluate and compare the concentration of the banking sectors in the Czech Republic, Poland and Slovakia. The first section will give an overview of the economic theory underlying the banks' concentration in these sectors; the second explains various concepts and quantification by applying two methods – the concentration ratio and the Herfindahl–Hirschman Index (HHI). The third section applies the above-mentioned methods to the Czech, Polish and Slovak banking sectors.

3.1 Concentration and economic theory

A number of authors focus attention on the analysis of concentration both on the theoretical and practical levels. A traditional paradigm giving emphasis to the dependence of performance (output) on the structure of the market (structure–conduct–performance – SCP) is in line with general opinion. In other words, a company's market force and the restriction of competition grow with concentration. The primary formulation of this hypothesis comes from Bain (1951). He concludes that a smaller number of selling companies in the market (that is, a more concentrated structure) restricts competitiveness in behaviour (as reflected in higher prices and restricted outputs) at the expense of a lower price for consumer's welfare. This hypothesis has been the result of empirical research, based on the analysis of American manufacturing industry. However, more precise methods and forms of expression were later sought. Empirical literature focuses in most cases on the examination of the effects of concentration on the output of industries and on the entire economy. The authors of the studies set their objective mostly to clarify whether the structural characteristics of the industry and its monopoly structure found practical fulfilment in the companies' behaviour and management. Attention is more and more drawn to the expression of concentration by means of indicators and their specifications.

A very apt survey of economic theory in the area of concentration is a study by Curry and George (1983). They emphasize that there is no ideal concentration index and, in accordance with Hall and Tideman (1967), they argue that there is a collection of desirable properties which each applied index of concentration might comply with:

- it should be a one-dimensional measure;
- concentration in an industry should be independent of the size of that industry;
- concentration should increase if the share of any firm is increased at the expense of a smaller firm;
- if all firms are divided into K equal parts, then the concentration index should be reduced by the proportion $1/K$;
- if there are N firms of equal size, then concentration should be a decreasing function of N;
- the concentration measure should be between zero and one.

They look through the prism of these principles at some of the indicators of concentration which are applied in economic theory (the Herfindahl–Hirschman Index, the K-firm concentration ratio, the Gini coefficient and others). They also pay attention to other factors which affect concentration, such as the average size of companies, the size of industries, developmental trends and mergers.

A series of research studies has confirmed that in some market situations, the SCP hypothesis holds true and the indicators of companies' performance prove to have a correlation with the indicators of concentration. The existence of dependence between concentration and performance is confirmed by the latest studies, although a number of them conclude that this relation may be noticeably modified by specific conditions in individual markets.

An alternative to this traditional interpretation of the relation between concentration, competitiveness and effectiveness is a hypothesis of an efficient structure held, for instance, by Berger and Hannan (1989). According to them, higher profits in concentrated markets are not a result of applying a privileged position of these companies in the non-competitive environment, but a consequence of their higher efficiency. According to the hypothesis of efficient structure, we can deal with considerably higher efficiency in some areas of business.[1] A higher efficiency of large companies may be a result of higher investments and innovations. Hyytinen and Toivanen (2000) arrive at the conclusion that banks which invest in the network of affiliated branches and human capital contribute to obtain information, but not to gain or to strengthen market force. Both obtaining of information and strengthening of market force require usually high fixed investments. Higher efficiency consequently means, for individual companies, a higher than average market efficiency. Wherever this company is located, more efficient companies gain a higher market share at the expense of smaller and less efficient companies, as expressed through direct proportion between profit and concentration.

From this perspective, the SCP hypothesis and the hypothesis of the efficient structure arrive at the same conclusion when analysing the relationship between concentration and profit, but they differ in substance and in their conclusions. First of all, it is very significant from the point of view of the approach to the role of the market and state in the economy: the SCP hypothesis implies a potentially positive role of the policy targeted at monopolies and concentration, as well as at the common procedure and secret companies' agreements, since the goal of this behaviour is to increase market force and to reduce total output. The hypothesis of efficient structure implies that the intention of concentration is the growth of efficiency, and, therefore, activities limiting concentration may have an adverse impact on companies' efficiency as well as on entire industries in an economy.

3.1.1 Economic theory and concentration in banking

Empirical studies which draw attention to the relation between profit and market concentration, or the relation between the level of prices and concentration, or which deal with the SCP hypothesis in the banking sector, are often done in developed countries. Many of them proceed from the traditional industrial organization rationale for competition in banking. Others highlight differences between banking and other industries of the economy (Allen and Gale, 2000). Among the most prominent studies are those by Alhadeff (1954), Guttentag and Herman (1967),

Mote (1967) and Gilbert (1984), who deal with the analysis of the profit-concentration equation, and as mentioned earlier, a study by Berger and Hannan focusing on the relationship between prices and concentration in banking. By and large, these studies find a positive correlation between the indicators of the market structure (for example, concentration or market share) on the one hand, and profits, returns or prices on the other. This proves that the structure of the banking sector affects both the price and the quantity of the banking services offered. Such concentrated banking markets could, as a result, be less efficient and less transparent. But the results of these studies are not often convincing, and in many cases, contradict each other (Fraser and Rose, 1971). For this reason their practical influence on the formation of the structure of the banking sector is very limited.

Gilbert's paper (1984) analyses the results of economic studies in the area of measuring market structure and performance (criteria for defining the most appropriate indicators, results of empirical studies of the relation structure–performance), regression equations and so on. Moreover, in the above-mentioned paper, Gilbert points out that very few studies deal with another very significant determinant of the banking sector – regulation.[2] According to his research, this has an essential influence on the structure–performance relationship.

Calem and Carlino (1991) pick up the threads of the study by Berger and Hannan and look for confirmation of the SCP hypothesis on small deposits in the American market. Unlike the other studies, theirs explicitly considers behaviour on the local deposit market to be determined by the relationship between structure and performance, and they conclude that banks usually act competitively or strategically, whether or not their behaviour is affected by the market concentration. Further, their study differs from analogical research in that their empirical research is based on the model of the market balance of small deposits. The authors come to the conclusion that strategic behaviour is common in all markets studied: in MMDAs (money market deposit accounts) and on three- and six-monthly deposit certificates.

Apart from that, Calem and Carlino conclude that there is a certain monopoly in deposit rates even in non-concentrated markets; the banks act strategically regardless of market concentration. They come to a somewhat different conclusion from most of the studies concerning the American market, arguing that there is a high level of competition in these markets. When competition is directly based on an analysis of the number of banks and their branches, the American market can be regarded as very competitive. Nevertheless, a relatively high number of banks and branches in the USA is not a result of competition but regulation, a consequence of the McFadden–Pepper Act (1927).

As early as the mid-1960s, Edwards (1965) dealt with the analysis of the relationship between concentration in banking and interest rates for small clients. He concluded that the bond existing is none the less not strong. Besides the above-mentioned relationship, Edwards analyses some drawbacks of the concentrated banking market, for instance, a strenuous application of monetary policy, provided that interest rates are not flexible. In his earlier paper (1964) he had tested two hypotheses: (1) that the level of business loan rates is higher in markets having relatively high concentration; and (2) that business loan rates are less flexible in markets having relatively high concentration. The conclusion is that there is a certain relationship between market structure and market performance in banking markets.

Bell and Murphy (1969) also analysed the influence of concentration on prices, which is, according to them, positive and significant. They point out the dilemma connected with mergers, that is, the average increase in company size may have a positive effect on cost efficiency, which can result in lowering prices. In addition, the other way round, mergers mean a growth of concentration and therefore an increase in prices, too. The final outcome depends on the relative size of both aforementioned effects.

Fraser and Rose (1971) selected in their analysis samples of small banks from the state of Texas, where they saw the relationship between the banking structure and banking performance. They concluded that the relation between concentration and company output is not statistically significant.

Galbraith (1967, chs 3 and 7) assigns a vital role to the mutual relation between uncertainty and market organization. According to him, a company's performance depends largely on how companies are organized and what their reciprocal relations are. He devotes his study to crucial but often ignored aspects of the behaviour of large companies. First of all, he shows that large companies are aware that they dispose of a larger market power than smaller companies and that elimination of uncertainty forms a significant part of potential profit (resulting from their market power). Therefore, these companies are willing to give up the extra profit for the benefit of 'a quiet life' and they become more risk-averse. Caves (1970, p. 284) expands on the idea and he makes the effort to define its validity. He points out that more risk-averse managers, who free themselves from stockholders' pressure (from those demanding to maximize the value of the company), could manage large companies.

Edwards and Heggestad (1973) test the Galbraith–Caves hypothesis, that is, the conclusion that a firm's risk-avoidance behavior varies directly with its degree of market power. The authors come to that conclusion, which is not identical with the stated hypothesis. The result of their analysis is a verification of a statistically significant inverse relation between the companies' market power and their profit margin ratio. Their analysis was derived from a sample of large banks. In their opinion, managers of large companies may be more risk-averse, as these banks have the advantage to exploit more market opportunities. However, the authors refer to certain deficiencies in the initial hypothesis, as there is no specification of preconditions and reasons which may lead to avoidance of uncertainty. This is precisely what Edwards and Heggestad regard as substantial. If managers of large companies are more risk-averse without using the above-mentioned market opportunities, then the Galbraith–Caves hypothesis has an essential importance. It applies first to a number of empirical studies devoted to the relationship between companies' (or industrial) performance and the market structure, as some analysts presuppose the same relationship towards risk in all the companies studied.

In comparison to previous studies which concentrate on examining the influence of concentration in the banking sector on the banking output, a rather different approach is applied by Cetorelli (2001). Cetorelli explores the effects of banking concentration on the market structure of the other industries of the economy. The results of this work illustrate a significant relationship – more concentrated banking is found to enhance industries' market concentration, especially in sectors highly dependent on external finance. The author has no reservations about the fact that banks with larger market power may concentrate lending to fewer firms with whom they have already established long-lasting relationships. This restricts extension of credit to new entrants. Cetorelli also refers to the fact that the effect of concentration in the banking sector is heterogeneous across countries, with a weaker effect in countries with a more efficient legal structure and more developed financial markets.

Conditions of entry and competitive conduct in highly concentrated banking markets are topics of another paper by Cetorelli (2002). Its methodology is based on the entry thresholds definition – the author estimates the minimum market size at which a second bank, a third, a fourth and so on can enter and maintain long-run profitability. The results suggest no evidence of cartel-like behaviour, where banks collude and maximize joint monopoly profits, even in highly concentrated US banking markets with only two or three banks.

One of the latest studies, which deals with the effect of concentration in banking on the structure of the other industries, is by Petersen and Rajan (1995). They argue that banks with larger market power facilitate access to credits by young and less-known companies with a conviction that they will be able to profit from future incomes of these companies, as they become profitable. It is obvious that a bank may be interested in continuing relations established this way, and at the same time refuse to grant credit to other new companies. The increase in market competition would lower profitability of their former (key) clients. This leads Petersen and Rajan to conclude that concentration in the banking sector may increase concentration in other industries of the economy. They also conclude that the top managers of banks, who are located in concentrated markets, may have closer ties to key clients. Therefore, governed by strategic decisions resulting from maximizing bank profitability, they continue to support these clients.

With reference to the credit crunch of the 1990s, numerous studies dealt with the analysis of the influence of concentration in the credit market and credit rationing. Pagano (1993) and Guzman (2000) concluded that concentration in banking limits balance in credit markets, resulting in credit rationing, and, subsequently, negatively influencing economic growth. Shaffer (1998) also claims that the average quality of the bank's credit portfolio is inversely proportional to the number of banks competing against each other, and that banking concentration has a negative influence on economic growth.

An empirical investigation of the relationship between market share or concentration and return on equity or assets in the European banking sector is a major feature of the study by Punt and van Rooij (1999). They come to the conclusion that the existence of the profit structure relationship and X-efficiency (managerial efficiency) is a crucial factor because it stimulates both profitability and market share.

The existence of the SCP hypothesis and empirical studies relating to concentration and competition in banking have likewise been considered in transition economies in recent years. In past decades, there has been an increase in concentration in the banking sector of these countries, owing to numerous factors, such as the decrease in the number of banks and an increase in their average size. At the same time, with the decrease in the quantity of banks, there has been a plunge in the number of banks' branches. While competition has primarily influenced concentration, closing branches reflects the banks' efforts to increase efficiency in their activities by closing non-profitable units, and simultaneously by offering products through electronic distribution channels (e-banking and others).[3] Of course, this trend is also strong due to pressure from competition.

A relatively high concentration of activities in the banking sector in the hands of a few banks in most of the countries around the world raises the question of whether the banking sector is efficient and if its profitability is not a result of returns gained because of monopolistic prices at the clients' expense. Due to high concentration, banks are conveniently able to make conditions setting and keeping higher interest margins, credit rationing, and, as is often the case, a strong negotiating position. Higher concentration also creates additional room for banks to collude, thus resulting in their higher profitability. In transition economies, a non-transparent environment as a result of, for instance, market imperfections, a non-developed capital market, and so on, has an indisputable effect on the banks' greater powers.

The SCP hypothesis and its defence for transition economies still has a great number of opponents. Risk of a negative influence of concentration on efficiency, in their opinion, does not loom large, provided that the banking sector is open, especially when dealing with a small open economy. In this case, then, banks face competition not only from other companies in the financial sector, but also from foreign banks. The globalization process, information technologies and a deregulation process would weaken the possibilities of misusing high concentration in any industry, particularly in banking. Punt and van Rooij (1999) provide evidence that there are no indications of unfavourable price-setting behaviour because of increased market power in the European banking sector. On the other hand, theory and experience demonstrate the significance of competition for efficiency, and confirm that a competitive environment requires a system that is open to competition, but not necessarily to a large number of institutions. A concentrated system can be competitive if it is contestable (that is, if competition is open). In addition, experience from many countries verifies the same fact, as attested by data from the Czech Republic, Slovakia and Poland.

3.2   The concept and measurement of concentration

The quantification of concentration belongs to the most significant and at the same time debatable areas of market analysis and market structure. Economists' attention was drawn to prices in the 1930s.

Lerner (1934) suggested that to express a deviation from the competitive ideal, the difference between price and marginal cost divided by price ([P − MC]/P) may be used. A disadvantage of this approach lies in the fact that this is essentially only a subsequent (*ex post*) measure of allocative inefficiency of an industry. It may also be influenced by factors other than the monopoly power of some firms. Moreover, it is rather hard to obtain necessary information on cost factors (Feinberg, 1980).

Kaldor (1935) proposed applying cross-elasticities of demand to express concentration, while Rothschild (1942) considered measurement based on the angle between the segments and a kinked demand curve. They mentioned ways of measuring market power which are theoretically quite interesting; nevertheless, a problem arises again in terms of the calculation and definition of data concerning the demand factor.

Gradually, economists' attention turned to the application of the size distribution of firms in industries – a method of measuring concentration which, according to numerous economists, is much easier to calculate (Curry and George, 1983). In this case, a number of methods can be applied for quantifying a level of concentration. In essence, all of these quantify an extent, in which an examined feature (in the banking sector, for instance, the volume of deposits, the volume of credits, capital, interest income, or expenses) of a particular company (a bank in the banking sector, an insurance company in the insurance market) accounts for the whole sum of values of this feature in the entire sector (banking sector, insurance sector and so on).

Depending on whether the indicators quantify a level of concentration with reference to all subjects of the banking (financial) sector, or should be regarded as a subset with a specific attribute, we can measure two kinds of concentration: absolute and relative. Relative concentration is expressed by means of the dispersal ratio or the variation coefficient. The dispersal ratio relates to the ratio of concentration corresponding to particular groups of subjects with the highest value of the examined indicator. The variation coefficient expresses the ratio of the composition of influences of all subjects from the point of view of the studied indicator. The expression of absolute concentration is applied in this chapter; it can be measured by means of the concentration ratio or by the Herfindahl–Hirschman Index (HHI).

It is essential to stress that it is very complicated to measure the above-mentioned outputs despite great developments in economic theory. The same applies to banking – mainly because of the variety of banking outputs: banks offer a wide spectrum of services and activities and costs are affected by many internal and external factors. According to some economists (Fraser and Rose, 1971), banks' efficiency should not be expressed by a simple production function, such as total credits or total deposits, but rather by total indicators, which take into consideration both internal and external bank's characteristics, that is, market structure, demand for banking services, significance of non-banking financial institutions, banking costs, credit structure, a bank's size. For this reason, as stated above, one would agree with Curry and George's opinion (1983) that there is no ideal indicator of concentration.

3.2.1   Concentration ratio

One of the oldest and most mentioned indices of market concentration is concentration ratio. It expresses a ratio of a defined number of ψ subjects (for instance 3, 4, 6, 10, 25, 50 or 100) with the highest value of the studied indicator for the industry's production, or for a production of a specifically defined group of companies. It is extremely simple to calculate, but the choice of ψ is somewhat arbitrary. The analytical expression of the concentration ratio is the following:

$$CR_\psi = \frac{1}{Q} \sum_{k=1}^{\psi} q_k \qquad (3.1)$$

where $\psi = (1, n)$, Q is production,
and for quantities of production of q_k companies

$$q_p > q_{p+1} \quad \text{for } p = 1, 2, \ldots, n-1.$$

The inequality expresses the fact that companies are arranged in descending order for the needs of an analysis according to the examined indicator. Coefficients of the ratio of concentration assume values from the interval

$$0 \leq CR_\psi \leq 100.$$

The ratio of concentration is usually measured in percentages – in this case, the following holds true:

$$CR_\psi = \frac{100}{Q} \sum_{k=1}^{\psi} q_k \qquad (3.2)$$

In the case of the equal division of the studied indicator among all subjects of the industry, that is, if the following holds true,

$$q_k = q_{k=1} = \frac{Q}{n} \quad \text{for } k = 1, 2, \ldots, n-1$$

the value of the concentration ratio for any grouping of products is expressed in the form

$$CR_\psi = \frac{1}{Q}\sum_{k=1}^{\psi} q_k = \frac{1}{Q}\sum_{k=1}^{\psi} \frac{Q}{n} = \frac{Q}{Q}\frac{\psi}{n} = \frac{\psi}{n} \tag{3.3}$$

and as a percentage expressing the ratio of concentration:

$$CR_\psi = \frac{100}{Q}\sum_{k=1}^{\psi} q_k = \frac{100}{Q}\sum_{k=1}^{\psi} \frac{Q}{n} = \frac{100Q}{Q}\frac{\psi}{n} = 100\frac{\psi}{n}. \tag{3.4}$$

3.2.2 Herfindahl–Hirschman Index

The Herfindahl–Hirschman Index (HHI) also expresses absolute concentration. It considers both the number of banks in a banking sector, and their share in the market. Its construction is based on the hypothesis that the bank's denotation is a function of the second power of its market share in the banking sector. This concept of concentration highlights the influence of economically 'small' banks. It allows us simultaneously to assess concentration if we do not have the data of a 'small' bank or when examining the influence of marginal or external companies which offer products of the considered industry. Banking belongs to the industries where a number of non-banking subjects offer products similar or close to the banks' products in past years.

HHI is defined as the sum of the squared market shares of all banks in the market. The analytical expression of HHI is the formula

$$H = h(q_1, q_2, ..., q_n) = \sum_{k=1}^{n}\left(\frac{q_k}{Q}\right)^2 = \sum_{k=1}^{n} r_k^2 \tag{3.5}$$

where

h is real function of n variables, $h: R^n \to R$;
n is number of banks in the banking sector;
q_k is production quantity of k-bank; $k = 1, 2, ..., n$;
Q is production quantity of banking sector;
r_k is share of k-bank in the production volume of the banking sector.

Extreme values of HHI are interesting. Should the division of the studied indicator be equal to particular banks, it would mean that

$$q_k = q_{k=1} = \frac{Q}{n} \quad k = 1, ..., n - 1. \tag{3.6}$$

In this case, the value of HHI is the lowest for any number of banks in the banking sector. The value is not always the same; it is a function of the number of banks in the banking sector. To put it differently, with the given number of banks, HHI reaches a minimum value H_d only when the market share of each bank is identical in the studied indicator, that is, when equation (3.6) holds true.

If we replace (3.6) by (3.5), then we obtain:

$$H_d = h(q_1, q_2, \ldots, q_n) = \sum_{k=1}^{n} \left(\frac{q_k}{Q}\right)^2 = \sum_{k=1}^{n} \left(\frac{\frac{Q}{n}}{Q}\right)^2 = \frac{1}{n^2} = \frac{1}{n} \qquad (3.7)$$

On the other side the upper maximum limit of HHI is $H^h = 1$; this extreme situation holds in the case of absolute monopoly. In this case, $n = 1$, $q = Q$ and after replacing it by (3.5) we obtain:

$$H^h = h(q) = \sum_{k=1}^{1} \left(\frac{q_k}{Q}\right)^2 = \left(\frac{Q}{Q}\right)^2 = 1 \qquad (3.8)$$

The HHI value comes near to the value 1 if there is a relatively low number of banks or if the relatively low number of banks realizes a substantial part of production in the corresponding market.

In many countries, HHI is used as one of the indicators when permitting mergers and acquisitions[4] – the levels and the marginal increase in the indicator are fixed, in which case the merger or takeover can be considered as a non-infringing environment for competition, and therefore, allowed (Ahi, 2002, p. 1013; Jackowicz and Kowalewski, 2002; Cetorelli, 2002, p. 18). These values are usually higher for banking than for other sectors of the economy. Principally, there are three basic levels of concentration: a non-concentrated market, a medium concentrated market and a concentrated market.[5] We are dealing here with very sensitive problems, for which an economic interpretation of the obtained data has a key meaning. The decisions of the European Court of First Instance are evidence of this (October 2002), ruling that the Merger Task Force (MTF), the body within the European Commission responsible for reviewing mergers, was wrong to block several mergers in 1999–2000. One of the reasons was, according to the European Court, that MTF's economic analysis of the relevant markets was marked by 'errors, omissions, and contradictions'. The MTF muddled its arguments and overestimated the combined group's likely economic power.

3.3 Concentration in the banking sectors of the Czech Republic, Poland and Slovakia

In transition economies, we can observe two fundamental developmental trends in the last decade. The transition to a market economy is principally linked with a distinct growth of the number of banks in all countries. This growth leads to a reduction of concentration, which is partly induced by the fact that new banks gain some of the clients of the formerly established banks. On the other hand, dynamic growth of the market takes place, and new banks gain most new clients. Owing to the fact that financial and banking sectors of transition economies are markedly underdeveloped,[6] we are dealing here with a relatively broad spectrum for further expansion and change.

The banks' and banking sector's difficulties, banks' collapses and banking crises, and much stricter regulation as well as the increasing openness of banking sectors and consequently rising foreign competition in a series of countries have, however, led to a decline in the number of banks after some time in all transition economies. Efficiency is slowly being pressured in these countries, and globalization tendencies related to mergers and acquisitions lead in a great number of cases to a noticeable decrease in the number of banks. This trend is associated with increasing competition in the banking sector, and in a number of transition economies means that, in comparison with other countries and regions, the banking sector is highly concentrated. Nevertheless, there is a tendency present throughout, which is also typical of developed countries. Suominen (1994) refers to the Finnish banking sector, which is a striking monopolistic environment. What is interesting is that, according to this study, the banks' non-competitive behaviour has been strengthened after deregulation. The financial market and the Finnish banking market until the mid-1980s used to be rather competitive.

The Department of Bank Supervision of the ČNB had, in its reports until 1999, given the status of banks in relation to large and small-sized banks. Since 2002, it has stated that an independent group of medium-sized banks and the uniform criterion for the banks' division according to the groups is the size of the total balance. The group of large-sized banks includes banks with a total balance higher than CZK 100 billion; among medium-sized banks are ranked banks, which administer a total balance in the vicinity of CZK 15–100 billion. The number of banks in this structure, as calculated, is given in Table 1.4 in Chapter 1.

The number of banks affects the analysis, since it is subject to change, and so does the structure of the largest three banks. Moreover, there are data in the Czech Republic pertaining to the banking sector which are noticeably influenced by the transfer of some selected activities into the Consolidation Bank, respectively into the Czech Consolidation Agency.[7]

If we look at the Czech banking sector by the ratio of concentration of the three largest banks (Komerční banka, Česká spořitelna and Československá obchodní banka) and HHI, we can see the results of the calculations in Table 3.1 and in Figures 3.1 and 3.2.

Table 3.1   Market share and Herfindahl–Hirschman Index of the banking sector in the Czech Republic (1994–2001)*

	Market share (%)			Herfindahl–Hirschman Index		
	Total balance	Clients' credits	Clients' deposits	Total balance	Clients' credits	Clients' deposits
1994: IV	56.32	53.74	75.41	1190.18	1187.20	2371.88
1995: IV	51.52	54.44	67.11	1013.23	1254.77	1803.38
1996: IV	51.71	55.55	68.48	1019.20	1271.42	1860.18
1997: IV	50.45	56.18	65.15	969.18	1208.00	1630.69
1998: IV	48.17	49.22	61.55	875.32	937.43	1443.79
1999: IV	43.13	42.90	61.12	722.65	763.76	1370.12
2000: IV	54.03	54.86	80.83	1036.41	1176.59	2202.98
2001: I	54.23	53.58	73.95	1047.23	1121.49	1858.96
II	54.55	52.72	72.21	1054.83	1076.21	1779.84
III	58.28	64.09	74.43	1186.87	1469.27	1892.13
IV	58.24	73.83	75.59	1185.27	1849.30	1952.87

* Czech accounting standards, non-consolidated data.

Source: Author's calculations based on data from banks and ČNB.

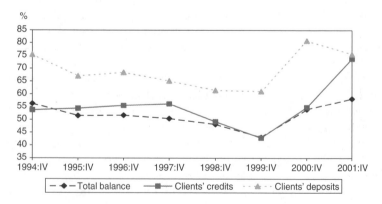

Figure 3.1   Market share of the three selected banks in the Czech Republic in relation to the selected indicators of the banking sector (1994–2001)

Source: Author's calculations based on data from banks and ČNB.

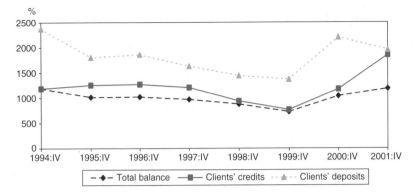

Figure 3.2   Herfindahl–Hirschman Index of the banking sector in the Czech Republic (1994–2001)

Source: Author's calculations based on data from banks and ČNB.

As is evident from the above data and figures, the situation in the Czech banking sector from 1994 to 2001 had not radically changed[8] from the point of view of concentration. It had gone through a relatively diverse development in the studied areas (assets, credits, deposits), which did not correspond to the changes in the number of banks in the banking sector. The number of banks increased until 1995, and then there was a steady decrease in number. The period of increase in the number of banks, as well as the following period of decrease, was accompanied by a reduction of concentration in the total balance of clients' deposits, until the year 1999, as shown by the market share of the three largest banks or by the HHI. On the contrary, concentration of credits markedly increased in 1994–97 and noticeably dropped in 1998–99. There was distinct concentration of credits in 2000–2001, which reflected credit rationing in the Czech Republic during this period.

Throughout this period, the increase in importance of medium-sized banks has been noticeable. Their shares in deposits and credits increased in 2000 due to a considerable change in the Czech banking market which took place that year because of privatization in the banking sector[9] and continuing mergers and acquisitions. Concentration in the banking sector in the Czech Republic is markedly influenced by changes in the number of banks and the collapse of relatively large ones.[10] Subsequently, in 2001, a merger of HypoVereinsbank CZ and Bank Austria Creditanstalt Czech Republic took place (which followed the merger of controlling companies of these banks), and a conversion of the Consolidation bank into a 'non-bank subject'. Because of this conversion, there was an increase in the HHI of customer credits and deposits in 2001, after several years of decrease.

In 2000, the takeover of Investment and Post Bank (which, by the end of 1999, was the third largest Czech bank in total balance and number four in total capital) by ČSOB (which, by the end of 1999, was the fourth largest Czech bank in total balance and number three in total capital) noticeably contributed to the increase in concentration in the Czech banking sector. Because of this takeover, ČSOB increased deposits and credits by more than 100 per cent and acquired more than a quarter share in the market.[11]

In any case, the values of the concentration ratio, as well as the HHI with all three indicators, markedly exceeded the recommended orientation values. There is also a relatively high concentration in the Czech Republic in other sectors of the financial market, for instance, in insurance, as demonstrated by data relating to the concentration ratio and HHI in Table 3.2 and Figure 3.3. Česká pojišt'ovna (the Czech Insurance Company) gradually lost its monopolistic (dominant) position as concentration in life insurance declined; nevertheless its market share is very high and the HHI in Czech insurance is well above the recommended value of 1,800.

The Slovak banking sector demonstrates similar tendencies, and its development is comparable to that of Czech banking. Three of its largest banks (Slovenská sporitel'ňa, Všeobecná úverová banka, Tatra banka) created a highly concentrated environment in the banking sector, as was the case in the Czech Republic. The growth of the number of banks in Slovakia is given in Table 1.5 of Chapter 1.

The concentration of the Slovak banking sector through the market shares of the three largest banks, and through HHI, is shown in the calculations of Table 3.3 and in Figures 3.4 and 3.5.

Table 3.2 Life insurance concentration ratio and Herfindahl–Hirschman Index in the Czech Republic (1997–2001)

	Total amount (CZK bn)	Share of Česká Pojišt'ovna (%)	Share of IPB Pojišt'ovna (%)	Share of Pojišt'ovna Kooperativa (%)	Total share (%)	HHI
1997	12.7	57.2	11.9	x	69.1*	3438.58
1998	15.0	52.6	14.3	2.7	69.6	3002.86
1999	19.9	42.8	22.2	3.7	68.7	2362.86
2000	22.8	41.2	15.8	6.6	63.6	2025.51
2001	28.4	42.3	11.3	7.3	60.9	2010.50

* Only Česká pojišt'ovna and IPB Pojišt'ovna.

Source: Czech Association of Insurance Companies.

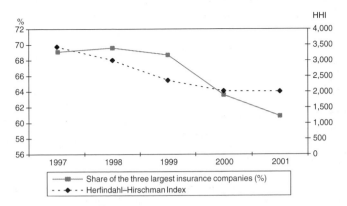

Figure 3.3 Herfindahl–Hirschman Index and concentration ratio of life insurance in the Czech Republic (1997–2001)

Source: Czech Association of Insurance Companies.

Table 3.3 Market share and Herfindahl–Hirschman Index of the banking sector in the Slovak Republic (1996–2001)*

	Market share (%)			Herfindahl–Hirschman Index		
	Total balance	Clients' credits	Clients' deposits	Total balance	Clients' credits	Clients' deposits
1996	52.50	49.96	60.71	1261.43	1299.51	1577.92
1997	48.86	48.61	61.44	1084.61	1205.65	1605.24
1998	46.87	50.27	64.95	1002.03	1219.04	1829.00
1999	50.08	43.64	62.20	1071.21	926.62	1611.94
2000	52.43	44.81	62.56	1132.52	923.18	1533.64
2001	54.72	32.30	63.47	1177.68	622.87	1547.91

* According to the Slovak accounting standards, non-consolidated data.

Source: Author's calculations based on data from banks and NBS.

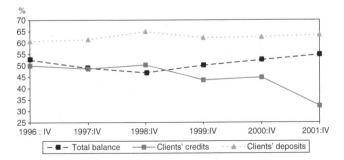

Figure 3.4 Market share of the three selected banks in the Slovak Republic in relation to the selected indicators of the banking sector (1996–2001)

Source: Author's calculations based on data from banks and NBS.

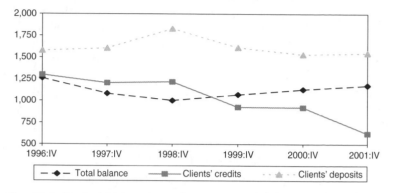

Figure 3.5   Herfindahl–Hirschman Index of the banking sector in the Slovak Republic (1996–2001)

Source: Author's calculations based on data from banks and NBS.

In Slovakia, the process of changes in concentration in the 1990s is analogous to that of the Czech Republic. A significant share in the market belongs to Slovenská sporitel'ňa, whereby its balance is made up of more than 20 per cent of the total balance of the Slovak banking sector, and still shows an increasing trend. The total of this bank's deposits is also high (reaching a third of total deposits), showing a very slight decreasing trend. The same tendency applies to Všeobecná úvěrová banka, whose shares are slightly lower than that of Slovenská sporitel'ňa. If we consider the relatively dynamic growth of the share of Tatrabanka in clients' deposits and a slight increase in the total balance, the outcome is that of mounting concentration in the banking sector. Note also that in these three banks, there is an unequivocally stagnating feature in clients' deposits in the years 1999–2001. In the case of total balances, the largest banks demonstrate an increasing trend. Concurrently, both indicators, with the exception of clients' credits, have exceeded the recommended values.

The Polish banking sector differs to some extent from the Czech and Slovak sectors, not only because the Polish economy is noticeably larger and there are naturally more banks in its banking sector. As data and a further analysis will show, there is a considerably lower concentration in the banking sector in Poland than in the above-mentioned countries. The standing of the largest banks is also different if we take into consideration the criteria of capital and assets, confirming the fact that there is not much difference in the size of these banks. The number of banks in Poland is given in Table 1.5 and Table 1.6 in Chapter 1.

Let us now look at the concentration in the Polish banking sector by the market share of the three largest banks and HHI,[12] as contained in Table 3.4 and Figures 3.6 and 3.7.

As the data and figures confirm, the changes in concentration in Poland were relatively small in the six-year period. It slowly decreased until 1997, and increased in subsequent years. The largest changes were clients' credits, the same situation in Poland as in the Czech Republic and Slovakia, with a significant difference – in comparison with the Czech Republic and Slovakia, it was markedly lower in Poland.

Table 3.4 Market share and the Herfindahl–Hirschman Index of the banking sector in Poland (1994–2000)

	Market share (%)			Herfindahl–Hirschman Index		
	Total balance	Clients' credits*	Clients' deposits*	Total balance	Clients' credits*	Clients' deposits*
1994: IV	42.19	40.37	47.66	850	878	1070
1995: IV	41.46	37.27	50.85	859	760	1227
1996: IV	39.91	32.33	48.59	788	625	1144
1997: IV	38.83	30.67	47.61	758	579	1129
1998: IV	43.07	37.33	51.24	883	706	1239
1999: IV	40.21	36.85	49.20	807	719	1136
2000: IV	42.13	40.40	48.46	834	776	1124

* Account receivables and clients' and state budget's deposits.

Source: Jackowicz and Kowalewski (2001).

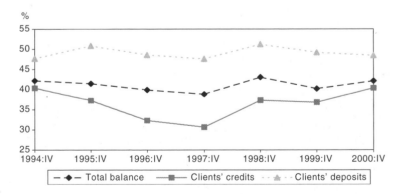

Figure 3.6 Market share of the three selected banks in Poland in relation to the selected indicators of the banking sector (1994–2000)

Source: Jackowicz and Kowalewski (2001).

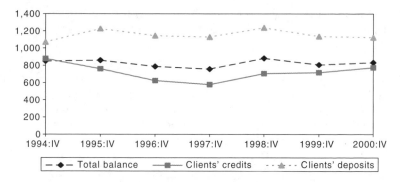

Figure 3.7 Herfindahl–Hirschman Index of the banking sector in Poland (1994–2000)

Source: Jackowicz and Kowalewski (2001).

3.4   Conclusion

Concentration in the banking sector has been relatively higher in the Czech Republic and in Slovakia than in banks of most developed countries and transition economies. This is evidenced by data in the Polish banking sector as well as other studies, which were elaborated in previous years by other authors (Table 3.5). A highly concentrated sector is usually considered one in which the share of the three largest banks (concentration ratio) is higher than 55 per cent in selected indicators, or where the HHI is higher than 1,800.

On the other hand, it is appropriate to note that among developed countries there are also economies where the share of the three largest banks is very high in certain indicators of the banking sector (Finland, Greece, the Netherlands, Denmark and others). In the 1990s, concentration has increased in all the major countries (Table 3.6).

The high level of concentration in the Czech Republic and in Slovakia is a result of the specific Czech and Slovak (Czechoslovak) development of banking after 1990. Nevertheless, the openness of both economies, relatively liberal entry into the banking sector and foreign competition form a relatively competitive environment in the banking sector.

All three economies demonstrate some similar tendencies. First and foremost, the concentration of clients' deposits is the highest in the indicators studied. It is evident that problems of the banking sector were reflected in small banks; as for savings, these were deposited in the large banks. After the initial stage of the concentration's weakening in all the countries, we can observe that in the second half of the 1990s,

Table 3.5 Structure and performance of the banking sector in some transition countries

	Number of banks	Total assets mean (USD thousand)	ROA (%) mean	Concentration*
Bulgaria	18	536,684.70	1.26	60.75
Croatia	23	502,256.20	0.28	70.43
Czech Republic	16	1,776,398.00	0.26	78.08
Estonia	9	57,758.01	1.54	71.57
Hungary	28	632,230.90	1.34	42.19
Latvia	8	77,419.50	2.68	54.07
Lithuania	7	83,280.86	0.23	66.83
Poland	31	922,551.60	2.36	45.73
Romania	9	926,777.80	3.30	72.56
Slovak Republic	13	1,688,554.00	0.74	63.40
Slovenia	7	336,435.80	0.92	89.10

* Three-bank asset concentration ratio.

Source: Mullineux and Green (1998, p. 151).

Table 3.6 Concentration in the banking industry (1992–2001)

	1992	1995		1998		2001	
	Number of participants	Number of participants	Number of banks covering 75%	Number of participants	Number of banks covering 75%	Number of participants	Number of banks covering 75%
United Kingdom	352	313	20[a]	293	24	257	17
United States	180	130	20[b]	93	20	79	13
Japan	330	345	24	356	19	342	17
Singapore	208	218	25	206	23	192	18
Germany	81	80	10	57	9	33	5
Switzerland	105	114	5	64	7	42	6
Hong Kong SAR	375	376	13–22[c]	366	26	272	14
Australia	72	75	10[b]	66	9	54	10
France	50	77	7–12[c]	84	7	113	6
Canada	45	38	6–7[c]	36	5–7[c]	28	4–6[c]

[a] 68%; [b] 70%; [c] Depending on the market segment.

Source: Triennial Central Bank Survey (2001, Table B.5, p. 10).

the banking sector stabilized with increasing concentration. This has a wholly different character from the concentration at the beginning of the 1990s, or in the period before the conversion of the centrally managed economies.

In the case of relatively small and open economies, high concentration has adverse effects on clients and on the banking sector's efficiency. Ahi states, for instance, in the case of the Estonian market, that even though the value of the HHI is relatively high and obviously clandestine, agreements among large banks take place, and as a result, external circumstances may limit monopolistic behaviour (principally, free access into and withdrawal from the sector). According to him, this was socially acceptable, profits were proportionate, and the banking sector worked effectively (Ahi, 2002, p. 1013). Cetorelli (2002) claims that the focus of his article is precisely on the markets that raise special anti-trust concerns: US local banking markets where the average HHI is about 4,000, and 90 per cent have the HHI greater than 1,800. Nevertheless, his conclusion is that in these markets there is no evidence consistent with collusive behaviour, and whether it exists or not improves market competition. In the Czech Republic, the low and decreasing value of the HHI is considered by the ČNB as evidence of deepening market conditions, although market shares of large banks in selected banking businesses demonstrate their unambiguous predominance.[13] A number of indicators in both the Czech and the Slovak markets still certify that increasing concentration is linked to the growth of stability and the banks' competitiveness when offering their services. Presumably, deregulation and elimination of important barriers to entry seem to enhance the conditions for market competition.

Notes

1. Chapter 4 deals with the efficiency analysis.
2. In the USA, for instance, interest ceilings (Regulation Q), or the McFadden–Pepper Act (Regulation Y) influencing bank branching, or the Glass–Steagall Act dividing commercial and investment banking.
3. Binda, J. 'Models of the distribution of products and banking facilities', *National Economic Horizons*, 2003, 3 (1), p. 3–10.
4. This index is also used by the ČNB, as well as by other central banks. More details in *Bank supervision 2000* (Prague: ČNB, 2001, p. 23); *Bank supervision 2001* (Prague: ČNB, 2002, p. 24) (http://www.cnb.cz). In the Czech Republic, not only the ČNB, but also the Office for the Protection of Competition takes this indicator into account in mergers and acquisitions valuation.
5. The obtained HHI value is usually multiplied by 100 or 10,000. Those markets whose HHI values are lower than 10 or 1,000 are regarded as non-concentrated and those markets whose HHI values are lower than 18 or 1,800 are regarded as medium-concentrated. Above this value, the market is regarded as concentrated.
6. More about typical features of banking sectors in transition countries can be found in Chapter 1.
7. As in many other countries, government steps to help banks with NPLs included the establishing of specialized institutions (consolidation or hospital banks) into which NPLs were transferred. In the Czech Republic, the Consolidation bank (Konsolidační banka) changed its status in 2001 and

became a non-bank institution – the Czech Consolidation Agency (Česká konsolidační agentura).

8. The level of concentration in the Czech banking sector has manifested moderate changes in the long term even if we apply other ways of measuring or if we take into account, for instance, the five largest banks. Towards 31.12.1993, the share of the five largest banks (Česká spořitelna, Komerční banka, Československá obchodní banka, Investiční banka, Agrobanka) amounted to 72 per cent with credits and 92 per cent with deposits. Ninety per cent shared in the number of banking employees with the given five banks. Data on the five banks (the stated banks without Agrobanka, but including Konsolidační banka) towards the end of 1997 was a bit lower in the stated shares, yet still high: in the case of the share in total balances, it came to 65.64 per cent (in 1995 it was 64.9 per cent, in 1996, 68.9 per cent), five largest banks shared in deposits with 74.2 per cent and, with credits, it was even more than the five banks' share in 1993 at 73.3 per cent. Towards the end of 1997, five banks (including Konsolidační banka) shared in the number of banking employees with 75.9 per cent and the share of the two largest banks summed to 56.7 per cent.

9. In 2000, the government stake was sold in Česká spořitelna, into which the affiliated bank Erste Bank Sparkassen (CR) was later integrated; in 2001, the government stake was sold in the large state-owned bank Komerční banka, into which the Société Générale – subdivision Prague – was subsequently integrated.

10. Section 1.2 deals with banking structure analysis. More about collapses of relatively large banks in Chapter 5.

11. The results of our analyses demonstrate a different trend from the data of the report of the Department of Bank Supervision for 2000, showing a noticeable increase in concentration. The concentration report of the Department of Bank Supervision was probably measured from the five largest banks, and not influenced (as it was in our case) by the takeover of IPB by ČSOB.

12. The values of indicators have been adopted from Jackowicz and Kowalewski (2002), very detailed and comprehensive publication devoted to concentration in the Polish banking sector.

13. *Banking supervision 2000*, Prague: ČNB, 2001, p. 23.

References

Ahi, K. 'Bank Competition and Monopoly Power in Transition Economies – the Case of Estonia', in *Finance* (Veliko Tarnovo: ABAGAR, 2002).

Alhadeff, D. *Monopoly, and Competition in Banking* (Berkeley: University of California, 1954).

Allen, F. and Gale, D. *Comparing Financial Systems* (London and Cambridge, MA: MIT Press, 2000).

Bain, J.S. 'Relation of Profit Rate to Industry Concentration: American Manufacturing, 1936–1940', *Quarterly Journal of Economics*, LXV, 3 (1951), 293–324.

Bell, F.W. and Myrphy, N.B. 'Impact of Market Structure on the Price of a Commercial Banking Service', *Review of Economics and Statistics*, 51, 2 (1969), 210–13.

Berger, A.N. and Hannan, T.H. 'The Price-Concentration Relationship in Banking', *Review of Economics and Statistics*, 71, 2 (1989), 291–9.

Calem, P.S. and Carlino, G.A. 'The Concentration/Conduct Relationship in Bank Deposit Markets', *Review of Economics and Statistics*, 73, 2 (1991), 268–76.

Caves, R.E. 'Uncertainty, Market Structure and Performance: Galbraith as Conventional Wisdom', in Markham, J. and Papanek, G. (eds) *Industrial Organization and Economic Development* (Boston, MA: Houghton Mifflin, 1970).

Cetorelli, N. 'Does Bank Concentration Lead to Concentration in Industrial Sectors?' (*Federal Reserve Bank of Chicago*, WP 2001-01, 2001).

Cetorelli, N. 'Entry and competition in highly concentrated banking markets', *Economic Perspectives, Federal Reserve Bank of Chicago*, XXXVI, 4 (2002), 18–27.

Curry, B. and George, K.D. 'Industrial Concentration: A Survey', *Journal of Industrial Economics*, 31, 3 (1983), 203–55.

Edwards, F.R. 'Concentration in Banking and its Effect on Business Loan Rates', *Review of Economics and Statistics*, 46, 3 (1964), 294–300.

Edwards, F.R. 'Concentration and Competition in Commercial Banking: A Statistical Study', *The Journal of Finance*, 20, 1 (1965), 101–2.

Edwards, F.R. and Heggestad, A.A. 'Uncertainty, Market Structure, and Performance: The Galbraith–Caves Hypothesis and Managerial Motives in Banking', *Quarterly Journal of Economics*, 87, 3 (1973), 455–73.

Feinberg, R.M. 'The Lerner Index, Concentration, and the Measurement of Market Power', *Southern Economic Journal*, 46, 4 (1980), 1180–86.

Fraser, R.D. and Rose, P.S. 'More on Banking Structure and Performance: The Evidence from Texas', *Journal of Financial and Quantitative Analysis*, 6, 1 (1971), 601–11.

Galbraith, J.K. *The New Industrial State* (Boston, MA: Houghton Mifflin, 1967).

Gilbert, R.A. 'Bank Market Structure and Competition', *Journal of Money, Credit, and Banking*, 16, 4 (1984), 617–45.

Guttentag, J.M. and Herman, E.S. 'Banking Structure and Performance', *The Bulletin, New York University, Graduate School of Business Administration*, 41/43 (1967), 105–25, 169–96.

Guzman, M. 'Bank Structure, Capital Accumulation, and Growth: A Simple Macroeconomic Model', *Economic Theory*, 16, 2 (2000), 421–55.

Hall, M. and Tideman, N. 'Measures of Concentration', *Journal of the American Statistical Association*, 62, March (1967) 162–8.

Hyytinen, A. and Toivanen, O. 'Monitoring and Market Power in Loan Markets', *Bank of Finland Discussion Paper*, 9 (2000).

Jackowicz, K. and Kowalewski, O. *Concentration of banking sector's activities in Poland in the years 1994–2000* (www.nbp.pl/publikacje/index.html) (2002).

Kaldor, N. 'Market Imperfections, and Excess Capacity', *Economica*, 2, February (1935), 33–50.

Lerner, A.P. 'The Concept of Monopoly and the Measurement of Monopoly Power', *Review of Economic Studies*, 1, 3 (1934), 157–75.

Mote, L.R. 'Competition in Banking: What is Known? What is the Evidence?', *Business Conditions, Federal Reserve Bank of Chicago* (1967), 7–16.

Mullineux, A.W. and Green, CH.J. (eds) *Economic Performance and Financial Sector Reform in Central and Eastern Europe. Capital Flows, Bank, and Enterprise Restructuring* (Cheltenham, UK and Northampton, MA, USA: Edward Elgar, 1998).

Pagano, M. 'Financial Markets, and Growth. An Overview', *European Economic Review*, 37 (1993), 613–22.

Petersen, M.A. and Rajan, R.G. 'The Effect of Credit Market Competition on Lending Relationship', *Quarterly Journal of Economics*, 90 (1995), 407–43.

Polouček, S. 'The Role of Banks and Capital Markets in Developed and in Transition Countries', in *Finance* (Veliko Tarnovo: ABAGAR, 2002).

Punt, L.W. and van Rooij, M.C.J. 'The Profit–Structure Relationship, Efficiency, and mergers in the European Banking Industry: an Empirical Assessment', *Research Memorandum WO&E*, (1999), 604.

Rothschild, K.W. 'The Degree of Monopoly', *Economica*, IX, February (1942), 24–39.

Shaffer, S. 'The Winner's Curse in Banking', *Journal of Financial Intermediation*, 7, 4 (1998), 359–92.

Suominen, M. 'Measuring Competition in Banking: A Two-Product Model', *Scandinavian Journal of Economics*, 1 (1994), 95–110.

Annual reports of ČNB, NBP and NBS (www.cnb.cz; www.nbp.pl; www.nbs.sk).

Bank supervision reports of ČNB, NBP and NBS (www.cnb.cz; www.nbp.pl; www.nbs.sk).

4
Efficiency and Profitability in the Banking Sector

Daniel Stavárek and Stanislav Polouček

Efficiency and profitability of banks and other financial institutions are very frequently discussed topics in economic literature. Harker and Zenios (2000) give a comprehensive and excellent analysis of the performance of financial institutions. Berger and Humphrey (1997) likewise surveyed 130 studies that apply frontier efficiency analysis to financial institutions in 21 countries. They report that the majority of these studies are confined to the US banking sector, and draw attention to the need for further research in this area outside the USA. This chapter aims to do precisely that.

The first section of this chapter presents a theoretical background in the efficiency and profitability area. Basic approaches towards understanding the topic are viewed, as well as specific aspects of links and typical differences. The methodology used in measuring efficiency and profitability as well as the underlying pros and cons of these methods form an integral part of this chapter.

Section 4.2 includes an original cross-border analysis of X-efficiency of banks in the CEC (Poland, the Czech Republic, Hungary and Slovakia) and in two EU countries (Finland and Belgium). The analysis is based on a method widely used nowadays – data envelopment analysis (DEA).

Section 4.3 presents an analysis of profitability, asset quality and bank capitalization in the Czech Republic, Poland and Slovakia based on ratio analysis. It focuses on establishing the influence of privatization on all basic aspects of banking activities.

The profitability of the banking sector is very seriously influenced by risk: the higher the risk, the higher the demanded yields (*ceteris paribus*) and the higher the profitability of the banking sector. This brings us to the fourth section of the chapter, which incorporates an analysis of five factors that affect the bank's profit in the Czech Republic, Poland and Slovakia: credit, liquidity, interest rates, capital and exchange rates.

The efficiency and profitability of banks are particularly important because of the unique circumstances in transition economies. The CEC are no exception. The establishment of a two-tier banking system based on market principles, the implementation of new methods and practices of banking regulation and supervision, a large amount of NPLs, financial or economic crises, the entry of foreign banks through the privatization process, or the creation of new banks, mergers and acquisitions, massive expansion of modern banking products and technologies – all these factors significantly affect the efficiency and profitability of the banking sector, and all these topics are analysed throughout this book. Banking regulation and supervision, along with its implications for NPLs, is studied in Chapter 2; banking crises in Chapter 5; some aspects of privatization are mentioned in this chapter (Section 4.3); and factors of development in the financial sector are discussed in Chapter 1.

However, the terms efficiency, profitability and productivity are often used interchangeably, and sometimes incorrectly. There are several differences among them. First, profitability measures the extent to which a business generates profit from factors of production. Profitability analysis focuses on the relationship between revenues and expenses and on the level of profits relative to the size of assets, capital or investments in the business. Efficiency measures the degree of the efficacious use of the factors of production. Efficiency analysis deals with the relationship between inputs and outputs. Next, efficiency and profitability represent different approaches and methodological concepts. Profitability and productivity can be characterized as performance indicators of a single unit calculated without the need for benchmarks. On the other hand, efficiency is based on relativity and can only be calculated with respect to a reference point. The differences are also very clearly apparent considering methods used in measuring both variables. Section 4.1.2 includes a detailed distinction and explanation. As a result, empirical findings evaluating efficiency and profitability of banks may differ, or even report absolutely contradicting values and trends.

4.1 The theoretical framework of efficiency

4.1.1 Types of efficiency

There are two types of bank efficiency. The first is operational efficiency as introduced by Farrell (1957) to measure general efficiency; and the second is X-efficiency, introduced by Leibenstein (1966) to explain differences in efficiency among banks; in other words, to measure relative efficiency. Operational efficiency studies estimate an average-practice frontier, which relates bank cost to output levels and input prices. The technique implicitly assumes that all banks in the sample use their inputs efficiently – there is no X-inefficiency – and that the banks are using the same production technology. Berger *et al.* (1993) review operational efficiencies of financial institutions and show how these compare to best frontier efficiencies. Studies concerned with X-efficiency estimate a best-practice frontier, which represents the predicted cost function of banks that are X-efficient, and then measure the degree of inefficiency of banks relative to this best-practice technology (Mester, 1993).

X-inefficiency comes in two varieties. A bank is technically inefficient if it uses too many inputs to produce its outputs. In this case, the bank would not be operating on its production frontier but at some point below the frontier. A bank is considered as allocatively inefficient if it is using the wrong mix of inputs to produce its outputs. In this case, the bank may be operating on its production frontier, but it is not minimizing its production costs. We will discuss X-efficiency further on.

In other words, technical efficiency reflects the ability of a bank to obtain maximal output from a given set of inputs, and allocative efficiency reflects the ability of a bank to use the inputs in optimal proportions given their respective prices and the production technology. These two components of X-efficiency are graphically demonstrated in Figure 4.1. We assume that a set of units (banks) use two inputs (x_1 and x_2) to produce a single output (y), under the restriction of constant returns of scale.

Knowledge of the unit isoquant of fully efficient units represented by SS' permits the measurement of technical efficiency. The unit uses quantities of inputs defined by, for example, point P. Technical inefficiency can be defined by the distance QP, which is the amount by which all inputs could be proportionally reduced without a reduction of the output level. Technical efficiency is then usually expressed in percentage

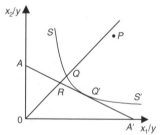

P = an inefficient unit
Q = a technically efficient unit
Q' = an allocatively (and technically) efficient unit
AA' = the isocost line
SS' = the isoquant of efficiency
R = a hypothetical point on the isocost line indicating equal to Q' costs

Figure 4.1   Technical and allocative efficiencies

terms by the ratio QP/OP, which represents the percentage by which all inputs need to be reduced to achieve technically efficient production. Technical efficiency is commonly measured by the ratio $0Q/0P$ which is equal to one minus QP/OP.

$$\text{Technical efficiency: } TE_i = 0Q/0P = 1 - QP/OP \qquad (4.1)$$

If the input price ratio represented by the slope of the isocost line AA' is also known, allocative efficiency may also be calculated. The allocative efficiency of the unit operational at P is defined to be the ratio $0R/0Q$ since the distance RQ represents the reduction in production costs that would arise if production were to occur at the allocatively (and technically) efficient point Q', instead of the technically efficient, but allocatively inefficient point Q.

$$\text{Allocative efficiency: } AE_i = 0R/0Q \qquad (4.2)$$

The total efficiency is defined as the ratio $0R/0P$, where the distance RP can also be interpreted in terms of cost reduction. We can show that the product of technical and allocative efficiency measures provides the measure of overall efficiency.[1]

$$\text{Total efficiency: } E_i = 0R/0P = (0Q/0P) \times (0R/0Q) = TE_i \times AE_i \qquad (4.3)$$

4.1.2 Measurement of efficiency

One of the most frequently and widely used methods of evaluating performance of banks is ratio analysis. However, this approach does not correspond with the defined concept of efficiency and in addition proves insufficient in efficiency calculations involving multiple input and output, because ratio analysis is defined as a ratio of one input and one output. When all input and output factors cannot be transformed into one aggregate input or output unit, the input and output factors involved in the measurement process need to be evaluated separately. This usually leads to meaningless results when ratios are analysed in isolation.[2] As the number of input and output factors increases, the vagueness in the analysis also increases because there are xy different ratios to be examined in the model where there are x input and y output factors.

Thus it is argued that the derivation of a single efficiency index will provide a more operational and practical basis for evaluating the relative efficiency of competing agencies. However, ratio analysis is still viewed as a good and reasonable approach to measure partial aspects of overall bank performance, such as profitability, cost-effectiveness, quality of a loan portfolio, liquidity, productivity and others. The third and fourth sections of this chapter use applications of ratio analysis in profitability evaluation.

We focus our study on frontier efficiency, which means how close banks are to a best-practice frontier. Efficiency literature reports that differences in frontier efficiency among banks exceed inefficiencies attributable to incorrect scale or scope of output. However, there is really no consensus on the preferred methods for determining the best-practice frontier against which relative efficiencies are measured, as is evident, for example, in Berger and Humprey (1997).

Two main empirical approaches to measure technical efficiency can be distinguished: the non-parametric (mathematical programming) approach and the parametric (econometric) approach. The first was developed by Charnes *et al.* (1978), while the second was initiated by Aigner *et al.* (1977). Each approach employs a different technique to envelop a data set with different assumptions for random noise and for the structure of production technology. These assumptions generate the strengths and drawbacks of both approaches, which can be grouped under two categories.

1. The parametric approach is stochastic and attempts to differentiate the effects of noise and the effects of inefficiency. The non-parametric approach is non-stochastic and commits the fault of not allowing for random error owing to luck, data problems, or other measurement errors. If random error exists, measured efficiency may be confused by these random deviations from the true efficiency frontier.
2. The parametric approach imposes a particular functional form (and associated behavioural assumptions) that presupposes the shape of the frontier. If the functional form is not specified, measured efficiency may be confused with the specification errors. The non-parametric approach imposes less structure on the frontier.

As we can see, the conflict between non-parametric and parametric approaches is important because the two types of methods tend to have different degrees of dispersion and rank the same financial institutions somewhat differently. It is not possible to determine which of these major concepts dominates the other since the true level of technical efficiency is unknown. Parametric approaches are represented mainly by SFA (stochastic frontier analysis) and non-parametric methods by DEA (data envelopment analysis). Non-parametric approaches also include the free disposal hull method,[3] whereas a functional form for the frontier is also specified by the distribution free approach and thick frontier analysis as representatives of parametric approaches.

SFA assumes that inefficiency follows an asymmetric half-normal distribution, while random fluctuations follow a symmetric normal distribution. The efficiency results depend critically on the distortion of the data – any inefficiency components that are more or less symmetrically distributed will tend to be measured as random error and any random error components that are more or less asymmetrically distributed will tend to be measured as inefficiency. The SFA results also depend on the arbitrary assumption that the X-efficiencies are orthogonal to the cost function exogenous variables, including those used to compute scale efficiency. According to the conventional scale economics literature, if X-efficient firms tend to compete well and become large, SFA may falsely attribute X-efficiency to scale efficiency. The major reason for this is that the coefficients on the output regressors pick up the correlation with the X-efficiency factors, which are in the composite error term. The SFA cost function coefficients may be biased, leading to miscalculations of X and scale efficiencies, if some of the input prices are correlated with X-efficiency. For example, this may occur if banks facing relatively high wages tend to innovate and become more X-efficient.

TFA (thick frontier analysis) assumes that deviations from predicted costs within the lowest average cost quartile of banks represent random error, while deviations in predicted costs between the highest and lowest quartiles represent inefficiency. The TFA estimates separate cost functions for the lowest and highest average-cost quartiles. The residuals for both functions are assumed to represent only random error, while the predicted difference between the two functions is assumed to represent X-efficiency differences. The measured efficiency under TFA is obviously sensitive to assumptions about which fluctuations are random and which represent efficiency differences. For example, TFA may mistake one for the other if random errors follow a thick-tailed distribution and tend to be large in absolute value while inefficiencies follow a thin-tailed distribution and tend to be small.

Figure 4.2 shows an input–output model of a set of units to be analysed and the application of three different approaches to the estimation of efficiency frontier: (a) an average practice function using least square estimators, (b) frontier estimated by a parametric approach using maximum likelihood estimators, (c) piece-wise linear convex frontier estimated by a non-parametric approach generated by linear programming.

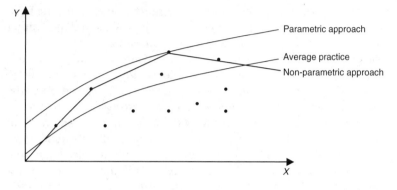

Figure 4.2   Approaches to frontier estimation

We will subsequently present the methodology, and in Section 4.2, the application and results of measuring efficiency using the non-parametric approach, that is, restricting ourselves to DEA.

4.1.3   Data envelopment analysis

Data envelopment analysis (DEA) is a mathematical programming technique that measures the efficiency of productive units (in DEA literature they are referred to as decision making units – DMUs) relative to other DMUs in the observed set, which means it estimates the relative efficiency of DMUs. DEA was first introduced by Charnes *et al.* (1978). Since then, its utilization and development have grown rapidly, and throughout the past two decades, hundreds of articles have developed the DEA methodology, and over a thousand papers have applied the method to different fields ranging from banking to education. Emrouznejad and Thanassoulis (1996 a, b, c) give a detailed review as well as a bibliography of DEA studies. A regularly updated list of DEA studies can also be accessed at http://www.deazone.com/bibliography/index.htm.

The most usual way to calculate relative efficiency is to form the ratio of a weighted sum of outputs to a weighted sum of inputs. Within the DEA approach, multiple inputs and outputs are reduced to a single virtual input and output and finally to a single summary relative efficiency score. The gradual development of DEA illustrates the difficulty in identifying a common set of weights of all examined DMUs. DEA allows each DMU to place importance on different inputs and outputs and consequently adopt different weights, showing the DMU in the most favourable light in comparison to other DMUs (Dyson *et al.*, 1990).

The weights for both outputs and inputs are selected to calculate the Pareto-efficiency measure of each DMU. Pareto-efficiency is attained when no input can be reduced without reducing the output, or when no output can be increased without increasing the input. The efficiency score of any DMU cannot be greater than one. The DEA calculations are designed to maximize the relative efficiency score of each DMU, subject to the condition that the set of weights obtained in this manner for each DMU must also be feasible for all the other DMUs involved in the calculation.

The reference points (relatively efficient DMUs) that define the efficient frontier (as the best-practice production technology) are identified in this way as well as interior points (relatively inefficient DMUs) that are below the frontier. If a DMU is not efficient, DEA suggests strategies required to increase the efficiency of this unit with reference to the DMUs selected as best-practice. In the light of these data, managers can evaluate the extent to which a less efficient unit underuses or overuses the input factors, how unproductive a unit is with respect to the output factors, and what needs to be done to improve the situation.

The DEA technique can be considered as an alternative approach to regression analysis. DEA is based on extreme observations, whereas regression analysis relies on central tendencies. While the regression approach assumes that a single estimated regression equation applies to each observation vector, DEA analyses each vector (DMU) separately, producing individual efficiency measures relative to the entire set under evaluation (Vujcic and Jemric, 2002).

A great number of models, specifications and versions of DEA can be found in the literature. We use the two most frequently applied models: the CCR model – after Charnes *et al.* (1978) and the BCC model – after Banker *et al.* (1984). The basic difference between these two models is the treatment of returns to scale. While the latter takes into account the effect of variable returns to scale, the former restricts DMUs to operate with constant returns to scale.

The CCR model

Under restriction that each DMU's efficiency is judged against its individual criteria (individual weighting system), efficiency of a target DMU_0

can be obtained as a solution to the following problem:

$$\max h_{0_{u,v}}(u,v) = \frac{\sum_{r=1}^{s} u_r y_{r_0}}{\sum_{i=1}^{m} v_i x_{i_0}} \tag{4.4}$$

subject to

$$\frac{\sum_{r=1}^{s} u_r y_{r_j}}{\sum_{i=1}^{m} v_i x_{i_j}} \leq 1, \quad j = 1,2,\dots,j_0,\dots,n \tag{4.5}$$

$$u_r \geq 0, \quad r = 1,2,\dots, s \tag{4.6}$$
$$v_i \geq 0, \quad i = 1,2,\dots, m, \tag{4.7}$$

where

h_0 is technical efficiency of DMU_0 to be estimated
u_r, v_i is weights (variables) to be estimated
y_{rj} is observed amount of output of the rth type for the jth DMU
x_{ij} is observed amount of input of the ith type for the jth DMU
r is indicates the different s outputs
i is indicates the different m inputs
j is indicates the different n DMUs

The weights u_r and v_i in the objective function are chosen to maximize the value of the DMU's efficiency ratio subject to the less-than-one constraint. These constraints ensure that the optimal weights for DMU_0 in the objective function do not imply an efficiency score greater than one, either for itself or for any of the other DMUs.

The DEA problem above is a fractional linear program in which the numerator has to be maximized and the denominator minimized simultaneously; that is, the problem has an infinite number of solutions. To solve the model, it is first necessary to convert it into linear form by following a transformation developed by Charnes and Cooper (1962) for fractional programming. It allows the introduction of a constant,

$$\sum_{i=1}^{m} v_i x_{i_0} = 1 , \tag{4.8}$$

meaning that the sum of all inputs is set to equal one. The obtained linear programming problem that is equivalent to the linear fractional programming problem (4.4–4.7) for DMU_0 can be written as:

$$\max_{u} z_0 = \sum_{r=1}^{s} u_r y_{r_0} \tag{4.9}$$

$$\sum_{r=1}^{s} u_r y_{r_j} - \sum_{i=1}^{m} v_i x_{i_j} \leq 0, \quad j = 1,2,\ldots,n \tag{4.10}$$

$$\sum_{i=1}^{m} v_i x_{i_0} = 1 \tag{4.11}$$

$$u_r \geq 0, \quad r = 1,2,\ldots,s \tag{4.12}$$

$$v_i \geq 0, \quad i = 1,2,\ldots,m, \tag{4.13}$$

For linear programs in general, it is true that the more constraints, the more difficult a problem is to solve. For any linear program, a dual (partner) linear program using the same data can be formulated. The solution of either primal (original) program or the dual (partner) program provides the same information about the program being modelled. In the case of DEA, switching to duality reduces the number of constraints in the model. Hence, for this reason, it is usual to solve the dual DEA model rather than the primal one. The dual model for the above linear programming problem[4] for DMU_0 can be written as:

$$\min_{\lambda} z_0 = \Theta_0 \tag{4.14}$$

subject to

$$\sum_{j=1}^{n} \lambda_j y_{r_j} \geq y_{r_0}, \quad r = 1,2,\ldots,s \tag{4.15}$$

$$\Theta_0 x_{i_0} - \sum_{j=1}^{n} \lambda_j x_{i_j} \geq 0, \quad i = 1,2,\ldots,m \tag{4.16}$$

$$\lambda_j \geq 0, \quad j = 1,2,\ldots,n \tag{4.17}$$

where
   Θ_0 is technical efficiency of DMU_0 to be estimated
   λ_j is an n-dimensional constant to be estimated
   y_{rj} is observed amount of output of the rth type for the jth DMU
   x_{ij} is observed amount of input of the ith type for the jth DMU

r is indicates the different s outputs
i is indicates the different m inputs
j is indicates the different n DMUs.

The optimal solution of Θ_0 represents the technical efficiency score of DMU_0. This result is usually referred to as technical efficiency, or CCR efficiency. Efficiency scores for all DMUs are obtained by repeating of solving the problem for each $DMU_j(j = 1,2, \ldots, n)$. While DMUs with efficiency score $\Theta_j < 1$ are relatively inefficient, the efficiency score $\Theta_j = 1$ indicates relatively efficient units occurring on the efficiency frontier. However, among inefficient DMUs there are cases when higher efficiency can be reached but not through a proportional reduction of all inputs. Rather, it is sufficient to reduce only one input. The problem arises because of the sections of the piecewise linear frontier that run parallel to the axes. The variable Θ_j as defined by the dual model cannot reflect this type of unproportional efficiency increase.

The solution is based on the identification of the extreme cases that should be included in the optimization program. This can be achieved by replacing the constraint that the weights are equal to or greater than quantity ϵ in order to avoid any input or output being totally ignored in determining the efficiency. This led to the modification of the primal model (4.9–4.13) and the dual model (4.14–4.17).

The modified primal model can be written as:

$$\max_{u} z_0 = \sum_{r=1}^{s} u_r y_{r_0} \tag{4.18}$$

$$\sum_{r=1}^{s} u_r y_{r_j} - \sum_{i=1}^{m} v_i x_{i_j} \leq 0, \quad j = 1,2, \ldots, n \tag{4.19}$$

$$\sum_{i=1}^{m} v_i x_{i_0} = 1 \tag{4.20}$$

$$u_r \geq \epsilon, \quad r = 1,2, \ldots, s \tag{4.21}$$

$$v_i \geq \epsilon, \quad i = 1,2, \ldots, m \tag{4.22}$$

And the modified dual model is defined as follows:

$$\min_{\lambda} z_0 = \Theta_0 - \left(\sum_{i=1}^{m} \epsilon s_{i_0}^{+} + \sum_{r=1}^{s} \epsilon s_{r_0}^{-} \right) \tag{4.23}$$

subject to

$$- y_{r_0} + \sum_{j=1}^{n} \lambda_j y_{r_j} - s_{r_0}^{-} = 0, \quad r = 1,2, \ldots, s \tag{4.24}$$

$$\Theta_0 x_{i_0} - \sum_{j=1}^{n} \lambda_j x_{i_j} - s_{r_0}^+ = 0, \quad i = 1,2,\ldots,m \tag{4.25}$$

$$\lambda_j \geq 0, \quad j = 1,2,\ldots,n \tag{4.26}$$

where ϵ is a marginally small, but positive quantity
s_r^+ is the slack variables for s outputs
s_j^- is the slack variables for m inputs.

The BCC model

The constant returns to scale assumption is only appropriate when all DMUs are operational at an optimal scale. Imperfect competition, constraints on finance, leverage concerns, certain prudential requirements, etc., may cause a DMU not to operate at optimal scale. The fact that banks face non-constant returns to scale has been documented empirically by, among others, McAllister and McManus (1993), and Wheelock and Wilson (1999). To overcome this problem, a DEA model with variable returns to scale has been developed. In the model below, the variables of technical efficiencies, which are compounded to scale efficiencies, are measured. This is done by adding the convexity constraint:

$$\sum_{j=1}^{n} \lambda_j = 1, \tag{4.27}$$

meaning that under variable returns to scale the λ adds up to one. This condition ensures that an inefficient bank is benchmarked against similar-sized banks. The input-oriented BCC model for the DMU_0 can be written formally as:

$$\min_{\lambda} z_0 = \Theta_0 \tag{4.28}$$

$$\sum_{j=1}^{n} \lambda_j y_{r_j} \geq y_{r_0}, \quad r = 1,2,\ldots,s \tag{4.29}$$

$$\Theta_0 x_{i_0} - \sum_{j=1}^{n} \lambda_j x_{i_j} \geq 0, \quad i = 1,2,\ldots,n \tag{4.30}$$

$$\sum_{j=1}^{n} \lambda_j = 1 \tag{4.31}$$

$$\lambda_j \geq 0, \quad j = 1,2,\ldots,n \tag{4.32}$$

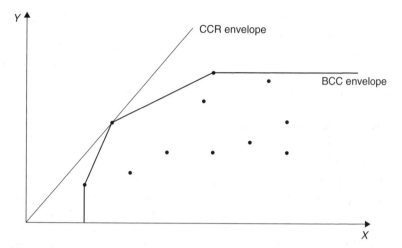

Figure 4.3 CCR and BCC envelope

The BCC efficiency scores are also called pure technical efficiency scores and they are obtained by running the above model for each DMU. The BCC model eliminates the scale part of efficiency from the analysis, and therefore, the CCR efficiency score for each DMU does not exceed the BCC efficiency score. This is evident since the BCC model analyses each DMU locally, meaning, compared to the subset of DMUs, they operate in the same region of returns to scale, rather than globally.

Graphical illustration is presented in Figure 4.3. The BCC model forms a convex hull of intersecting planes which envelopes the data points more tightly than the CCR's conical hull, and thus provides technical efficiency scores greater than or equal to those obtained using the CCR model.

4.2 Cross-country analysis of relative efficiency

DEA was used extensively in studies of the banking industry in developed market economies, and US data alone show that the method was used in more than 30 published articles (Berger and Humprey, 1997). The method was also applied in Norway and other Nordic countries, as well as Spain, the UK, Croatia, Poland and several other countries. There is still a lack of literature which uses DEA for cross-country comparisons[5] including an analysis of banks from transition countries.

This chapter therefore aims to fill the gap to include banks from the CEC. The rationale for this selection is the fact that these countries started the restructuring of their banking sectors around same time, and they were affected during the transformation process by broadly similar factors. These counties also belong to the group of accession countries (ACC), in line to become members of the European Union in 2004. Comparing their banking sectors with those of the EU is also an important consideration. The Finnish and Belgian banks were selected to represent the banks from EU countries in evaluating their relative efficiency with banks from the selected CEC. The Belgian banking sector is perceived to be developed and stable, whereas the Finnish banking sector is representative of a banking industry which has suffered from banking crises, resulting in loss of confidence, but eventually recovering, as described in Chapter 1, Section 1.2.

4.2.1 Methodology and selection of variables

The function of commercial banks is generally defined as collecting the savings of households and other agents to finance the investment needs of firms and consumption needs of individuals and providing transactions (document) processing services.[6] Banking literature distinguishes four approaches that discuss the activities of these banks. They are: (i) the production approach; (ii) the operational approach; (iii) the intermediation approach; and (iv) the modern approach. The first three approaches apply the traditional microeconomic theory of the firm to banking and differ only in the specifics of banking activities and operations. The fourth approach goes one step further by incorporating banking classical theory in specific activities and hence, modifying these banking activities. We estimate the relative efficiency in the analysis by the traditional approaches only.

In the production approach, banks are described as producers of services to depositors and borrowers (account holders). Banks employ traditional production factors, that is, land, labour and capital, to produce desired outputs, such as loan applications, credit reports, cheques or other payment instruments. This approach suffers from the basic problem of measuring outputs. Should the number of accounts, the number of operations on these accounts, or the financial value of accounts and transactions for measurement be used? The generally accepted methodology is to use financial value because of the availability of such data.

The operational approach evaluates the efficiency of a bank from the perspective of cost/revenues management. It covers all significant costs of basic banking activities on the side of inputs and main sources of bank revenues on the side of outputs. Usually, the interest expenses, along with personal costs, capital costs as well as fees and commissions paid are considered as inputs, while interest revenues with fees and commissions received are considered as outputs. Some studies combine both the production and operational approaches (Denizer *et al.*, 2000, among others).

The intermediation approach is complementary to the production and operational approaches, and describes such banking activities as transforming money borrowed from depositors into money lent to borrowers. This transformation activity originates from the different characteristics of deposits and loans. Deposits are typically divisible, liquid and free of risk, whereas loans are indivisible, illiquid and risky. In this approach, inputs include financial capital, particularly the deposits collected and funds borrowed from financial markets, whereas the volume of loans and investment outstanding measures outputs.

As it is obvious from the above definitions, none of these three approaches is perfect because none fully captures the whole role of commercial banks. The best solution we would consider is applying two of the approaches because it is assumed that banking is a simultaneously occurring two-stage process. This allows us to evaluate banking comprehensively and compare maybe different findings from the same estimated set of DMUs.

It is commonly acknowledged that the choice of variables in efficiency analysis significantly affects the results. A number of studies present results that differ due to variable selection (see Favore and Pappi, 1995; Hunter and Timme, 1995). However, certain limitations on variable selection exist due to the reliability of the data. For example, the variables may present different information, although they carry the same label, or the same information may be reported under different labels. This variation stems from the lack of reporting standards in the banking industry. On the other hand, the use of unnecessary variables clutters the analysis and makes it difficult to interpret. The variable selection for this study relied mainly on classical banking theory.

After surveying a number of similar studies, we decided to use these sets of inputs and outputs for the two approaches in estimating relative efficiency. For the operational approach as well as for the intermediation approach, all data were extracted from the banks' end-of-year unconsolidated balance sheets and financial statements based on international accounting standards. All data are reported in EUR as the reference currency, and have been converted using official exchange rates. To convert values from local currencies we used either the official exchange rate or the purchasing power parity rate as computed by the OECD. According to Berg *et al.* (1993), the two approaches seem to yield very similar results.

For the intermediation approach, four inputs were selected for each (jth) bank:

- total deposits received from clients (x_{1j}) representing the main source for lending operations;
- receivables from other credit institutions (x_{2j}) representing sources from the interbank market;
- personal costs (x_{3j}) representing labour inputs;
- fixed assets and software (x_{4j}) representing necessary preconditions for intermediary activities;

and two outputs:

- net loans to clients (y_{1j}) representing direct use of funds in intermediation process;
- claims on other credit institutions (y_{2j}) representing indirect use of funds in the intermediation process through interbank loans and deposits.

In the case of the operational approach, for each (jth) DMU the input data (x_{ij}) were:

- interest and related expenses (x_{1j}) representing funds used by the bank;
- commissions and fees for services and related expenses (x_{2j}) representing cost of other financial services;
- personal costs (x_{3j}) representing labour inputs;
- tier 1 capital (x_{4j}) representing input of shareholders' sources;

while the output data (y_{ij}) were:

- gross interest incomes (y_{1j}) representing output of lending activities;
- fee and commission incomes (y_{2j}) representing output of other banking services.

In our empirical study we used 2000 and 2001 data to calculate the relative efficiency of banks of six European banking industries. After carefully checking the data for consistency, we evaluated a fairly representative set of DMUs including 64 banks in the year 2000 and 65 banks in 2001,[7] which represents more than 90 per cent of the total assets in the banking sector of each country excluding foreign bank branches. We foresaw arguments concerning the reliability of some of the indicators in an environment where serious false reports and non-compliance could take place. This is why the choice of countries (those with relatively advanced banking sectors and relatively similar overall population) and the sample period (the end period as opposed to the early or mid-transition period) for this study was made to reduce the extent of these problems.

We have pooled the cross-country data and have used them to define a common best-practice frontier. This has allowed us to focus on determining the relative differences in performances across banking industries. The same approach was previously followed by Berg *et al.* (1993), Fecher and Pestieau (1993), Bukh *et al.* (1995), Allen and Rai (1996), Pastor *et al.* (1997), Bergendahl (1998) and Dietsch and Weill (2000). For a better comparison, we have also computed a separate frontier for each country. It should be noted that, more importantly, this type of cross-border comparison may be difficult to interpret because the regulatory and economic environments faced by banks are likely to differ across nations; and furthermore, the level and quality of services associated with deposits and loans in different countries may differ in ways that are hard to measure. Such cross-country differences were not specified when a common frontier was being estimated, and this may affect the cross-country results.

However, cross-country studies can provide valuable information regarding the competitiveness of banks in different countries, an issue of particular importance in the increasingly harmonized European market for banking services and, perhaps, the globalized financial markets of the future (Berger and Humprey, 1997). In addition, the selection of countries in our study guarantees relatively similar conditions for banks within the regulatory and supervision framework. This similarity is based on the process of legislative harmonization with EU standards in transition countries (Nicastro *et al.*, 2002, among others). The quality of banking services in the CEC has also been improving noticeably, and does not lag behind the quality in EU so dramatically as was the case several years ago. Improvements were stimulated mainly by the effects of privatization and activities of foreign banks, as described in Chapter 1. Therefore we do not consider the differences among the selected countries as sufficiently significant to reduce the reliability, consistency and comparability of the cross-country results.

4.2.2 Empirical findings

Following the methodology described, we evaluated the efficiency of all banks in the estimation set and calculated DEA efficiency scores obtained by running separate programs (4.14)–(4.17) for the CCR model or (4.28)–(4.32) for the BCC model. The list of all banks included in the study along with their efficiency scores is provided in the Appendix. The results of the analysis via the operational as well as the intermediation

Table 4.1 Summary statistics (%)

	Intermediation approach				Operating approach			
	CCR model		BCC model		CCR model		BCC model	
	2000	2001	2000	2001	2000	2001	2000	2001
No. of efficient DMUs	14	17	26	34	25	23	36	31
Average efficiency (M_T)	75.08	78.49	83.39	86.03	89.86	87.10	94.24	92.30
Adj. avrg. efficiency (AM_T)	73.63	75.92	90.76	97.40	88.84	88.27	99.00	98.60
Standard deviation (σ_T)	0.2078	0.1959	0.1973	0.1887	0.1088	0.1242	0.0945	0.1062
Interval I	0.5430	0.5891	0.6366	0.6716	0.7898	0.7468	0.8479	0.8167
$[M_T - \sigma_T; M_T + \sigma_T]$	0.9585	0.9808	1.0312	1.0490	1.0074	0.9952	1.0369	1.0292
Percentage of DMUs in I	53.13	45.54	81.25	76.92	87.50	47.69	82.81	83.08

Source: Authors' calculations.

approach (for both CCR and BCC models) are summed up in Table 4.1. The average efficiency (M) stands for the average of all optimal values Θ_0 of banks from each country. We are aware that averaging without any respect to the size of banks causes loss of information, and therefore, we implemented in our analysis an adjusted average efficiency (AM) calculated as:

$$AM = \sum_{j=1}^{n} w_j \Theta_j \qquad (4.33)$$

where

AM is the adjusted average efficiency;

w_j is the weight computed as a share of jth DMU's assets on total assets of all estimated DMUs;

Θ_j is the observed efficiency for the jth DMU; and

j indicates the different n DMUs.

The average efficiency of all banks, depending on treatment of returns to scale and year, varies from 75.08 to 86.03 per cent for the intermediation approach, and from 87.10 to 94.24 per cent for the operational approach. In comparison with findings of Berger and Humprey (1997), the figures show signs of good performance. They surveyed, as mentioned earlier, 130 studies (122 of which were focused on depository financial institutions), applying frontier efficiency analysis (using parametric as well as non-parametric methods) to financial institutions in 21 countries. They drew the conclusion that the mean value of average efficiencies was 79 per cent, with a standard deviation of 0.13, and a range of 31 per cent to 97 per cent. The interval formed by the mean plus and minus one standard deviation would cover efficiency values from 66 per cent to 92 per cent and capture 82 per cent of observations. Results of our study are not very different. Considering only 69 applications of non-parametric techniques, the mean average efficiency was 72 per cent, with a standard deviation of 0.17 and a range of 31 to 97 per cent.

The intermediation approach's average efficiency scores of the banking sectors, with the exception of Finland, as well as the total efficiencies are significantly lower than the operational approach's efficiency scores. Similarly, the variability of efficiency scores recorded higher levels in the intermediation approach than in the operational approach, as evidenced from the computed standard deviations. The efficiency fluctuated from 19.70 per cent to 100.00 per cent in the intermediation approach compared to the fluctuation from 52.35 per cent to 100.00 per cent in the operational approach.

The results obtained in the next feature show differences between efficiencies allowing variable returns to scale (BCC model) and efficiencies based on constant returns to scale (CCR model). Recall that the CCR efficiency score is a product of technical and scale efficiency, and BCC measures purely technical efficiency; thus, the ratio of the efficiency scores,

$$S_n = \frac{\Theta_{n,CCR}}{\Theta_{n,BCC}}, \tag{4.34}$$

yields a measure of the relative scale efficiency of bank n, if $S_n = 1$. This means that bank n is operational at the most efficient scale size. If it is less than one, this means there is scale inefficiency for bank n. Thus, $(1 - S_n)$ represents the relative scale inefficiency of a bank. The units that are CCR-efficient will also be scale-efficient, since scale was already factored in the CCR model. Thus the two are equal. The units that are BCC-efficient, but inefficient in the CCR model, have a scale inefficiency. Since they were technically efficient, all the inefficiencies picked up by CCR are due to scale. Those units that are CCR-efficient are considered the most productive scale sizes, as the average productivity of each of those units is maximized. Average scale inefficiencies of all banking sectors are presented in Table 4.2.

As is evident in Table 4.2, all banking industries suffer from scale inefficiency that is to a larger degree concentrated, in the majority of cases,

Table 4.2 Average scale inefficiency (%)

	Intermediation approach		Operating approach	
	2000	*2001*	*2000*	*2001*
Belgium	10.82	14.85	2.47	2.62
Czech Republic	14.27	8.00	5.74	7.82
Finland	2.53	1.89	8.06	9.30
Hungary	6.71	3.72	2.93	2.55
Poland	11.52	11.42	5.47	5.88
Slovakia	9.15	9.04	5.19	7.85
Total	9.97	8.76	4.65	5.63

Source: Authors' calculations.

in the intermediation part of banking process. Finland, inversely, is an exception to the rule, reaching the lowest scale inefficiency in the intermediation approach and the highest scale inefficiency in the operational approach. The issue of bank size can also be analysed by comparing average efficiency scores and adjusted average efficiency scores.

Considering constant returns to scale, in both intermediation and operational approaches, the adjusted average efficiency is lower than the simple average efficiency in Belgium, the Czech Republic, Slovakia and, partly, in Finland. This indicates that the smaller banks perform better than the larger ones. Hence, in the case of common efficiency analysis, we can generalize that larger banks mainly operate at the wrong scale in the aforementioned countries. Their size and capital equipment are not fully utilized and thus exceed the total volume of products and services provided. On the contrary, the scale inefficiency in Poland and, to a lesser extent, Hungary stems from a great number of relatively small banks which perform badly due to their high fixed costs in relation to their limited market shares. More detailed efficiency analysis of Polish banks was recently published by Mielnik and Lawrynowicz (2002). This finding corresponds to the rather low concentration of Polish and Hungarian banking sectors as computed in Section 3.3. A summary of the results for all banking sectors is presented in Tables 4.3 and 4.4. We computed four separate measurements of relative efficiency for both intermediation and operational approaches generated by CCR and BCC models for years 2000 and 2001. Consequently, we ranked the countries eight times for each approach (four times according to average efficiency scores and four times using adjusted average efficiency scores). The Finnish banking sector appeared as the most efficient in the intermediation approach, topping it six times, while Belgium was placed

Table 4.3 Summary results – intermediation approach with constant returns to scale (grey part) and variable returns to scale (white part) (%)

Variable returns to scale (white part)

	Belgium		Czech Republic		Finland	
	2000	2001	2000	2001	2000	2001
No. of DMUs	11	11	13	14	6	6
No. of efficient DMUs	3	4	2	4	3	3
Average efficiency (M)	77.54	78.91	76.83	81.71	90.88	83.87
Adj. avrg. efficiency (AM)	68.83	70.95	74.22	80.95	90.09	97.28
Standard deviation (σ)	0.2557	0.2500	0.1201	0.1530	0.1316	0.2476
Percentage of DMUs in I	36.36	36.36	84.62	64.29	50.00	16.67

	Hungary		Poland		Slovakia	
	2000	2001	2000	2001	2000	2001
No. of DMUs	11	11	13	13	10	10
No. of efficient DMUs	2	3	3	2	1	1
Average efficiency (M)	73.58	83.10	75.66	72.32	61.49	73.26
Adj. avrg. efficiency (AM)	73.81	88.23	76.82	70.79	70.34	64.96
Standard deviation (σ)	0.1903	0.1755	0.1918	0.1466	0.2299	0.1898
Percentage of DMUs in I	54.55	45.45	61.54	61.54	50.00	30.00

Constant returns to scale (grey part)

	Belgium		Czech Republic		Finland	
	2000	2001	2000	2001	2000	2001
No. of DMUs	11	11	13	14	6	6
No. of efficient DMUs	6	8	7	7	4	4
Average efficiency (M)	86.95	92.67	89.62	88.82	93.24	85.49
Adj. avrg. efficiency (AM)	87.74	98.88	95.13	92.80	95.36	97.67
Standard deviation (σ)	0.2249	0.2205	0.1237	0.1411	0.1309	0.2119
Percentage of DMUs in I	90.91	90.91	92.31	85.72	100.00	83.33

	Hungary		Poland		Slovakia	
	2000	2001	2000	2001	2000	2001
No. of DMUs	11	11	13	13	10	10
No. of efficient DMUs	2	6	5	5	2	3
Average efficiency (M)	78.87	86.31	85.51	81.64	67.68	80.54
Adj. avrg. efficiency (AM)	80.85	90.39	90.14	87.81	74.03	72.10
Standard deviation (σ)	0.1933	0.1778	0.1702	0.1736	0.2117	0.1834
Percentage of DMUs in I	72.73	72.73	84.62	69.23	50.00	60.00

Source: Authors' calculations.

Table 4.4 Summary results – operating approach with constant returns to scale (grey part) and variable returns to scale (white part) (%)

Grey part (constant returns to scale)

	Belgium		Czech Republic		Finland	
	2000	2001	2000	2001	2000	2001
No. of DMUs	11	11	13	14	6	6
No. of efficient DMUs	7	8	4	5	1	2
Average efficiency (M)	97.01	97.05	89.83	86.49	87.65	84.92
Adj. avg. efficiency (AM)	92.54	92.27	84.54	89.84	80.77	76.87
Standard deviation (σ)	0.0499	0.0536	0.0898	0.1158	0.0843	0.1143
Percentage of DMUs in I	100.00	27.27	92.31	42.86	83.33	50.00

	Hungary		Poland		Slovakia	
	2000	2001	2000	2001	2000	2001
No. of DMUs	11	11	13	13	10	10
No. of efficient DMUs	5	5	5	2	3	1
Average efficiency (M)	91.22	91.34	89.62	85.30	82.15	75.98
Adj. avg. efficiency (AM)	90.54	92.61	94.65	92.78	83.91	74.68
Standard deviation (σ)	0.0919	0.0996	0.0924	0.1158	0.1659	0.1270
Percentage of DMUs in I	90.91	45.45	92.31	61.54	60.00	60.00

White part (variable returns to scale)

	Belgium		Czech Republic		Finland	
	2000	2001	2000	2001	2000	2001
No. of DMUs	11	11	13	14	6	6
No. of efficient DMUs	10	10	8	7	2	3
Average efficiency (M)	99.47	99.66	95.30	93.83	95.33	92.63
Adj. avg. efficiency (AM)	99.93	99.95	92.41	95.81	97.33	94.54
Standard deviation (σ)	0.0166	0.0108	0.0681	0.0766	0.0566	0.0815
Percentage of DMUs in I	100.00	100.00	84.62	85.71	83.33	83.33

	Hungary		Poland		Slovakia	
	2000	2001	2000	2001	2000	2001
No. of DMUs	11	11	13	13	10	10
No. of efficient DMUs	5	6	7	3	4	2
Average efficiency (M)	93.97	93.73	94.81	90.63	86.65	82.45
Adj. avg. efficiency (AM)	91.78	93.88	97.80	95.43	89.12	80.02
Standard deviation (σ)	0.0791	0.0870	0.0698	0.1128	0.1629	0.1397
Percentage of DMUs in I	72.73	81.82	84.62	76.92	70.00	70.00

Source: Authors' calculations.

first twice. One can consider this result as an empirical justification of the comment pointed out in Chapter 1, Section 1.1 that the size of a market does not directly affect the efficiency of intermediation. In Finland, the banking sector represents the smallest part of the financial sector relative to all countries analysed (see Figure 1.5 and Figure 1.6). Hence, it does not suffer from an extensive amount of deposits and inadequate volume of loans as do the banking sectors of traditionally B-system transition countries (Czech Republic, Slovakia) in a period of calm and limited lending activity.[8]

On the other hand, the last place was held seven times by the Slovak banking sector and the sixth position went once to Belgium. The Czech banking sector showed itself as the most aligned banking industry among transition countries, as evidenced in the fluctuation of its ranking. The Czech Republic was in second place three times and was ranked third five times. The Hungarian banking sector most often had third, fourth and fifth placing and Polish banks were on average ranked primarily fourth and fifth. These results allow us to conclude that the final ranking in the intermediation approach was Finland in first place, followed by the Czech Republic, Belgium,[9] Hungary, Poland and without doubt, the worst, Slovakia in last place.

The explanation of generally lower intermediation efficiency in the CEC can be found in a couple of factors mentioned in Chapter 1, Section 1.1, above all, past NPLs, low credit scores of the majority of potential borrowers, the dormant capacity of lending to households. In 2001, loans to households amounted to 6.5 per cent of GDP in the Czech Republic and 6 per cent of GDP in Hungary, while it was 30 per cent of GDP in Austria. In addition, much of the investment in transition countries has been realized by foreign investors either with their own financial resources, or with connections to foreign banks and foreign capital. As a result, potential borrowers and clients of the first quality have brushed aside the banks as well as capital markets in transition countries regardless of the method of investment (privatization, merger and acquisition or 'green-field' investment). As a consequence of high interest rates, a considerable number of domestic companies have decided to finance their business activities from abroad, obtaining resources from foreign banks and thus reducing capital costs. The indebtedness of companies at home as well as abroad had the same levels only in the Czech Republic; with the rest of the V4 countries, indebtedness abroad was substantially higher.

The average efficiency scores obtained from the operational approach are, with the exception of Finland, distinctively higher than the scores of the intermediation approach. Hence, the country ranking changed considerably. In measurements using adjusted average efficiency, Belgium was in first place six times and Poland was ranked first twice. It is valuable to note, however, that Poland had fourth and fifth places when ranked by average efficiency. The results for Hungary and the Czech Republic were quite similar to Poland, with less than notable differences. Finnish banks suffered from scale problems in the operational approach, as illustrated by their fifth and sixth positions in the CCR model, whereas in the BCC model, the Finnish banking sector was placed second, third and fourth. Probably, the only common characteristic of the results of the intermediation and operational approaches was the poor performance of Slovak banks, which on average had last ranking seven times and fifth once. Accordingly, the operational approach was led by Belgium, followed by the group of three transition countries, namely Poland, the Czech Republic and Hungary, whose results did not differ significantly. Fifth place went to Finland and in the unfavourable sixth place was Slovakia.

The inefficiency of the Finnish banking sector may have been caused by the inadequate size of banks in relation to the size of the market characterized by a sparse population dispersed in a large area. Finnish banks usually establish branches at places that do not create a real potential for sufficient profit, resulting in the deterioration of the operational efficiency of the whole bank and banking system. All six banks had capital higher than EUR 60 million in 2001, and four of them even higher than EUR 150 million.

The lower operational efficiency of banks in transition countries is brought about, among other factors, by the deficient use of banking services. While a bank account and associated products belong among standard and widely used services of almost every citizen older than 15 years in developed European countries, in the analysed V4 countries the share is significantly lower. In the Czech Republic and Hungary, roughly 70 per cent of the adult population own and use a current bank account and in Poland and Slovakia, 60 per cent. The distribution and use of saving accounts or payment instruments are even less evident. Banking sectors in transition countries have also witnessed a rapid expansion of the medium-sized banks (mainly subsidiaries of foreign banks) in the retail market as described in Chapter 1, Section 1.3. This increase has been accompanied by investment in information technologies, formation of branch networks, engagement of new employees, factors which have negatively affected the operational efficiency in the period analysed.

We can find studies estimating the efficiency frontiers for banks in a country or in several countries. Those studies analysing several countries must deal with differences in economic development, legislative framework or institutional environment of the relevant countries. There are two possible approaches to solving the problem. One group of economists incorporate into efficiency frontier estimation some specific variables that aim to compensate the aforementioned differences. The other one also constructs, apart from the common frontier, particular country frontiers. There are not many cross-country studies using this approach (e.g. Berg *et al.*, 1993 applies it). However, we have followed it in this section and interesting results obtained are reported in Table 4.5. The lower the difference between the 'country' average efficiency (only banks from one country are analysed) and 'common' average efficiency (all banks analysed), the fewer banks from other countries are more efficient than domestic banks.

The banking sectors can be grouped into three pairs. The first pair with the lowest difference consists of EU members' banking sectors (Belgium and Finland). There is no serious difference between the efficiency computed for banks from a particular country and the efficiency computed for a group of all analysed banks. Belgium and Finland are followed by the pair Hungary and the Czech Republic and the pair Poland and Slovakia, whose efficiency scores vary in some cases by more than 20 percentage points. Such a picture hides one of the conclusions from Chapter 1 that only a few banks from the CEC are performing better than banks from EU member countries.

One of the strengths of DEA is its ability to provide information about sources of inefficiency in both input and output. This information is extremely useful for managers in improving organizational performance. We have already established that the banking sectors analysed struggled with serious scale problems, which, in turn, negatively affected the efficiency of the industry. However, even after the scale effect had been removed by using the BCC model, some of the banking sectors still suffered from high technical inefficiency. This indicates an excess use of resources, output shortfalls, or a combination of the two.

Regarding the intermediation approach, in both years, the inefficiency of all Belgian banks on the input side stemmed from high labour costs and from too many clients' deposits that were not used effectively. On the output side, the results show that banks performed relatively well in providing loans to customers, but some area for improvement existed in providing loans to other financial institutions. Many common sources of banking inefficiency from the CEC are visible in the

Table 4.5 Comparison of average efficiency calculated by country or common frontier estimation (%)

	Belgium 2000		Belgium 2001		Czech Republic 2000		Czech Republic 2001	
	Country	Common	Country	Common	Country	Common	Country	Common
CCR – intermediation	82.78	77.54	84.09	78.91	96.99	76.83	95.24	81.71
CCR – operating	98.19	97.01	98.54	97.05	99.59	89.83	97.63	86.49
BCC – intermediation	95.42	86.95	99.98	92.67	98.02	89.62	96.33	88.82
BCC – operating	100.0	99.47	100.0	99.66	99.73	95.30	100.0	93.83

	Finland 2000		Finland 2001		Hungary 2000		Hungary 2001	
	Country	Common	Country	Common	Country	Common	Country	Common
CCR – intermediation	94.68	90.88	89.08	83.87	90.58	73.58	92.64	83.10
CCR – operating	99.24	87.65	98.28	84.92	95.89	91.22	94.26	91.34
BCC – intermediation	95.87	93.24	96.46	85.49	93.19	78.87	95.65	86.31
BCC – operating	100.0	95.33	100.0	92.63	97.74	93.37	96.81	93.73

	Poland 2000		Poland 2001		Slovakia 2000		Slovakia 2001	
	Country	Common	Country	Common	Country	Common	Country	Common
CCR – intermediation	96.93	75.66	93.34	73.32	87.21	61.49	93.29	73.26
CCR – operating	96.79	89.62	94.15	85.30	95.27	82.15	95.19	75.98
BCC – intermediation	100.0	85.51	97.87	81.64	92.98	67.68	98.75	80.54
BCC – operating	98.70	94.81	95.46	90.63	96.57	86.65	98.85	82.45

Source: Authors' calculations.

results. Czech, Hungarian, Polish and Slovak banks suffered in both years from the low efficiency of fixed assets' usage. As the comparison of financial and banking sectors from Chapter 1 and the characteristics mentioned above might suggest, inefficiency of Czech and Slovak banks in the intermediation process is also caused by redundant or surplus amount of deposits in relation to their insufficient level of lending activities. On the other hand, high labour costs appeared as a considerable source of inefficiency in Poland and Hungary. This finding reminds us of the conclusions of Chapter 3, where we reported low concentration of these banking sectors and identified them as overbanked because of a great number of active banks. Hence more employees must be employed in the banking industry, but their working capacity is wasted and they do not contribute to the bank's profitability and efficiency at the appropriate level. The most significant source of inefficiency of Hungarian banks on the output side is the inadequately small amount of loans to other depository institutions.

Concerning the operational approach and excluding Belgium as the most efficient banking sector, the inefficiency of the rest of the banking sectors, mainly the big banks from transition countries, is on the input side due to the less efficient usage of the banks' own resources (capital) more than the other three inputs, namely interest expenses, fees and commissions paid, and labour costs. The inefficiency on the output side of the operational process was determined especially from low incomes in fees and commissions. Despite the introduction of new products and services and changes to their charging policy, and even though these banks increasingly receive fees and commissions, they are still not maximizing to their full capacity.

After analysing banking sectors according to country, we now turn to the structural insight of efficiency evaluation. In Tables 4.6 and 4.7 banks are classified into peer groups according to their size and results are presented separately for each group. While interpreting the data, it is necessary to note that composition of the peer groups changed slightly over the period analysed because banks moved from one group to the other. The results show that the largest banks were the most efficient, reaching the highest average efficiency score in six out of eight measurements, using the BCC model. It is quite a common finding of many studies that smaller banks dominate the frontier in the CCR model, while in the BCC model, frontier banks are on average much larger. Berg *et al.* (1993) and Vujcic and Jemric (2002) came to the same conclusion as our study, as is evident from the Appendix.

Table 4.6 Efficiency of banks grouped by size (tier 1 capital) – intermediation approach with constant returns to scale (grey part) and variable returns to scale (white part) (%)

	Over EUR 1bn				EUR 150mn–1bn				EUR 30mn–150mn				Less than EUR 30mn			
	2000		2001		2000		2001		2000		2001		2000		2001	
	No. of DMUs	Average effic.	No. of DMUs	Average effic.	No. of DMUs	Average effic.	No. of DMUs	Average effic.	No. of DMUs	Average effic.	No. of DMUs	Average effic.	No. of DMUs	Average effic.	No. of DMUs	Average effic.
Belgium	4	87.23	4	100.0	1	100.0	1	100.0	3	100.0	3	98.96	3	77.31	3	75.64
Czech Republic	0	–	0	–	4	100.0	5	96.70	3	81.66	4	84.11	6	95.44	5	95.96
Finland	2	98.06	2	100.0	2	100.0	2	85.14	3	89.09	2	67.92	0	–	0	–
Hungary	0	–	0	–	4	95.05	5	91.38	6	77.66	6	87.20	1	100.0	0	–
Poland	0	–	0	–	7	92.12	8	76.73	4	90.99	3	83.71	2	100.0	2	100.0
Slovakia	0	–	0	–	1	50.39	2	80.40	5	78.69	6	83.34	4	74.47	2	84.54
TOTAL	6	90.84	6	100.0	18	93.08	23	86.32	24	84.82	24	85.15	16	87.65	12	89.65
Belgium	4	87.78	4	100.0	1	100.0	1	100.0	3	100.0	3	100.0	3	77.49	3	75.81
Czech Republic	0	–	0	–	4	100.0	5	96.99	3	91.28	4	91.56	6	95.57	5	97.77
Finland	2	100.0	2	100.0	1	100.0	2	89.31	3	100.0	2	89.70	0	–	0	–
Hungary	0	–	0	–	4	96.06	5	95.09	6	81.58	6	87.73	1	100.0	0	–
Poland	0	–	0	–	7	92.99	8	88.64	4	97.61	3	84.69	2	100.0	2	100.0
Slovakia	0	–	0	–	1	100.0	2	100.0	5	94.11	6	90.73	4	81.28	2	98.86
TOTAL	6	91.85	6	100.0	18	96.40	23	93.40	24	92.68	24	90.44	16	89.44	12	92.83

Source: Authors' calculations.

Table 4.7 Efficiency of banks grouped by size (tier 1 capital) – operating approach with constant returns to scale (grey part) and variable returns to scale (white part) (%)

	Over EUR 1 bn				EUR 150 mn.–1 bn				EUR 30 mn.–150 mn				Less than EUR 30 mn			
	2000		2001		2000		2001		2000		2001		2000		2001	
	No. of DMUs	Average effic.	No. of DMUs	Average effic.	No. of DMUs	Average effic.	No. of DMUs	Average effic.	No. of DMUs	Average effic.	No. of DMUs	Average effic.	No. of DMUs	Average effic.	No. of DMUs	Average effic.
Belgium	4	100.0	4	99.14	1	100.0	1	100.0	3	100.0	3	98.96	3	97.90	3	100.0
Czech Republic	0	–	0	–	4	94.35	5	95.02	3	87.93	4	84.11	6	99.16	5	97.43
Finland	2	100.0	2	100.0	1	100.0	2	96.84	3	96.28	2	67.92	0	–	0	–
Hungary	0	–	0	–	4	94.25	5	97.10	6	97.62	6	87.20	1	100.0	0	–
Poland	0	–	0	–	7	97.14	8	91.99	4	97.66	3	83.71	2	89.99	2	100.0
Slovakia	0	–	0	–	1	89.95	2	91.88	5	84.53	6	83.34	4	91.77	2	100.0
TOTAL	6	100.0	6	99.43	18	95.80	23	94.52	24	93.82	24	85.15	16	95.98	12	98.93
Belgium	4	100.0	4	100.0	1	100.0	1	100.0	3	100.0	3	100.0	3	98.07	3	100.0
Czech Republic	0	–	0	–	4	97.21	5	96.89	3	100.0	4	91.56	6	100.0	5	100.0
Finland	2	100.0	2	100.0	1	100.0	2	100.0	3	100.0	2	89.70	0	–	0	–
Hungary	0	–	0	–	4	96.06	5	97.24	6	99.47	6	87.73	1	100.0	0	–
Poland	0	–	0	–	7	97.35	8	94.87	4	100.0	3	84.69	2	92.76	2	100.0
Slovakia	0	–	0	–	1	96.17	2	95.71	5	94.34	6	90.73	4	91.98	2	100.0
TOTAL	6	100.0	6	100.0	18	97.37	23	93.57	24	98.69	24	90.44	16	96.73	12	100.0

Source: Authors' calculations.

Although it seems that the variable returns to scale model is a more plausible choice for banking efficiency analysis, we should point out that Peer Group 1 consisted of only the six largest banks from Belgium and Finland, and they might appear efficient simply because there are no more good reference banks for them. The same limitation was also referred to by Vujcic and Jemric (2002). On the other hand, Peer Group 3 was likely to represent the worst group since it was placed last six times. Hence it seems that the most efficient banks are either the smallest or the largest, while, on average, the most dangerous or slippery territory belongs to medium-sized banks. However, the results of Peer Group 2, which includes the largest banks from transition countries, were considerably worse in the period 1993–99 because they were extremely overstaffed and burdened with NPLs.

Ownership is thought to be related to a financial institution's performance, because the incentives for managers to allocate resources efficiently might differ under different ownership arrangements. If owners do not have the incentive or capability to monitor the activity of management, then agency problems and subsequent costs are expected to increase. In particular it is expected that privately owned banks are more efficient than state-owned banks, and that foreign banks will be relatively more efficient, because their corporate governance is of international standards. This conclusion was reported, among others, by Laeven (1999).

We do not attempt to average the efficiencies of state-owned banks and privately owned banks and try to test the hypothesis that privately owned banks outperform the state-owned ones. The reason is that the period analysed represents the final stage of the privatization process in the banking sectors of all the transition countries when the sample of state-owned banks amounted to very few institutions. This set would not be representative, and results might be irrelevant. However, this approach was followed by Denizer *et al.* (2000), Grigorian and Manole (2002), Laeven (1999) and Vujcic and Jemric (2002). All these studies confirmed the hypothesis, reporting higher efficiency scores for privately owned banks.

Hence, we distinguished domestic ownership and foreign ownership regardless of state or private ownership. Banks were not grouped into peer groups but the average efficiencies were obtained from the whole set estimation. Banks owned by investors from any other transition country were considered domestic-owned. This approach was viewed as a good method to restrict foreign ownership only on investors from developed countries. Table 4.8 reports the results.

Table 4.8 Efficiency of banks by ownership status (%)

	Intermediation approach				Operating approach			
	CCR model		BCC model		CCR model		BCC model	
	2000	2001	2000	2001	2000	2001	2000	2001
Czech Republic								
2000: 6 domestic-owned, 7 foreign-owned					2001: 5 domestic-owned, 9 foreign-owned			
Efficiency of domestic	86.26	92.15	91.31	93.41	90.72	86.64	96.07	92.23
Efficiency of foreign	70.33	75.90	88.17	86.27	89.06	86.35	94.63	94.71
Hungary								
2000: 4 domestic-owned, 7 foreign-owned					2001: 3 domestic-owned, 8 foreign-owned			
Efficiency of domestic	70.57	75.44	74.05	77.14	91.66	93.68	92.11	96.04
Efficiency of foreign	75.29	85.97	81.62	89.74	90.97	90.46	93.95	92.86
Poland								
2000: 5 domestic-owned, 8 foreign-owned					2001: 4 domestic-owned, 9 foreign-owned			
Efficiency of domestic	91.61	84.89	94.63	90.11	91.25	90.08	98.07	95.92
Efficiency of foreign	65.69	66.73	79.81	77.88	88.60	83.17	92.77	88.27
Slovakia								
2000: 4 domestic-owned, 6 foreign-owned					2001: 3 domestic-owned, 7 foreign-owned			
Efficiency of domestic	56.05	55.76	68.85	71.02	77.40	73.75	87.40	84.49
Efficiency of foreign	65.12	80.76	66.90	84.62	85.32	77.37	86.14	81.57

Source: Authors' calculations.

The most significant finding suggests that, with the exception of Slovakia and the intermediation approach in Hungary, the foreign banks did not reach higher efficiency than domestic banks. Our findings of the Hungarian banks' efficiency are in total accord with the results of Hasan and Marton (2000). This result does not conform with the widely held belief of higher efficiency in foreign banks. There are several reasons for this.

First, foreign banks entered the banking markets of the CEC at the beginning of the transformation process and the boom of their activities began in the middle of the 1990s. Foreign banks influenced the new markets significantly, as described in Chapter 1. They were almost certainly more efficient than domestic banks during this period. However, the gap in quality of banking services, know-how, risk management and production technology started to narrow gradually, and today the difference is not as dramatic.

Second, medium-sized banks completely owned, for instance, by Citibank, ErsteBank, Raiffeisenbank, HVB, Volksbank and others have recently started to expand their activities in the retail market and they are forming and building up their market positions. Associated necessary investment worsens efficiency in a short-term horizon.

The third reason stems from the structure of the domestic-owned banks' group. Small banks that dominate the efficiency frontier but not the banking market represent the majority of domestic-owned banks and this affects average efficiency. The largest banks were considered as foreign-owned because of privatization; however, almost all of them suffered from scale inefficiency. In addition, private ownership and strategic investments did not bring in positive effects due to the very short period since privatization took effect. Only some of them, which were privatized last, belonged to the group of domestic-owned banks in 2000.[10]

If we compare the results obtained from both approaches, there are smaller differences between efficiency of domestic-owned and foreign-owned banks in the operating approach than in the intermediation approach. This supports our hypothesis that the quality of cost/revenues management of banking activities does not differ according to type of ownership. Only Slovakia, from the results, shows foreign-owned banks as more efficient in most cases.

4.3 Privatization and banking sector profitability

In EU countries as well as in the CEC, banking sectors have seen important changes during recent years. Privatization is one of the most important steps in transition countries, inevitable for changing centrally planed economies to market economies (Fuchs, 2002). The improvement of the banking sector's profitability is one of the main positive aspects of privatization of Central European banks. Other positive aspects are that foreign investors have brought in additional capital, skills, experience and managerial capability. An important benefit should also be a higher level of competition in the banking sector and elimination of political pressures on banks (Turnovec, 2000). The result is that privatization has strengthened the banking sectors of the CEC as well as increased their profitability.

Generally it is difficult to separate a privatization impact on banks' profitability from other factors. Financial liberalization, globalization and technological changes over recent years have challenged banks' competitive pressures, and the approaching privatization of these banks pressed them to react strongly. The region's economic recovery helped banks' profitability while NPLs worsened it.

The relationship between ownership structure and performance of industrial companies is mostly covered by an interesting literature. Many fewer papers concerning the banking sector can be found – one of rare exceptions is that of Altunbas *et al.* (2001). They find little evidence to suggest that privately owned banks are more efficient than their mutual and public sector counterparts, which entirely corresponds with results of our study presented in Section 4.2.2. On the other hand, it is generally agreed that privatization improves the profitability of the banking sector and strengthens its stability in transition countries. On the basis of several indicators, the analysis in this section confirms this in the case of the Czech Republic, Slovakia and Poland. Data for developed countries are given as a benchmark.

This section first explains the basic features of the privatization process in the Czech Republic, in Slovakia and in Poland (Section 4.3.1). Then we explain why privatization could be seen as one of the most important factors strengthening stability of the banking sector on the basis of profitability (Section 4.3.2), asset quality (Section 4.3.3) and bank capitalization (Section 4.3.4).

4.3.1   Privatization of banks in the Czech Republic, Slovakia and Poland

Privatization in major European countries started in the mid-1980s (for instance with the sale of Société Générale in France), but acquired momentum only in the 1990s. Many banks (for instance Italian savings banks) changed their ownership structure from exclusively 'foundation-owned' to more open, shareholder-based, entities (Belaisch *et al.*, 2001).

Banking sector privatization in the Czech Republic, Slovakia and Poland started during the 1990s and was completed (partly) only recently. Privatization influences on the composition of foreign ownership may vary considerably. The pioneer foreign banks such as Bank Austria Creditanstalt, Citibank or Raiffeisenbank, which established their subsidiaries as brand new banks in the first half of the transformation process in transition countries, are gradually losing their positions. Table 4.9 illustrates this development and shows only three pioneer banks among the top 20 foreign banks in the CEC region. On the other hand, the most active foreign banks in the privatization process (for

Table 4.9   Top 20 foreign banks in Central and Eastern Europe*

Bank	Country	Regional market share (%)	Total assets in region (EUR bn)
KBC	Belgium	11.29	24.29
BA/CA	Austria	10.30	21.58
Erste	Austria	9.47	20.37
Unicredito	Italy	8.41	18.09
Citibank	USA	6.92	14.89
Société Générale	France	6.83	14.69
ING	Netherlands	5.78	12.44
Raiffeisen	Austria	5.17	11.13
Banca Commerciale Italina/Intesa	Italy	4.61	9.92
Commerzbank	Germany	3.64	7.84
ABN AMRO	Netherlands	2.53	5.45
Allied Irish Bank	Ireland	2.33	5.00
Deutsche Bank	Germany	2.25	4.84
GE Capital	USA	2.09	4.45
Bayersiche Landesbanken	Germany	1.62	3.48
Banco Commercial Portugues	Portugal	1.57	3.37
Crédit Lyonnais	France	0.98	2.11
Bankgesellschaft Berlin	Germany	0.90	1.95
Volksbank	Austria	0.66	1.40
Hypobank	Austria	0.66	1.40

* Assets to 31 December 2001 based on ownership interests as at June 2002.

Source: Bank Austria Creditanstalt.

instance KBC, Erste Bank, UniCredito Italiano or Société Générale) gained the highest positions in the ranking after acquisitions of the largest CEC banks. Above all, Belgian KBC continues to be the bank with the largest volume of assets and market share in Central and Eastern Europe.

In the Czech Republic the privatization of large state-owned banks started in 1998 with the Investiční a poštovní banka (Investment and Post Bank), followed by ČSOB (Czechoslovak Trade Bank) in 1999 and by Česká spořitelna (Czech Savings Bank) in 2000. The last of the large state-owned banks – Komerční banka – was privatized in 2001 and only some specialized banks (Czech and Moravian Guarantee and Development Bank, Czech Export Bank) remain in state hands. The share of private banks in various indicators of the banking sector exceeds 90 per cent (depending on the particular indicator) and is a bit higher than in Slovakia or in Poland. Also credit ratings of privatized banks have improved (Table 4.10). We can expect serious but probably only gradual improvement in banking sector profitability in the future. On the other hand the improvement in asset quality and bank capitalization should come in the near future.

In Poland privatization in the banking sector started in 1993 with WBK (Wielkopolski Bank Kredytowy) and the relatively large Bank Sląski (Silesian Bank) in Katowice in 1993. The main steps in privatization were taken during 1996–99. The increase of the private sector in banking was relatively slow in 2000 and in 2001 (partly as a result of the parliamentary elections in 2001) and in the end the privatization strategy was overestimated. For the time being 68 per cent of banking sector assets and 79 per cent of own funds are in the hands of banks with a majority of foreign capital (see Ogrodnik, 2001). Two large banks remain (2003) in the hands of the government: Poland's largest savings bank, PKO Bank Polski, which is the only locally owned bank in the top 10 Central European banks. The Ministry of Finance now guarantees 90 per cent of the bank's low-cost loans to housing cooperatives (as from 1965–92).

Banking sector privatization in Slovakia started only recently and most of our expectations concerning profitability must be confirmed in the future. Nevertheless the privatization process in Slovakia is very rapid. There are 20 banks in Slovakia, 17 of them in the hands of foreign investors (83 per cent of assets). The only large state-owned bank – Banka Slovakia – has not been sold so far; 55 per cent of Poštová banka (Post Bank), another large state-owned bank, was sold in 2002.

Table 4.10 Credit ratings of ČSOB, ČS and KB

Agency	ČSOB					
	Before privatization (31. 12. 1997)		*After privatization (15. 4. 2000)*		*At present (31. 12. 2002)*	
	Long-term liabilities	*Short-term liabilities*	*Long-term liabilities*	*Short-term liabilities*	*Long-term liabilities*	*Short-term liabilities*
FITCH					BBB+	F2
Moody's Investors	Baa2	Prime−2	Baa1	Prime−2	A1	Prime−2
Standard & Poor's	BBB−	A−3	BBB−	A−3	BBB	A−2
Capital Intelligence	BBB−	A2	BBB−	A3	BBB	A3

Agency	Česká spořitelna					
	Before privatization (31. 12. 1999)		*After privatization (31. 12. 2000)*		*At present (31. 12. 2002)*	
	Long-term liabilities	*Short-term liabilities*	*Long-term liabilities*	*Short-term liabilities*	*Long-term liabilities*	*Short-term liabilities*
FITCH	BBB	F2	BBB	F2	BBB	F2
Moody's Investors	Baa2	Prime−2	Baa1	Prime−2	A2	Prime−1
Standard & Poor's	BB	B	BB	B	BBB−	A3

Agency	Komerční banka					
	Before privatization (31. 12. 2000)		*After privatization (18. 10. 2001)*		*At present (31. 12. 2002)*	
	Long-term liabilities	*Short-term liabilities*	*Long-term liabilities*	*Short-term liabilities*	*Long-term liabilities*	*Short-term liabilities*
FITCH	BBB	F2	BBB+	F2	BBB+	F2
Moody's Investors	Baa2	Prime−2	Baa1	Prime−2	A1	Prime−1
Standard & Poor's	BB	B	BB+	B	BBB−	A3

Source: Annual reports of ČSOB, ČS and KB.

4.3.2 Profitability

Banks in CEC have focused on improvement of profitability, measured in terms of return on assets (ROA, the ratio of pre-tax profits to assets) and return on equity (ROE, the ratio of pre-tax profits to equity), only recently.

The new products offered to clients, huge investments in information technologies and staff reductions are some of the factors that supported ROA and ROE growth during bank privatization in the transition countries. Without any doubt all investors underlined this strategy and all the above-mentioned steps. That is why the profitability of the banking sector has been growing relatively rapidly during recent years in Poland, Slovakia and the Czech Republic.

Over the transition process all Central European banks (even before privatization) started with the development of non-interest-income activities. These may have a positive effect on banks' performance and non-interest income has been the most dynamic component in banks' income as a whole. It can be confirmed for the industrial countries that, where the contribution of non-interest income remains small (Germany, Austria), profitability measured by ROA actually declined (Belaisch *et al.*, 2001, p. 32). The Czech, Slovak and Polish banks belong to those banks in which non-interest-income earnings grew rapidly during the 1990s.

Data from industrial countries generally show an increase in ROA and a very marked increase in ROE in 1990s (Table 4.11). This confirms growing competition in the banking sector, globalization of banking services and focus on the owner's earnings in companies. The comparison of industrial countries data on profitability with the same data in Poland, Slovakia and the Czech Republic (Table 4.12) suggests that further improvement in profitability in transition countries can be expected. Also higher stability of indicators is desirable. What is striking is that the indicators of ROA in Slovakia are very high – this is the result of under-capitalization of large Slovak state-owned banks. Capital support of banks given by the government in 1999 made the ROE indicator more

Table 4.11   Profitability of banks in some industrial countries (%)

	France	Italy	Spain	Belgium	Finland	Ireland	Portugal
1992							
ROA	0.2	0.3	0.2	0.3	−1.0	0.9	0.7
ROE	3.9	5.0	2.6	9.1	−21.7	14.9	10.3
1995							
ROA	0.3	0.3	0.7	0.3	−0.1	1.1	0.7
ROE	6.0	4.7	12.4	10.9	−1.4	14.9	12.2
1998							
ROA	0.3	0.5	0.9	0.6	0.7	1.1	0.8
ROE	8.0	7.6	14.5	17.5	14.0	17.7	14.8

Source: Belaisch *et al.* (2001).

Table 4.12 Profitability of banks in the CEC (%)

	1993	1994	1995	1996	1997	1998	1999	2000	2001	2002
Czech Republic										
ROA	0.75	0.41	0.07	0.56	negative	negative	negative	0.57	0.93	1.59
ROE	9.53	5.32	0.97	11.32	negative	negative	negative	13.08	14.41	22.05
Poland										
ROA	negative	0.30	1.94	2.25	1.81	0.54	0.85	0.99	0.89	0.85**
ROE	negative	3.52	23.29	26.89	21.13	6.39	10.05	12.09	12.27	9.90**
Slovakia										
ROA	4.66	5.54	5.02	3.69	4.03	4.01	3.46	3.91	3.70	2.61*
ROE	175.43	176.04	148.60	125.21	127.32	115.07	58.13	70.81	87.18	68.31*

* 3Q; ** 2Q.

Source: ČNB, NBP, NBS, authors' calculations.

reliable. Nevertheless the ROA and ROE data development in all three countries confirms our expectations – privatization means ROA and ROE growth; privatization means improvement in banks' profitability.

4.3.3 Asset quality

Asset quality can be measured by the NPLs of banks. Some countries do not publish figures on the level of NPLs (Germany, Austria, Luxembourg, the Netherlands), but in most of the Central European countries these figures are easily available for recent years. Moreover, the indicator of NPLs is unique.

In the Czech Republic and Slovakia NPLs are one of the typical and persistent features of banking sector transformation. The share of NPLs is much higher than in any other industrial or transition countries (see Table 4.13). In the Czech Republic the situation worsened after the banking crises in 1997–98. NPLs require high provisions to protect depositors from losses.

In Poland, Slovakia and the Czech Republic the asset quality in banks has markedly improved through the transfer of bad loans of privatized banks into the specialized institutions (Consolidation or Hospital Bank). The same way of cleaning bank portfolios was used in some industrial countries (Crédit Lyonnais in France, Banco di Napoli in Italy and so on). Nevertheless in industrial countries the share of NPLs in total loans remains very low (Table 4.14) in comparison with Slovakia and the Czech Republic (Table 4.15). After privatization this indicator shows a gradual tendency to improve in the Czech Republic, but the NPLs/loans indicator has grown surprisingly in Poland.

Table 4.13   Non-performing loans during financial crises in some countries (% of total loans)*

	Crises in 1980s		Crises in 1990s			
	Peak of the crises	*NPLs*	*1990*	*1994*	*1995*	*1996*
Korea	1986	6.7	2.1	1.0	0.9	0.8
India	–	–	–	23.6	19.5	17.3
Hong Kong	–	–	–	3.1	2.9	2.7
Taiwan	1986	5.5	1.2	2.0	3.1	3.8
Indonesia	–	–	4.5	12.0	10.4	8.8
Malaysia	1988	32.9	20.6	10.2	6.1	3.9
Thailand	1983–88	15.0	9.7	7.5	7.7	?
Argentina	1985	30.3	16.0	8.6	12.3	9.4
Brazil	–	–	4.7	3.9	8.9	5.8
Chile	1983	15.5	2.1	1.0	1.0	1.0
Colombia	1984	25.3	2.2	2.2	2.7	4.6
Mexico	1982	4.1	2.3	10.5	19.1	12.5
Venezuela	1983	15.4	3.0	24.7	10.6	3.8
USA	1987	4.1	3.3	1.9	1.3	1.1
Finland	1992	8.0	–	4.6	3.9	2.7
Norway	1992	9.1	–	25.4	4.5	3.2
Sweden	1992	11.0	6.0	4.0	3.0	–
Czech Republic	–	–	–	38.8	33.6	30.7

* Data are not fully comparable due to different accounting standards.

Source: Jonáš (1998).

Table 4.14   Asset quality – non-performing loans in selected industrial countries (% of total loans)

	France	*Italy*	*Spain*	*Belgium*	*Finland*	*Ireland*	*Portugal*
1995	8.5	9.0	6.0	4.0	6.0	n.a.	5.9
1998	6.3	8.9	1.7	3.2	1.8	2.1	2.8

Source: Belaisch *et al.* (2001).

Table 4.15   Asset quality – non-performing loans in the CEC (% of total loans)

	1993	*1994*	*1995*	*1996*	*1997*	*1998*	*1999*	*2000*	*2001*	*2002*
Czech Republic	13.41	24.20	30.50	28.80	28.30	28.80	33.50	29.83	21.53	16.89*
Poland	31.02	28.52	20.9	13.20	10.50	10.90	13.70	16.27	17.73	20.99**
Slovakia	11.82	28.43	40.26	32.08	33.09	37.95	34.88	23.92	24.31	11.54*

* 3Q; ** 2Q.

Sources: ČNB, NBP, NBS, authors' calculations.

4.3.4 Bank capitalization

In order to be competitive, banks in the CEC have no other choice than to boost their capitalization. Growing activities and thus growing assets demand more and more capital. Greater capitalization also helps to reduce the costs of borrowed funds for banks. This is very important for the CEC, where capital markets are underdeveloped and a large share of savings is not saved in banks. To improve capitalization, banks started to issue hybrid instruments (quasi-equity) and subordinated debt.

At the beginning of the 1990s the Capital Adequacy Directive and the Basel Committee's recommendations on bank soundness were accepted by the Czech Republic as well as by Slovakia and Poland. This was the only way to make the banking sector more credible. Nevertheless the basic reason for the growth of capital in banks was to fulfil the criteria demanded by central banks. But this process would be impossible without government help. To boost banks' capitalization was very expensive for government budgets, and also had a marked impact on bank privatization (Polouček *et al.*, 2001). Government budget deficits and persistent inefficiency of banks were among the major reasons for privatization. In the Czech Republic the costs of keeping government banks working and of selling them later were much higher than the price these banks were sold for. Details are reported in Table 4.16, nevertheless some studies estimate even higher costs (Matoušek and Taci, 2000).

Data in Tables 4.17 and 4.18 confirm that there is no important difference between capitalization measured by equity/total assets or BIS ratio in developed countries and in Poland, respectively in Slovakia and in the Czech Republic. The equity/total assets indicators are slightly higher in the case of Poland than in industrial countries, while they are slightly lower in the case of the Czech Republic. Further capitalization can be expected in all these countries. The new owners should be guarantors of this development.

4.4 Risk and profitability of banks in the CEC

This section determines risk factors by incorporating them into the banking sector in Poland, Slovakia and the Czech Republic. The basic idea is that the stability of the banking sector relates closely to its risk and profitability. Higher risk is usually related to higher profitability and the quality of banks' management is reflected in how they manage to optimize profitability and risk. To define risk factors, which affect profitability, is also a rather complex issue, both theoretically and practically.

Table 4.16   Costs and incomes of the Czech banking sector (CZK bn)

	Costs paid from government budget	Income	Expected income*	Total income	Share sold (%)	Overvaluation of the net present value
Investiční a poštovní banka	95.0 **	3.0	10.0	−82.0	36.00	n.a.
ČSOB	56.4					
capital increase	56.4	40.047		−15.953	65.69	2.2
NPLs (PTS)						
Česká spořitelna						
capital increase	4.5	19.0	6.9	−3.0	52.07	1.8
NPLs (PTS)	3.0		20.1			
NPLs	41.5 ***					
Komerční banka						
capital increase	6.8	40.00	13.0	1.4	60.00	3.2
NPLs (PTS)	11.8		35.5			(2.6)
NPLs	68.5					
Small banks	73.0	n.a.	n.a.	n.a.	n.a.	n.a.
Agrobanka	42.0	n.a.	n.a.	n.a.	na.a	n.a.
TOTAL	402.5	102.047	85.5	−99.553	n.a.	n.a.

* Expected income or payment of NPLs.
** Estimation.
*** 8 bn of that estimation.

Sources: ČNB, Internet sites of particular banks.

Table 4.17   Capitalization in selected industrial countries in 1998 (%)

	France	Germany	Italy	Spain	Austria	Belgium	Finland	Ireland	Portugal
BIS ratio 5 largest banks	11.0	10.1	9.6	12.0	12.7	11.0	11.9	12.5	11.4
Equity/total assets	4.4	3.4	6.3	6.4	4.0	3.5	5.0	6.1	5.3

Source: Belaisch *et al.* (2001).

In Section 4.4.1, profitability and risk are defined. Section 4.4.2 offers presuppositions and hypotheses, from which the analysis proceeds, and model relations are expressed among variables. Hypotheses are tested and results are commented on Section 4.4.3. The analysis is carried out in the banking sectors of three CEC (the Czech Republic, Slovakia and Poland) in 1993–2001. Conclusions and the final summary are contained in the last section of the chapter.

Table 4.18 Capitalization of banks in transition countries (%)

	1993	1994	1995	1996	1997	1998	1999	2000	2001	2002
Czech Republic										
BIS ratio 3 largest banks			10.58	10.58	10.32	12.31	14.71	13.78	14.78	15.40*
Equity/total assets	7.89	7.67	7.55	4.98	4.87	5.37	5.30	4.56	4.75	5.79
Poland										
BIS ratio 3 largest banks			17.6	13.85 *	11.80 *	12.20	13.37	13.85	18.65	15.80
Equity/total assests	7.70	8.66	8.34	8.36	8.55	8.46	8.50	8.21	7.31	18.10
Slovakia										
BIS ratio 3 largest banks			13.55	12.12	11.31	12.37	14.02	13.01	21.89	23.65
Equity/total assets	2.66	3.15	3.38	2.94	3.17	3.49	5.96	5.53	4.24	5.12

* Only two of the three largest banks.

Sources: CNB, NBP, NBS and Internet sites of particular banks.

In Poland, there were 71 commercial banks and 680 cooperative banks towards the end of 2001 (maximum 87 or 1,653 in the year 1993) – the analysis is based on the data concerning commercial banks. In Slovakia, there were 21 commercial banks towards the end of 2001 (maximum 29 in 1996–97) and in the Czech Republic there were 38 banks towards the end of 2001 (maximum 55 in 1994 and 1995) – the analysis is based on the data for these banks.[11]

4.4.1 Definition of risk and profitability

Economic theory and research studies offer a variety of definitions and concepts of risk (Jilek, 2000). These definitions distinguish:

- quantifiable and non-quantifiable risks;
- covered and non-covered risks;
- systemic and firm-specific risk;
- liquidity risk, interest rate risk, credit risk, capital risk + operational risk;
- liquidity risk, operational risk, transaction risk (that is, credit risk and price risk, price risk = interest rate risk, hedging risk, market liquidity risk and so on);
- credit risk, credit exposures and market risk = interest rate risk, stock, currency, commodity risk, and risk resulting from option contracts;

- financial risk = credit risk + market risk + liquidity risk + operational risk + trade risk;
- credit risk, interest rate risk, liquidity risk, capital risk, exchange rate risk, territorial and counter-party risk;
- credit risk, market risk, liquidity risk, interest rate risk, operational, cross-border, call, legislation, reputation risk.

Banks' profitability is a complex expression of their economic results. A number of risks affect it, above all by credit risk (CR), liquidity risk (LR), interest rate risk (IRR), capital risk (QR) and exchange rate risk (ERR). In recent years it has been stated that banks are very much influenced by operational risk, too. However, due to its nature and forms, this type of risk is quite difficult to quantify. This can be shown by discussions associated with the formation of Basel II rules of banking supervision and regulation (Lewandowski, 2001). A regression analysis can be applied to identify which of the given risks influences significantly the banking sectors' profitability (Günay, 2000) in Poland, Slovakia and the Czech Republic. We apply it to determine how indicators reflecting five of the stated risks (independent variable) affect profitability (ROE) (dependent variable) in the years 1993–2001.

Variables are defined as follows.[12]

Banks' profitability

Banks' profitability is mostly expressed by proportional indicators, which reflect a share in returns on assets or capital. In this chapter, we define banks' profitability generally as a share in net returns on equity (ROE). Similarly, all textbooks and a series of research articles pay attention to the analysis of profitability and the definition of factors which affect it. Banks' profitability is reflected both in the interest of shareholders and public investments into a bank, and it is a significant resource of settlement for a bank's possible losses.

Capital risk

For banks, the returns, and also provisions for NPLs and capital, give some protection against losses. An indicator of capital adequacy, that is, the share of equity in assets, in addition to it, expresses the strength of the bank. This indicator has been discussed comprehensively within the BIS.[13] There is no doubt that an inadequate amount of equity may even lead to the bank's insolvency. We are defining capital risk (QR) as a share in equity and net returns on total assets in this section.

Credit risk

Credit risk (CR) reflects the fact that banks' debtors in some cases do not repay all credits or they do not pay at all in accordance with the conditions agreed upon, and the bank sustains a loss. Predominantly banks with a high share of credits in assets are exposed to such a risk. It is generally known that NPLs represent a serious problem, particularly for the Czech and Slovak banking systems (Polouček, 1999). In this section, the share of NPLs in credits is used as an indicator of credit risk.

Liquidity risk

Liquidity risk (LR) reflects a danger that the bank will not have enough liquid assets to meet the immediate demand for deposits or any other sources of its creditors or depositors. We are dealing with the immediate endangering of the bank's existence and management if, in the case of such a threat, it has to limit granting credits instantaneously, sell some liquid (more liquid) assets, gain sources on the interbank market or ask the central bank for help as a lender of last resort. We define liquidity risk as a liquidity assets share in total assets.

Exchange rate risk

The bank is exposed to exchange rate risk (ERR) when the amount of its assets in foreign currency does not correspond to the amount of its liabilities in foreign currency. This is the case of the vast majority of banks at some stage. Change in the exchange rate presents a potential danger of losses for the bank, which can even lead to its insolvency. We define exchange rate risk by the foreign currency assets share in the foreign currency liabilities.

Interest rate risk

Interest rate risk (IRR) can be defined as an unexpected change of interest rates, which may affect the bank's future income. In this section, the interest income share in the total assets of banks is used as an indicator of interest rate risk.

For measuring particular kinds of risks a series of further standard and specific indicators is used, which are contained in the References section. In our opinion, the indicators applied in research correspond best to the particularities of the CEC, and therefore they confirm most of the following hypotheses.

4.4.2   Hypotheses and suppositions

We define and subsequently test five hypotheses:

H_1: There is a direct proportional relation between capital risk and profitability.

H_2: There is a direct proportional dependence between credit risk and profitability.

H_3: There is an inverse proportional dependence between liquidity risk and profitability.

H_4: There is a direct proportional dependence between exchange rate risk and profitability.

H_5: There is a direct proportional dependence between interest rate risk and profitability.

The suppositions of the analysis are the following. Banks' profitability in the examined period is dependent on only five of the above stated factors. The changes are homogeneous.

To give a picture of the development of the dependent variable by means of the multi-linear regression it is supposed that this variable (banks' profitability) is linearly dependent on each of the explanatory variables (capital risk, credit risk, liquidity risk, exchange rate risk, interest rate risk) and these variables are reciprocally independent (or at least they affect the changes of the dependent variable in one direction).

Data were analysed by means of the statistical software SPSS (Statistical Package for the Social Sciences), which contains various data files and modules. In our research, the module BASE (basic statistical analysis) and the module Advanced Statistics (multidimensional analysis) were applied.

Figure 4.4 demonstrates the structure of variables which affect banks' profitability. It proceeds from the assumption that five independent variables affect banks' profitability both independently and reciprocally. There is commonly a correlation among dependent variables. If the correlation is high, it may lead to multicollinearity with the regression analysis. This fact is considered when testing by way of the correlation analysis and if at least one non-diagonal component of the diagonal matrix is higher than 0.85, we left out the explanatory variable from the model, which is its source.

The aim of the analysis can be defined as follows:

1. To identify risks which affect banks' profitability.
2. To find out how much the dependent variable (ROE) will change (increase or decrease) if we increase or reduce the selected

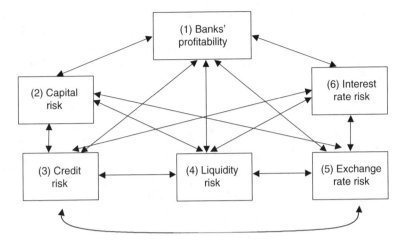

Figure 4.4 Relations among variables of the model

independent variable by one unit while leaving the other variables constant.
3. To identify by means of the regression analysis how strong the dependence between the indicators of risk and profitability is.
4. To formulate the regression equation expressing the relation of the dependent to the independent variables.

4.4.3 Test of the hypotheses by the multicorrelation analysis and the multiregression analysis

The results of the first regression analysis are specified in the following three tables (Tables 4.19 to 4.21). It is apparent from data that the *F* value, which expresses probability, in which the examined factors are most likely to affect profitability, is 95.2 per cent in the case of Poland, 94.3 per cent in the case of Slovakia, and 92.2 in the case of the Czech Republic. The *R*-squared value amounts to more than 90 per cent – in the case of Poland, it is 93.9, in the case of Slovakia, it is 93.2 per cent, and in the case of the Czech Republic, it is 91.5 per cent. This proves that independent variables (credit risk, liquidity risk, interest rate risk, capital risk and exchange rate risk) account for 91.5–93.9 per cent of the changes in the dependent variable (ROE).

In the case of Poland, it is noteworthy from the perspective of the statistical interpretation that three out of five hypotheses are confirmed by the regression analysis. There is a direct proportional dependence

Table 4.19   First regression analysis – Poland

	Coefficients	p-values	Regression statistics	
Constant	0.103	0.774	R:	0.969
Capital risk	4.160	0.209		
Credit risk	−1.218	0.118	R-squared	0.939
Liquidity risk	−0.248	0.659		
Exchange rate risk	−0.171	0.382		
Interest rate risk	0.278	0.825	F-value:	0.048

Source: Authors' calculations.

Table 4.20   First regression analysis – Czech Republic

	Coefficients	p-values	Regression statistics	
Constant	0.861	0.102	R:	0.957
Capital risk	3.662E-02	0.979		
Credit risk	−1.162	0.163	R-squared	0.915
Liquidity risk	−0.634	0.167		
Exchange rate risk	4.082E-03	0.984		
Interest rate risk	−5.424	0.018	F-value:	0.078

Source: Authors' calculations.

Table 4.21   First regression analysis – Slovakia

	Coefficients	p-values	Regression statistics	
Constant	−9.115	0.294	R:	0.965
Capital risk	−5.428	0.682		
Credit risk	1.852	0.551	R-squared	0.932
Liquidity risk	19.761	0.166		
Exchange rate risk	4.990	0.289		
Interest rate risk	28.618	0.062	F-value:	0.057

Source: Authors' calculations.

between capital risk and profitability and between interest rate risk and profitability. There is an inverse proportional dependence between liquidity risk and profitability. Therefore, it is possible to accept H_1, H_3 and H_5 for Poland. Another statistically noteworthy result is the confirmation of the strong dependence of returns of the Polish banks on capital risk: its increase by one unit leads to an increase in profitability of almost 4.2 units.

In the case of the Czech Republic, as well as in the case of Poland, three out of five hypotheses were proved. There is a direct proportional dependence between capital risk and profitability and an inverse proportional dependence between liquidity risk and profitability. It means that H_1 and H_3 can be accepted. H_4 can also be accepted since the increase in exchange rate risk leads to an increase in profitability. However, *p*-values indicate that in none of these cases was a markedly higher or significant dependence of returns on one of the risks confirmed.

In the case of Slovakia, three out of five hypotheses were also confirmed. From the standpoint of the statistical interpretation of the results, it is important to note that by using the regression analysis a significant impact of interest rate risk, credit risk and exchange rate risk on profitability was proved. The increase in interest rate risk by one unit enhanced profitability by 28.6 units. The increase in credit risk by one unit enlarged profitability by almost two units. In both cases, we are dealing with the direct proportional dependence between profitability and the considered quantities. It means that H_2 and H_5 can be accepted. H_4 can be also accepted because the increase in exchange rate risk by one unit increased profitability by almost five units.

With the intention of ruling out multicollinearity in the regression analysis, we shall consider the correlation matrix of independent variables and the dependent variable. Data for particular analysed economies are contained in Tables 4.22, 4.24 and 4.26.

In the case of Poland (Table 4.22), there is a statistically significant correlation between exchange rate risk and liquidity risk at 84.7 per cent. In addition to this, the correlation between credit risk and exchange rate risk is 71.2 per cent. Furthermore, there is a statistically significant correlation of 68.5 per cent between exchange rate risk and interest rate risk. These results indicate the existence of multicollinearity among these variables. For that reason, it is necessary to carry out the second regression analysis with the elimination of credit risk from the regression equation.

In the case of Poland, the results of the second regression analysis are shown in Table 4.23. It is evident that the *F*-value gains a higher value

Table 4.22 Correlations (Poland)

	Profitability	Capital risk (QR)	Credit risk (CR)	Liquidity risk (LR)	Exchange rate risk (ERR)	Interest rate risk (IRR)
Profitability	1.000					
Capital risk	0.894**	1.000				
Credit risk	−0.683*	−0.649	1.000			
Liquidity risk	0.090	0.262	−0.629	1.000		
Exchange rate risk	−0.038	0.125	−0.712*	0.847**	1.000	
Interest rate risk	−0.129	−0.058	0.625	−0.390	−0.685*	1.000

* Correlation is significant at the 0.05 level (2-tailed).
** Correlation is significant at the 0.01 level (2-tailed).

Source: Authors' calculations.

Table 4.23   Second regression analysis – Poland

	Coefficients	p-values	Regression statistics	
Constant	−0.485	0.136	R:	0.919
Capital risk	8.912	0.011		
Liquidity risk	−0.317	0.676	R-squared	0.844
Exchange rate risk	−9.57E-03	0.966		
Interest rate risk	−0.791	0.614	F-value:	0.065

Source: Authors' calculations.

Table 4.24   Correlations (Czech Republic)

	Profitability	Capital risk (QR)	Credit risk (CR)	Liquidity risk (LR)	Exchange rate risk (ERR)	Interest rate risk (IRR)
Profitability	1.000					
Capital risk	0.211	1.000				
Credit risk	−0.359	0.713*	1.000			
Liquidity risk	−0.043	−0.617	0.615	1.000		
Exchange rate risk	0.200	0.538	0.896**	−0.514	1.000	
Interest rate risk	−0.407	0.555	−0.638	−0.751*	0.647	1.000

* Correlation is significant at the 0.05 level (2-tailed).
** Correlation is significant at the 0.01 level (2-tailed).

Source: Authors' calculations.

than in the first regression analysis and the R-squared result (determinative coefficient) is 84.4 per cent, which is not a very successful result from the statistical point of view. Following the elimination of credit risk from the regression equation, the increase in capital risk by one unit leads to an increase in profitability by almost nine units, however. Also other regression analyses bear out a very noticeable dependence of profitability on capital risk in Poland. From the economic point of view, we are talking here about the substantiation of the strong thesis that in the CEC capital risk and banks' capital provision had a significant impact on the stability of the banking sector.

In the Czech Republic, there is a statistically significant correlation of 89.6 per cent between credit risk and exchange rate risk, a further one of 75.1 per cent between interest rate risk and liquidity risk and 71.3 per cent between credit risk and capital risk (Table 4.24). These results indicate a problem of multicollinearity between these variables. Thus, it is necessary to carry out the second regression analysis in the case of the Czech Republic, this time eliminating credit risk from the regression equation.

The results of the second regression analysis for the Czech Republic are shown in Table 4.25. The F-value gains a higher value than in the first model and the R-squared result (determinative coefficient) is

Table 4.25   Second regression analysis – Czech Republic

	Coefficients	p-values	Regression statistics	
Constant	0.240	0.273	R:	0.905
Capital risk	1.319	0.393		
Liquidity risk	−0.780	0.143	R-squared	0.819
Exchange rate risk	0.304	0.079		
Interest rate risk	−5.772	0.015	F-value:	0.086

Source: Authors' calculations.

Table 4.26   Correlations (Slovakia)

	Profitability (QR)	Capital risk (QR)	Credit risk (CR)	Liquidity risk (LR)	Exchange rate risk (ERR)	Interest rate risk (IRR)
Profitability	1.000					
Capital risk	−0.104	1.000				
Credit risk	−0.427	−0.311	1.000			
Liquidity risk	−0.513	0.407	−0.366	1.000		
Exchange rate risk	0.439	−0.607	−0.005	−0.691*	1.000	
Interest rate risk	0.824**	−0.155	−0.034	−0.862**	0.520	1.000

* Correlation is significant at the 0.05 level (2-tailed).
** Correlation is significant at the 0.01 level (2-tailed).

Source: Authors' calculations.

81.9 per cent, which is statistically a worse result. Following the elimination of credit risk from the regression equation, the most noticeable impact of capital risk on banks' profitability has been proved though, as is the case with Poland: the change of capital risk by one unit leads to a change of profitability of 1.3 units. Taken as a whole, however, the results of the second regression analysis confirm the first regression analysis and they do not prove any substantial influence of any of the examined variables (with the exception of capital risk) on profitability.

In the case of Slovakia (Table 4.26), the correlation matrix shows a statistically significant correlation of 86.2 per cent between interest rate risk and liquidity risk, and 69.1 per cent between exchange rate risk and liquidity risk. These results indicate a problem of multicollinearity among these variables. As a result, it is essential to carry out the second regression analysis in the case of Slovakia, this time with the elimination of liquidity risk from the regression equation.

The results of the second regression analysis for Slovakia are shown in Table 4.27. The F-value, which gains a slightly higher value than in the first model, shows that we are dealing here with improvement of the model. Moreover, following the elimination of liquidity risk from

Table 4.27   Second regression analysis – Slovakia

	Coefficients	p-values	Regression statistics	
Constant	2.933	0.450	R:	0.925
Capital risk	−10.030	0.533		
Credit risk	−2.821	0.092	R-squared	0.856
Interest rate risk	11.225	0.022		
Exchange rate risk	−0.977	0.729	F-value:	0.056

Source: Authors' calculations.

the regression equation, interest rate risk has a *p*-value of 2.2 per cent and the increase in interest rate risk by one unit increases profitability by more than 11 units. Only the *R*-squared result (determinative coefficient) is 85.6 per cent, which is not a very satisfactory result from the statistical point of view. But generally, we are dealing here with statistically acceptable results. Hence the second regression analysis is statistically more precise than the first regression analysis.

If we look at the first and the second regression analysis in all three analysed countries, while considering the obtained *p*-values, we can note that the results do not allow us to accept any of the hypotheses without reservation. None of the hypotheses has been proved for all three examined economies, either. This just proves that despite overall identical starting conditions for transformation in the countries under consideration and relatively similar transformation steps, there were differences among them: profitability of banks had been generally influenced by the same factors; the meaning of those factors in particular countries was nevertheless rather different. The results can be summarized as follows:

1. In Poland and in the Czech Republic, the direct proportional dependence between profitability and capital risk was proved. In Poland, this dependence turned out to be a very strong one. The conclusion is interesting from the viewpoint of the Basel requirements for capital adequacy, and it does not support opinions asking for weakening the weight of this indicator in the banks' regulation. If we increase capital risk by one unit, profitability will increase by 1.32 units in the Czech Republic and by 8.91 units in Poland (with the second regression analysis). H_1 is confirmed for the Czech Republic and for Poland. In the case of Slovakia, the direct proportional dependence between profitability and capital risk has not been proved.

2. Only in the case of Slovakia was H_2 substantiated, which confirmed the dependence of returns on credit risk. At the same time, in the case of

Slovakia, we are not dealing with a significant dependence. Generally we are talking here about the result, which contradicts the usually accepted opinions and realities (in particular in the Czech Republic and in Slovakia), that there were NPLs and therefore a high credit risk in the CEC, one of the main causes for the instability of the banking sector and banking crisis. On the other hand, in spite of a large number of NPLs, the state-owned banks showed a relatively high profit at the beginning of the 1990s – maybe because banks with NPLs were protected by the government. And before privatization NPLs were taken out of the banks. From that perspective, these are exactly the reasons why this hypothesis was not proved.

3. The existence of the inverse proportional dependence between profitability and liquidity risk was confirmed for Poland and the Czech Republic. The dependence is relatively weak and p-values are high. The hypothesis was not proved in the case of Slovakia.

4. H_4 was proved for the Czech Republic and Slovakia, that is the direct proportional dependence between exchange rate risk and banks' profitability. In particular, in the case of Slovakia a relatively strong dependence was proved: if exchange rate risk increases by one unit, profitability increases by almost five units. This indicates that banks in Slovakia had more assets than liabilities in foreign currency and nominal depreciation of the SKK increased incomes from foreign assets in SKK and reduced costs of liabilities (again in SKK). Thus profitability was positively influenced. But unfortunately, the same is not true for Poland, where the gap between assets in foreign currencies and liabilities in foreign currencies is even larger.

5. For Poland and Slovakia, H_5 was proved, that is the direct proportional dependence between profitability and interest rate risk. Principally in the case of Slovakia, a relatively strong relation was proved: if we increase interest rate risk by one unit, profitability increases by 28.6 units. This result (the confirmation of the hypothesis for Poland and Slovakia and not for the Czech Republic) is among other things affected by the fact that banks with a high share of credits in assets and deposits in liabilities or banks with a high interest margin are primarily affected by interest rate risk. In Slovakia and also in Poland, the interest margin was noticeably higher than in the Czech Republic during the transformation period.

Based on the calculations carried out, it is possible to formulate the regression equation, which takes into account the given risk factors and profitability. If we denote profitability *ROE*, capital risk *QR*, credit risk *CR*, liquidity risk *LR*, exchange rate risk *ERR*, interest rate risk *IRR* and constant value k, the regression equations have the following form:

$ROE = -0.485k + 8.912QR - 0.317LR - 9.57e^{-3}ERR - 0.791IRR$ (Poland)
$ROE = 0.24k + 1.319QR - 0.78LR + 0.304ERR - 5.772IRR$ (Czech
        Republic)
$ROE = 2.933k - 10.03QR - 2.821CR - 0.977ERR + 11.225IRR$ (Slovakia)

The aims of the analysis, as defined in Section 4.4.2, have been accomplished. The total results show that the analysed CEC and their banking sectors not only have a series of similar features but also considerable differences. The common feature is above all the fact that we are dealing here with unstable economies in the transformation period and the analysis of the banking sectors supports such a conclusion. In all three countries, three hypotheses out of five were proved, but mostly with a low dependence, and concurrently the same three dependencies were not proved in any of the three countries.

When managing assets and liabilities, management in banks should consider these results. They also allow us to assess whether the bank has appropriate capital adequacy, liquidity, implements a suitable credit policy and takes further steps in banking activities so that it optimizes all risks, hence also capital risk, credit risk, liquidity risk, interest rate risk and exchange rate risk.

4.5   Relationship between efficiency and profitability

The theoretical difference between efficiency and profitability was discussed in Section 4.1. The next three sections provided empirical applications, and the findings can now be used for an analysis of the relationship between efficiency and profitability. Deregulation, which was introduced in European banking markets, pursued the goal of increasing efficiency of financial services by increasing competition. However, the empirical results from the recent cross-country studies indicated a worsening (for detailed information, see Turati, 2001) or just a slight improvement of mean efficiency in developed as well as transition European countries in the 1990s (see Casu and Molyneux, 2000; Grigorian and Manole, 2002; Stavárek, 2002, among others). On the other hand, with the sampling of six countries, it was shown that profitability (measured by ROE) increased sharply in the past decade, as illustrated in Section 4.3. These contrasting trends call for more precise explanation.

Table 4.28 Correlation coefficients between efficiency and ROE

Intermediation approach				Operating approach			
CCR model		BCC model		CCR model		BCC model	
2000	2001	2000	2001	2000	2001	2000	2001
0.8282	0.6799	0.5477	0.7085	0.5427	−0.1512	−0.1486	−0.1524

Source: Authors' calculations.

At least two possible scenarios can be distinguished, both of them discussed in Section 3.1.1. The first one suggests that efficiency is the driving force in shaping the structure of a market. Higher efficiency extends possibilities of earning higher profits and increasing profitability. Market principles consequently guarantee that more profitable banks gain higher market shares and this in turn will lead to market concentration. In this case, there is evidence of a positive relationship between efficiency and profitability. The second scenario suggests that in a concentrated industry where firms hold market power, banks will earn monopoly rents. This clearly reduces consumers' welfare, since banks increase prices and reduce the quantity of financial services supplied. The lack of competitive pressures in a more concentrated market reduces banking efficiency. Managers abandon efforts to minimize costs and prefer to have a 'quiet life', converting the higher inefficiencies to higher prices, as discussed in Section 4.3.

We now explore the relationship between efficiency and profitability (ROE) by computing correlation coefficients. The results are reported in Table 4.28.

Correlation coefficients between ROE and efficiency scores are relatively low for all the models, except in one case (intermediation approach, CCR model, 2000). However, we can see a much stronger relationship in the intermediation approach than in the operational approach, where the absence of a linear relationship between profits and efficiency scores can be considered as evidence of market power in favour of European banks and the SCP hypothesis of the European banking market. Inefficient banks can simply translate their higher costs to higher prices of services and thus earn positive profits, due to a very high level of customer loyalty and their reluctance to change banks. Previous findings, for example, by Dietsch and Weill (2000), emphasize an increase in profit efficiency linked with a decrease in cost efficiency for continental European banks. The findings for European markets are completely different from the results of Berger (1995) for the US banking market, where X-efficiencies are consistently associated with higher profitability.

On the other hand, although the correlation coefficients in the intermediation approach are only partly statistically significant, they indicate certain relationships between profitability and efficiency. Banks reporting higher profitability ratios are usually seen by clients as preferential and therefore attract the biggest share of deposits as well as the best potential borrowers. Such conditions create a favourable environment for the profitable banks to be more efficient from the point of view of financial intermediation.

When looking at assets and liabilities, bank management may consider the results of these studies which enable us also to assess whether the bank has appropriate capital adequacy, liquidity, and implementation of a suitable credit policy. Management can go even further by taking steps in banking activities so that it optimizes all risks, including capital risk, credit risk, liquidity risk, interest rate risk and exchange rate risk.

4.6   Conclusion

From our results, we may conclude that the banking sectors of the CEC are less efficient than their counterparts in EU member countries. In addition, even transition banking industries can be distinguished as more or less efficient. Generally, the Hungarian and Czech banking sectors were on average evaluated as the most efficient, followed, with a marginal distance, by the Polish banking industry. The Slovak banking sector stands apart, with a substantial gap in efficiency scores. This finding was enhanced by the value of differences between efficiencies computed using common and national efficiency frontiers.

Despite privatization, and the dominance of foreign banks, the banking industries in the CEC remained underdeveloped in terms of provision of credit to enterprises and households. The depth of financial intermediation was quite low in the CEC. This implies that all the banking sectors with the exception of Finland reported substantially lower efficiency in the intermediation approach than in the operational approach. However, efficiency is expected to improve with the development of the economy in general, and likewise, the development of small and medium enterprises in particular. Loans to households are also expected to rise as a consequence of growth in household incomes as well as efforts of banks to expand and diversify their activities.

Another of the study's essential findings is the refutation of the conventional wisdom of higher efficiency from foreign-owned banks than from domestic-owned banks, and as shown in our hypotheses, size is one of the factors that determine efficiency. To achieve high efficiency, a bank should either be large, well known, easily accessible and offering a wide range of products and services, or if small, must focus on specific market segments, offering special products. Any other structure or shape of a bank almost always leads to lower relative efficiency.

Privatization and, consequently, change of ownership are certainly among the most important factors behind serious shifts in the banking sector during the last ten years. In Poland, Slovakia and the Czech Republic, the restructuring and privatization of the banking sector improved bank profitability, capitalization and asset quality. Although the positive effects of privatization on bank profitability are evident, we consider them to be rather indirect in these countries.

The improvement does not fully arise from the benign actions of foreign ownership, but mainly from the state-guaranteed pre-privatization clean-up of the largest banks' asset portfolios of their non-performing assets. Hence banks need not cover the NPLs by provisions and reserves that previously changed a high operational profit into a net loss. However, massive government help (including the NPLs' transfer into the Consolidation Bank, respectively into the Consolidation Agency) was unavoidable. Without it the banks' privatization with a strategic foreign investor would have no chance to succeed. Data and comparison with developed countries show that improvement in asset quality and partly in capitalization can be expected in the near future while profitability has already started to increase in all three considered countries during the privatization process. Nevertheless further improvement in profitability, measured by ROA or ROE, can be expected.

Numerous factors and risks usually affect the development of profitability. According to empirical findings of regression analysis, it can be concluded that no such risk exists where there is a significant influence on profitability in all the countries analysed. While there is certain evidence of common features like relatively strong dependence of profitability on capital risk or interest rate risk, the group of the CEC does not represent the homogeneous club of identical economies that they are often supposed.

Appendix

Table 4A.1   Efficiency scores of analysed banks (%)

	Intermediation approach				Operating approach			
	CCR model		BCC model		CCR model		BCC model	
	2000	*2001*	*2000*	*2001*	*2000*	*2001*	*2000*	*2001*
			Belgium					
Fortis Banque	72.61	69.66	100.00	100.00	84.92	82.90	100.00	100.00
KBC Bank	52.35	58.08	73.09	99.51	89.89	91.40	100.00	100.00
Dexia Banque	100.00	100.00	100.00	100.00	100.00	100.00	100.00	100.00
CBC Banque	96.01	76.35	100.00	100.00	100.00	100.00	100.00	100.00
Banque Bruxelles Lambert	43.38	55.13	71.20	100.00	100.00	100.00	100.00	100.00
Banque Degroof	89.91	92.43	100.00	100.00	100.00	100.00	100.00	100.00
Bank J. van Breda & Co.	88.07	96.70	92.97	96.82	100.00	100.00	100.00	100.00
Bank Delen	100.00	100.00	100.00	100.00	100.00	100.00	100.00	100.00
BKCP Bank	100.00	100.00	100.00	100.00	100.00	100.00	100.00	100.00
VDK Spaarbank	21.71	19.70	23.76	22.99	93.52	93.29	94.21	96.23
Banque Belgolaise	88.93	100.00	95.46	100.00	98.79	100.00	100.00	100.00
			Czech Republic					
ČSOB	68.65	79.61	100.00	100.00	87.07	86.04	91.84	100.00
Česká spořitelna	86.56	71.60	100.00	84.02	89.04	100.00	100.00	100.00
Komerční banka	73.77	97.26	100.00	100.00	83.70	84.13	95.17	88.02
GE Capital Bank	73.46	87.26	83.82	100.00	100.00	100.00	100.00	100.00
HVB Czech Republic	n.a.	73.72	n.a.	91.61	n.a.	84.86	n.a.	92.23
Union banka	83.30	100.00	84.41	100.00	79.16	80.84	81.27	81.25
Živnostenská banka	70.98	100.00	70.99	100.00	80.28	81.85	82.38	85.85
Raiffeisenbank CZ	79.05	71.60	81.91	71.76	86.63	72.58	88.21	77.05
Volksbank CZ	70.78	81.58	100.00	92.80	97.31	85.19	100.00	97.29
eBanka	62.90	63.50	63.49	67.05	100.00	68.77	100.00	91.89
První městská banka	100.00	100.00	100.00	100.00	92.45	100.00	100.00	100.00
Plzeňeská banka	100.00	100.00	100.00	100.00	100.00	100.00	100.00	100.00
J&T Bank	62.07	61.80	100.00	79.15	72.20	66.61	100.00	100.00
Citibank CZ	67.32	55.94	80.46	57.08	100.00	100.00	100.00	100.00
			Finland					
Nordea	93.18	99.35	100.00	100.00	76.15	72.23	100.00	100.00
OKO Bank	100.00	100.00	100.00	100.00	94.60	100.00	97.60	100.00
Sampo bank	89.13	100.00	95.20	100.00	80.70	75.85	96.66	91.05
Aktia Savings Bank	62.94	69.54	64.23	71.07	91.96	85.73	94.20	85.75
Evli Bank	100.00	34.35	100.00	41.86	100.00	100.00	100.00	100.00
Bank of Aland	100.00	100.00	100.00	100.00	82.47	75.71	83.49	79.00
			Hungary					
General Banking & Trust	76.51	71.40	77.25	74.24	81.34	94.34	82.35	100.00
Budapest Bank	59.06	91.21	75.66	100.00	94.56	100.00	95.81	100.00

Table 4A.1   contd.

	Intermediation approach				Operating approach			
	CCR model		BCC model		CCR model		BCC model	
	2000	*2001*	*2000*	*2001*	*2000*	*2001*	*2000*	*2001*
CIB Bank	87.02	86.97	87.80	95.70	100.00	100.00 ·	100.00	100.00
Citibank HU	100.00	100.00	100.00	100.00	100.00	100.00	100.00	100.00
Hungar. Foreign Trade Bank	52.88	58.03	54.88	60.61	74.85	71.13	83.23	77.78
OTP Bank	79.96	100.00	91.30	100.00	100.00	100.00	100.00	100.00
Daewoo Bank	81.71	93.38	95.29	100.00	86.76	87.66	98.76	96.06
Raiffeisenbank HU	100.00	100.00	100.00	100.00	100.00	100.00	100.00	100.00
Kereskedelmi & Kitelbank	79.88	98.49	88.99	100.00	80.65	75.19	80.87	76.26
Postabank	38.82	54.93	39.86	57.17	85.29	86.69	86.09	88.12
Erste Bank Hungary	53.49	59.71	56.49	61.64	100.00	89.70	100.00	92.77
			Poland					
Bank PEKAO	70.15	67.70	100.00	100.00	100.00	100.00	100.00	100.00
Bank Handlowy	65.62	74.67	79.49	83.80	77.17	88.77	90.33	100.00
Bank Przemyslowo Handlowy	63.61	72.06	78.35	81.09	91.88	91.41	100.00	97.44
PKO Bank Polski	100.00	79.12	100.00	100.00	100.00	100.00	100.00	100.00
BIG Bank	54.72	52.00	82.68	56.92	100.00	63.68	100.00	67.28
Kredyt Bank	44.06	57.19	44.61	61.11	89.98	89.86	98.65	99.30
Bank Zachodni	67.99	74.45	88.59	85.01	79.93	75.51	87.18	76.90
Bank Ochrony Srodoviska	92.42	60.44	93.67	60.45	100.00	93.70	100.00	95.74
Bank Gospodarswa Krajovego	100.00	100.00	100.00	100.00	100.00	87.67	100.00	88.51
Bank Przemyslowy	100.00	100.00	100.00	100.00	79.08	78.96	100.00	99.44
BRE Bank	49.84	53.22	56.08	54.74	87.92	97.44	92.80	98.05
AmerBank	87.31	71.04	100.00	100.00	79.48	70.39	83.79	82.25
LG Petro Bank	87.80	78.23	88.18	78.25	79.62	71.47	79.75	73.23
			Slovakia					
Všeobecná úverová banka	38.23	56.03	42.93	56.07	80.78	76.82	95.28	84.16
Tatrabanka	76.50	56.45	76.66	59.46	58.57	62.22	58.72	62.79
Slovenská sporitel'ňa	95.60	63.32	100.00	81.89	88.02	77.18	90.62	83.52
Prvá komunálna banka	55.92	98.30	62.21	100.00	100.00	83.62	100.00	89.78
L'udová banka	74.01	87.40	77.09	89.82	59.65	52.35	64.41	57.31
Citibank SK	100.00	100.00	100.00	100.00	100.00	100.00	100.00	100.00
Pol'nobanka (UniBanka)	32.75	98.25	33.83	99.15	100.00	84.33	100.00	86.94
Istrobanka	51.54	61.62	51.62	61.99	93.72	81.89	93.73	90.67
Poštová banka	55.87	55.47	56.92	56.98	62.84	64.88	63.70	69.32
Komerční banka Bratislava	34.50	55.77	75.56	100.00	77.94	76.54	100.00	100.00

Notes

1. In Figure 4.1 we used an input-oriented model, which involves an isoquant representing constant output (y) determined through the quantities of two inputs (x_1 and x_2). Alternatively the output-oriented model can be used. In this case a production possibility isoquant has to be determined representing output quantities (y_1, y_2) achieved with a constant input of (x).

2. To illustrate, while bank A has achieved a certain level of fee and a commission income using high technology and a small number of branches and tellers, bank B has preferred a more labour-intensive model and has reached the same level of income using more personnel rather than modern technologies. In this case, the productivity (no efficiency) of bank A will be higher than of bank B when personnel expenditures are considered. However, when we take into account investments, bank B will appear more productive.

3. The free disposal hull approach (FDH) is a special case of the DEA model where the points on lines connecting the DEA vertices are not included in the frontier. Instead, the FDH production possibilities' set is composed only of the DEA vertices and the FDH points interior to these vertices. Because the FDH frontier is either congruent with or interior to the DEA frontier, FDH will typically generate larger estimates of average efficiency than DEA.

4. Equations 4.9–4.13 represent an input-oriented CCR model, in which the maximization is focused on seeking such weights as produce the greatest rate of virtual output per unit of virtual input. The second possible CCR model is output-oriented. It can be analogously obtained by output normalization in the Charnes–Cooper linearization.

5. Berg *et al.* (1993) evaluated the efficiency of Scandinavian banks and was followed by Bukh *et al.* (1995) and Bergendhal (1998). Pastor *et al.* (1997) applied DEA to a wide set of 427 banks from eight developed countries. The recent studies are Casu and Molyneux (2000) or Grigorian and Manole (2002).

6. On this basis financial systems are very often classified as in Chapter 1.

7. The observed set covers 11 banks from Belgium, six from Finland, 13 from Poland, 13 from the Czech Republic, 10 from Slovakia and 11 from Hungary in 2000 and one more Czech bank in 2001.

8. In 2001 total deposits in the Czech Republic represented 59.1 per cent of GDP whereas total loans amounted to 36.9 per cent of GDP. The difference was even greater in Slovakia, where total deposits equalled 67.8 per cent of GDP and total loans represented 34.8 per cent of Slovak GDP.

9. The average intermediation efficiency of the Belgian banking sector is significantly influenced by the extremely low efficiency score of VDA Spaarbank, a savings bank providing almost no loans at all. Except for this bank, the average Belgian efficiency score rose to 83.13 per cent and 93.27 per cent in 2000 and 84.84 per cent and 99.63 per cent in 2001 using the CCR and BCC model respectively.

10. They are Česká spořitelna in the Czech Republic, CIB Bank in Hungary, Bank Handlowy in Poland and Slovenská sporitel'ňa in Slovakia. Czech Komerční banka was considered as domestic-owned in both 2000 and 2001, because its sale to Société Générale was announced in June 2001.

11. More detailed data on the development of the banks' number in these countries are contained in Chapter 1.

12. Orientation values of some of the variables in transition economies and in some developed countries are part of the analysis of banks' efficiency in Section 4.3.
13. See for instance discussions and materials at http://www.bis.org and further studies in the list of literature.

References

Aigner, D.J., Knox Lovell, C.A. and Schmidt, P. 'Formulation and Estimation of Stochastic Frontier Production Function Models', *Journal of Econometrics*, VI (1977), 21–37.

Allen, L. and Rai, A. 'Operational Efficiency in Banking: An International Comparison', *Journal of Banking and Finance*, XX (1996), 655–72.

Altunbas, Y., Evans, L. and Molyneux, P. 'Bank Ownership and Efficiency', *Journal of Money, Credit, and Banking*, XXXIII (2001), 926–54.

Banker, R., Charnes, A. and Cooper, W.W. 'Some Models for Estimating Technical and Scale Efficiencies in Data Envelopment Analysis', *Management Science*, XXX (1984), 1078–92.

Belaisch, A., Kodres, L., Levy, J. and Ubide, A. *Euro-Area Banking at the Crossroads* (Washington, DC: International Monetary Fund, 2001).

Berg, A., Forsund, F.R., Hjarmarsson, L. and Suominen, M. 'Banking Efficiency in the Nordic Countries', *Journal of Banking and Finance*, XVII (1993), 371–88.

Bergendahl, G. 'DEA and Benchmarks – An Application to Nordic Banks', *Annals of Operations Research*, LXXXII (1998), 233–49.

Berger, A.N. 'The Profit–Structure Relationship in Banking-Tests of Market Power and Efficient-Structure Hypotheses', *Journal of Money, Credit, and Banking*, XXVII (1995), 404–31.

Berger, A.N. and Humprey, D.B. 'Efficiency of Financial Institutions: International Survey and Directions for Future Research', *European Journal of Operations Research*, IIC (1997), 175–212.

Berger, A.N., Hunter, W.C. and Timme, S.G. 'The Efficiency of Financial Institutions: A Review of Research Past, Present and Future', *Journal of Banking and Finance*, XVII (1993), 221–49.

Bukh, P.N.D., Berg, S.A. and Forsund, F.R. *Banking Efficiency in the Nordic Countries: A Four-Country Malmquist Index Analysis* (Aarhus: University of Aarhus, 1995).

Casu, B. and Molyneux, P. *A Comparative Study of Efficiency in European Banking* (Philadelphia: The Wharton School, University of Pennsylvania, 2000).

Charnes, A. and Cooper, W.W. 'Programming with Linear Fractional Functionals', *Naval Research Logistics Quarterly*, IX (1962), 165–83.

Charnes, A., Cooper, W.W. and Rhodes, E. 'Measuring the Efficiency of Decision Making Units', *European Journal of Operations Research*, II (1978), 429–44.

Denizer, C.A., Tarimcilar, M. and Dinc, M. *Measuring Banking Efficiency in the Pre- and Post-Liberalization Environment: Evidence from the Turkish Banking System* (Washington, DC: World Bank, 2000).

Dietsch, M. and Weill, L. 'The Evolution of Cost and Profit Efficiency in the European Banking Industry', in Hasan, I. and Hunter, C. (eds) *Advances in Banking and Finance, vol. 1* (London: JAI Press, 2000), 52–69.

Dyson, R.G., Thanassoulis, E. and Boussofiane, A. *A Data Envelopment Tutorial* (Warwick: Warwick Business School, 1990).

Emrouznejad, A. and Thanassoulis, E. 'An Extensive Bibliography of Data Envelopment Analysis (DEA)' (*Working Papers*, Warwick Business School, I, 1996a).

Emrouznejad, A. and Thanassoulis, E. 'An Extensive Bibliography of Data Envelopment Analysis (DEA)' (*Journal Paper*, Warwick Business School, II, 1996b).

Emrouznejad, A. and Thanassoulis, E. 'An Extensive Bibliography of Data Envelopment Analysis (DEA)' (*Supplement I*, Warwick Business School, III, 1996c).

Farrell, M.J. 'The Measurement of Productive Efficiency', *Journal of the Royal Statistical Society (Series A)*, CXX (1957), 253–81.

Favore, C. and Pappi, L. 'Technical Efficiency and Scale Efficiency in the Italian Banking Sector. A Non-parametric Approach', *Applied Economics*, XXVII (1995), 349–66.

Fecher, F. and Pestieau, P. Efficiency and Competition in O.E.C.D. Financial Services, in Fed, H.O. and Lovell, C.A.K. and Schmidt, S.S. (eds) *The Measurement of Productive Efficiency: Techniques and Applications* (Oxford: Oxford University Press, 1993).

Fisher, S. and Sahay, R. *The Transition Economies After Ten Years* (Washington, DC: International Monetary Fund, 2000).

Fuchs, K. 'Some Problems of Czech Privatization', in *Transition Countries Joining European Union* (Canakkale, Karviná: COMU, SUO, 2002).

Grigorian, D.A. and Manole, V. *Determinants of Commercial Bank Performance in Transition: An Application of Data Envelopment Analysis* (Washington, DC: World Bank, 2002).

Günay, S.G. 'An Ex Post Analysis about Risk Factors Which Have an Effect on Profitability of Private Banking Sector in Turkey', in *Future of the Banking after the Year 2000 in the World and in the Czech Republic. V. Audit and Rating in Banking Sector. Proceedings from the International Conference* (Karviná: SBA SU, 2000).

Harker, P.T. and Zenios, S.A. (eds) *Performance of Financial Institutions* (New York: Cambridge University Press, 2000).

Hasan, I. and Marton, K. *Development and Efficiency of the Banking Sector in Transitional Economy: Hungarian Experience* (Helsinki: Bank of Finland, 2000).

Hölscher, J. (ed.) *Financial Turbulence and Capital Markets in Transition Countries*. (Macmillan Press, 2000).

Hunter, W.C. and Timme, S. 'Core Deposits and Physical Capital: A Reexamination of Bank Scale Economies and Efficiency with Quasi-Fixed Inputs', *Journal of Money, Credit, and Banking*, XXVII (1995), 165–85.

Jílek, J. *Finanční rizika* (Praha: Grada Publishing, 2000).

Jonáš, J. *Bankovní krize a ekonomická transformace* (Praha: Management Press, 1998).

Laeven, L. *Risk and Efficiency in East Asian Banks* (Washington, DC: World Bank, 1999).

Leibenstein, H. 'Allocative Efficiency vs. "X-Efficiency"', *American Economic Review*, LVI (1966), 392–415.

Lewandowski, D. 'Operational Risk in Banking Activities: New Challenges, Urgent Call for Management', *Bank i Kredyt*, XXXII, 5 (2001), 29–35.

Matoušek, R. and Taci, A. 'The Assessment of the Costs and Benefits of the Small and Medium Commercial Banks within the Czech Banking Sector', in Hölscher, J. (ed.) *Financial Turbulence and Capital Markets in Transition Countries* (London: Macmillan Press, 2000).

McAllister, P.H. and McManus, D. 'Resolving the Scale Efficiency Puzzle in Banking', *Journal of Banking and Finance*, XVII (1993), 389–405.

Mester, L.J. *Efficiency of Banks in the Third Federal Reserve District* (Philadelphia: The Wharton School, University of Pennsylvania, 1993).

Mielnik, M. and Lawrynowicz, M. 'Badanie efektywnosci technicznej bonkow komercyjnych w Polsce metoda DEA', *Bank i kredyt*, XXXIII, 5 (2002), 52–64.

Nicastro, R., Steinbichler, A. and Revoltella, D. 'Banking Sectors in Transition: Comparisons, Experiences and Results', *BIATEC*, X, 3 (2002), 23–7.

Ogrodnik, M. 'Bank Privatization with Foreign Capital in Poland – Pros and Cons', in *Future of the Banking after the Year 2000 in the World and in the Czech Republic. VI. Privatization in the Banking Sector* (Karviná: SBA SU, 2001).

Pastor, J.M., Perez, F. and Quesada, J. 'Efficiency Analysis in Banking Firms: An International Comparison', *European Journal of Operational Research*, IIC (1997), 395–407.

Polouček, S. *České bankovnictví na přelomu tisíciletí* (Ostrava: Ethics, 1999).

Polouček, S., Kulhánek, L. and Fleissig, S. (eds) *Future of the Banking after the Year 2000 in the World and in the Czech Republic. VI. Privatization of the Banking Sector* (Karviná: SBA SU, 2001).

Stavárek, D. 'Comparison of the Relative Efficiency of Banks in European Transition Countries', *Finance* (Veliko Tarnovo: Abagar, 2002) 955–82.

Turati, G. *Cost Efficiency and Profitability in European Commercial Banking* (Milan: Universita Cattolica del S. Cuore, 2001).

Turnovec, F. 'Privatization and Transparency: Evidence from the Czech Republic', in Hölscher, J. (ed.) *Financial Turbulence and Capital Markets in Transition Countries* (London: Macmillan Press, 2000).

Vujcic, B. and Jemric, I. 'Efficiency of Banks in Croatia: A DEA Approach', *Comparative Economic Studies*, XLIV (2002), 169–93.

Wheelock, D.C. and Wilson, P.W. 'Technical Progress, Inefficiency, and Productivity Change in U.S. Banking, 1984–1993', *Journal of Money, Credit, and Banking*, XXXI (1999), 212–34.

5
Costs of Macroeconomic Instability in Accession Countries

Jan Frait, Luboš Komárek and Martin Melecký

The aim of this chapter is to show the impact of macroeconomic and financial instabilities on the CEC in the last ten years whereby financial crises and swings in macroeconomic conditions were among the most important driving forces of changes in reform strategies. This chapter proceeds as follows. The first section will show some of the main revisions of the transition process. The next section will provide some generalizations and facts concerning the activities of the fundamental indicators among selected countries that are crucial for financial instability. Section 5.3 will analyse the effect of currency crises on investment and economic performance for CEC, as well as other selected ACC. And finally, the chapter will conclude with a summary of our findings as well as some issues to consider for future research.

5.1 Overview of features of the transition process in the ACC

The 1980s and 1990s were very rich in events resulting in both positive and negative effects and consequences for the world economy. This period experienced several wide-ranging reforms. Some were structural – privatization and liberalization of domestic capital markets and capital transactions, with portfolio investment gaining in significance – while others, macroeconomic and cyclical, including increased openness to developing economies. Growing importance of institutional investors and securitization were also visible in this period.

During this period, a renewal of capital flows into developing and emerging market economies occurred. These flows accelerated sharply in the mid-1990s, triggering financial crises with devastating consequences, particularly in South East Asia. These crises became some of the most important events from the viewpoint of macroeconomics of that period, and attracted unprecedented attention from economists as well as the mass media. Financial crises, often comprising currency and banking crises, became significant determinants of economic development in the post-socialist economies of Central and Eastern Europe (CEE). These crises often led to deep structural and institutional reforms as well as programmes aimed at the privatization and restructuring of bank sectors in the countries affected (see Chapters 1 and 3). The fear of financial crises led most of the ACC economies to switch from fixed exchange rate arrangements to much more flexible patterns, thus constituting one of the main arguments for early substitution of the euro for national currencies (see Chapter 6).

5.1.1   Transition, macroeconomic instability and research challenges

Ever since the currency crisis occurred, which was brought about chiefly by speculative attacks on officially controlled exchange rates, and thus catching the attention of the world public, research has been ongoing to explain these events. These currency crises have often made policy-makers abandon pegging their currency, thus resulting in large exchange rate depreciations and sharp reductions in current account imbalances, or so-called reversals. Such reversals are then most probably connected with a depressed economic performance of the affected country. Recently, some work has been done on this topic (see, e.g., Milesi-Ferretti and Razin, 1997 and 1998; Barro, 2001; Edwards, 2001; Hutchison, 2001 or Loayaza and Ranciere, 2002). They mainly concentrate on the following questions: are these reversals costly in terms of output performance? How should these reversals be measured? Can some general quantification of their costs be made? Is economic performance affected directly by the reversal, or mainly indirectly through its effect on investment?

The aforementioned papers operate mainly in the framework of a panel and cross-country regression using large data sets. Estimations are then made for a group of countries that sometimes have very different characteristics. Nevertheless, some general results can be attained. Most results suggest that there are significant effects of reversals both direct and indirect (through investment) on economic performance measured by real output. Researchers have used different determinants in estimated equations, and the quantification is generally made from a broad point of view for all transition countries. We expect an analysis of similar questions, under the regional specifics of the ACC, to provide slightly different results. Furthermore, the quality and consistency of acquired results should be relatively enhanced considering the high homogeneity of such a sample.

In the twentieth century, the rise and subsequent fall of the socialistic central planning systems was an interesting episode, posing enormous challenges to economic theory and policy. The general absence of market-generated signals significantly distorted almost every economic category, and increased the gap between centrally planned and advanced market economies. The key economic objectives of the transition were to raise economic efficiency and promote GDP growth per capita. The main parts of the transition process included macroeconomic stabilization, price and market liberalization of the domestic sector and international trade, privatizing and restructuring state enterprises, and redefining the role of the non-socialistic state.

However, despite the similarity of general objectives and basic direction of changes necessary for successful transformation of the current ACC, strategies and experiences have differed according to both policies implemented and results achieved up to now. The main explanations for these differences were the initial conditions of these countries at the start of the transition period, the implementation of macroeconomic and microeconomic policies, and the pressures of external factors.

5.1.2   Macroeconomic stabilization process and the external environment

The first decade of transition of the ACC was characterized by economic and political changes with the aim of aligning themselves with Western European countries. Generally, all the ACC have made significant progress from centrally planned to market economies, although the macroeconomic stabilization process was not equally smooth for all of them. The main positive economic results of this process were published by the IMF (2000): (i) almost 75 per cent of the output was produced by the private sector; (ii) generally successful liberalization of trade and the foreign exchange system; (iii) resumed economic growth; and (iv) visible decline in inflation. On the other hand, the IMF also made mention of the main negative tendencies, which included: (i) a high external current account deficit; (ii) a high government fiscal deficit; and (iii) a high propensity for external factors to influence the domestic economy (notably, external shocks, for instance, the Gulf War at the beginning of 1990s, the regional war in the Balkans, the impact of events in the USA after 11 September 2001).

The macroeconomic development, including the history of the basic tenets and indicators of currency crises, during the transition process of the six most developed ACC,[1] generally considered as the 'front runners', will be discussed in the next section. The comparison of these countries will show a large array of both common and contrasting features. For instance, Hungary, Poland and Slovenia had experienced high initial inflation, which led to a sharp reduction of values of assets and liabilities. In the case of Poland and Czechoslovakia, on the eve of the transition, the Polish business sector's net position *vis-à-vis* domestic commercial banks was slightly more positive than Czechoslovakia's, especially at the end of 1989. Another crucial difference was a large foreign debt (Hungary, Poland) that rebounded from the 1970s borrowing episode (even though these countries benefited from a 50 per cent reduction in their debts in 1991). Furthermore, different exchange rate strategies (to be described below) and the 'split-away' experience (Estonia, Slovenia) as well as the break-up of Czechoslovakia, had significant influence on the economic development of these countries.

Admission of the CEE to the European community and to the market economy meant opening up these economies to international competition, and adopting the principles of EU-led competition. This meant no government bailouts to businesses, regulating monopolies, and strict limitations on public services. The free movement of goods, services, persons and capital within the EU characterized this intended free market.

5.1.3 The role of exchange rates and exchange rate regimes

The role of exchange rates and exchange rate regimes was very important during the initial phase of the transformation process, but not crucial enough to determine success or failure of the transition process. Although the exchange rate strategies varied across ACC, all of them were able to bring inflation down rapidly, while keeping the development of the other main fundamental variables under control. Estonia had operated under a currency board regime for more than ten years. The Czech Republic, the Slovak Republic, Hungary and Poland first introduced a pegged rate. This initial choice was slowly modified to more flexible systems in the course of the transition (due to concerns about potentially destabilizing effects of large capital inflows). The inverse process occurred in the other ACC. They had originally introduced the flexible exchange rate due to a lack of sufficient foreign exchange reserves. Later on Latvia pegged its currency and Bulgaria and Lithuania shifted to currency boards. More facts about exchange rate policies are presented in Chapter 6.

5.2   Facts on financial instability

In this section, we will discuss the main indicators related to our analysis of currency crises for selected ACC, including the CEC. We will present some facts on fundamental indicators of currency crises, applying these to selected ACC. We will focus on the development of indicators based on: (i) the real exchange rates, indicators of under-/overvaluation of currency); (ii) the balance of payments (current account/GDP ratio, foreign direct investment/GDP ratio); and (iii) the real economic variables (gross fixed capital formation/GDP ratio, real GDP growth).[2] Finally, we will summarize the main impacts of the currency crises in the 1990s (especially on real variables) and calculate the exchange market pressure index for our selected group of countries.

5.2.1   Exchange rate development in selected transition economies

For an assessment of the exchange rate developments in selected transition economies with the aforementioned theoretical and empirical information, we present monthly real (CPI-based) exchange rate indices against the ECU and EUR in Figure 5.1 and Figure 5A.1 in the Appendix. Throughout this chapter we will use the Czech Republic data as an example while referring to data of the remaining countries presented in the appendices. The sources of data are the same as for the Czech Republic.

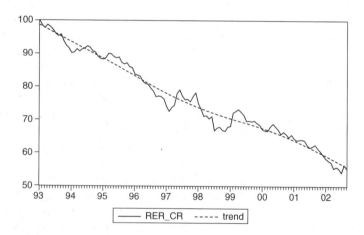

Figure 5.1   Real exchange rate of the Czech koruna (January 1993 = 100)

Source: Authors' calculations based on ČNB database and IMF-IFS database.

Figure 5.1 and the numbers in Figure 5A.1 show a clearly distinguishable continuous appreciation trend in the real exchange rate of all six currencies. Tendencies towards relatively fast real appreciation repeatedly created the fear of a large external deficit followed by a balance-of-payments crisis. The reason why the real exchange rate is a very important indicator of a potential speculative attack is that, as a key relative price, it summarizes several other fundamental factors. Goldfajn and Valdés (1997) note that a medium to large overvaluation is rarely eliminated without step devaluation. Investors are well aware of this and incorporate the strong correlation between overvaluation and subsequent devaluation into their exchange rate expectations. However, the problem is that, although overvaluation is a systemic indicator of a possible crisis, it is very difficult to distinguish the fundamentally appreciating currencies from fundamentally overvalued currencies in countries like the ACC. We are thus unable to anticipate a crisis, and in particular the timing of it. This is why it is very important for the authorities to monitor whether the currency is appreciating 'too much' and strive to reduce any resulting overvaluation in a timely fashion. Countries whose statistics are underdeveloped (that is, the majority of the transition countries) have no option but to monitor the scope of overvaluation using very simple indicators. DARER (debt-adjusted real exchange rate) would be one of such indicators.[3] The estimates of this indicator are shown in the next section.

5.2.2   Indicators of exchange rate overvaluation

The three estimated indicators of overvaluation of the currency that proceed from the DARER concept are demonstrated in Figure 5.2 and other computations in Figure 5A.2. The first indicator deflated by CPI (The Debt Overvaluation Index, DO_(CPI)) identifies the currency overvaluation due to the very existence of the debt. The second indicator (The Trend Overvaluation Index, TrO_(CPI)) uses the Hodrick–Prescott filter to determine the 'trend overvaluation'.[4] The third indicator (The Total Overvaluation Index, TO_(CPI)) combines the two concepts to express the overvaluation/undervaluation of the exchange rate from a 'broader' perspective. The Appendix provides a detailed description of each indicator, together with its formal notation.

The fact that the Czech koruna started to be overvalued in 1995 is illustrated in Figure 5.2. Here we can see the total, debt and trend overvaluation indicators, showing broadly similar dynamics, except for the period between 1996:2 and 1997:3, when a large current account deficit

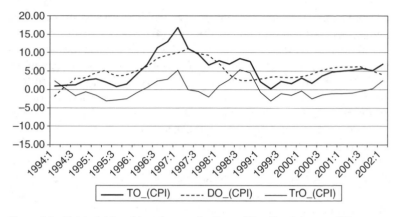

Figure 5.2   Total, debt and trend overvaluation of the Czech koruna (%)
Source: Authors' calculations based on ČNB database and IMF-IFS database.

and, simultaneously, swings in the real exchange rate occurred. The data set contains 34 observations between 1994:1 and 2002:2. Consequently, it is difficult to draw exact conclusions regarding the actual overvaluation, undervaluation or equilibrium of the real exchange rate of the Czech currency. Nevertheless, we believe – and the recent exchange rate trend and the current account figures bear this out – that the koruna found its equilibrium level during the first half of 1999 (after a nominal depreciation in 1999:1). However, it is evident that the real exchange rate of the Czech currency is again becoming modestly overvalued at the beginning of the new millennium.

The risk of a speculative attack is not the only danger stemming from the overvaluation of the currency. Overvaluation also has its adverse effects on the long-term growth of the economy. There is a general belief that an overvalued currency leads to lower growth, but that an undervalued currency has an equivocal effect (see Razin and Collins, 1997). There are two basic channels through which a misalignment (overvaluation or undervaluation) might influence growth. First, it could influence domestic and foreign investment, thereby influencing the process of capital accumulation. Second, it could affect the competitiveness of the trading sector, thereby affecting net exports, which is an important component of economic activity. Another potential channel is the volatility of misalignment.

Much of the subsequent empirical work that aimed to identify the main factors of an economy's vulnerability to currency crisis concluded that the overvaluation of the real exchange rate is indeed the most important indicator (see Goldfajn and Valdés, 1997; Kaminski *et al.*, 1997; IMF, 1998). For example, the International Monetary Fund (IMF, 1998, pp. 89–94) reported that, in examples of earlier crises, a real appreciation of the domestic currency relative to the average for the previous two years, signals the possibility of the outbreak of a crisis, on average, a year before it actually happens. Moreover, this signal persists until the crisis erupts. Around 24 months before the crisis, the real exchange rate is, on average, about 7 per cent higher than its normal level. But about three months earlier, it begins to decline, that is, it depreciates, towards its normal level. In the second year after the crisis, the real exchange rate is, on average, 7 per cent below the average for the normal period.

5.2.3 Indicators of balance-of-payments data

From Figure 5.3 below and Figure 5A.3 we can infer that all countries have experienced higher CA/GDP ratios in current prices. The first country with a CA/GDP ratio above the 'safe' threshold of 5 per cent was Hungary (1994: 1–1995: 4) followed by the Czech Republic (1996: 3–1998:1), Slovakia (1996: 3–1998: 4 and 2001: 2–2002: 1) and Estonia (1994: 4–1995: 2, 1996: 1–1999: 2 and 2000: 4–2002: 1). Poland has been the most successful country from this point of view, with the lowest value of this ratio. Nevertheless, Poland has recently reached higher values of this ratio as well (1999: 2–2001: 1). External adjustment policies introduced after the Russian crisis have narrowed the current account deficits in ACC, but in the case of Estonia, Slovakia and the Czech Republic, they are still above the 'safe level'.

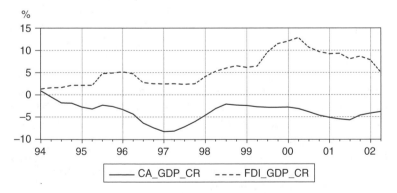

Figure 5.3 Ratio of current account and FDI inflows relative to GDP (%)

Source: Authors' calculations based on ČNB database and IMF-IFS database.

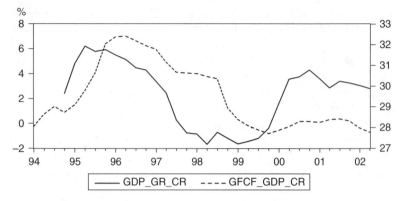

Figure 5.4   Real GDP growth and investment ratio in the Czech Republic (%)
Source: IMF-IFS database.

5.2.4   Indicators based on real economic activity

Figure 5.4 describes the movements in real economic growth as measured by GDP for the Czech Republic. Figure 5A.4 in the Appendix provides plots of GDP growth rates for the other countries in our group under consideration.

5.2.5   Financial crises and their impact on selected ACC

In the 1990s, currency crises occurred first in Europe in the 1992–93 period during the European Exchange Rate Mechanism (ERM) break-up. This was followed by the peso crisis in Mexico (1994), the crisis in East Asia (1997–98), the Russian crisis during the second half of 1998, and quite recently the crisis in Argentina (2001–2002). The general structure of those financial crises is summarized in Table 5.1. The 1992–93 ERM crisis was essentially a currency crisis, although the Nordic countries that experienced a currency crisis also experienced domestic banking crises roughly around the same time. Banking crises have often preceded currency crises, especially in less developed countries.[5] The typical examples are situations in Turkey and Venezuela in the mid-1990s. All three categories of financial crises (banking, currency and debt crisis) may be present simultaneously, as in the East Asia crisis and in the Mexican crisis. Financial (currency) crises have a large negative impact on the real economy, especially in terms of output losses, and are therefore likely to spill over to other economies.

In this section, a currency crisis is defined similarly as in Edison (2000), that is, an episode during which an attack on the currency leads

Table 5.1 Crises beyond Central and Eastern Europe territory

Time period	Place/territory	Main type of crisis and its development
1992–93	ERM crisis	Currency crisis
1994–95	Mexico	Currency crisis → banking crisis → debt (credit) crisis
1997–98	East Asia	Currency crisis → banking crisis → debt (credit) crisis
1998	Russia	Debt (credit) crisis
2001	Argentina	Debt (credit) crisis → currency crisis

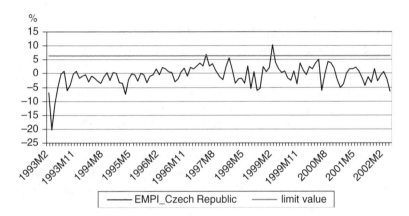

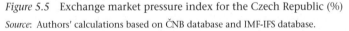

Figure 5.5 Exchange market pressure index for the Czech Republic (%)

Source: Authors' calculations based on ČNB database and IMF-IFS database.

to a sharp depreciation of the currency, a large decline in international reserves, or a combination of the two. The definition is intended to be comprehensive, including both successful and unsuccessful adjustments on the currency under different exchange rate regimes.

For a less abstract definition and identification of currency crisis, we will attempt to calculate, based on the work of Edison (2000) and Edwards (2001), an Exchange Market Pressure Index (EMPI). The index is calculated as the weighted average of percentage changes in the bilateral nominal exchange rate and the percentage changes in foreign reserves, such that the two components of the index have equal sample volatility,

$$EMPI_t = \text{per cent } \Delta NER_t - \alpha \text{ per cent } \Delta R_t, \tag{5.1}$$

where NER_t denotes nominal exchange rate of selected Central European economies against ECU/EUR; R_t denotes foreign reserves at time t; and α is the ratio of the standard deviation of the exchange rate changes to the standard deviation of changes in foreign exchange reserves, that is, σ_{NER}/σ_R.

Figure 5.5 and Figure 5A.5 in the Appendix include estimates of the exchange market pressure index. The thin line represents the exchange rate pressure variable. The straight line is the threshold above which the exchange rate pressure indicates a crisis. This limit value is different for each country and is calculated as a mean of the pressure variable plus 2.5 times the standard deviation of the country sample.

5.3   An empirical analysis of potential costs associated with macroeconomic instability

Recent research suggests that currency crises have a significant negative effect on economic growth. Nevertheless, there is a suspicion that currency crises may mainly affect investment through large currency devaluation (see Barro, 2001 or Edwards, 2001). Investment is, in turn, one of the most important determinants of economic growth.

The up-to-date results of research on effects of currency crises are associated with a use of a large data set comprising low- and higher-income countries and/or different regions. Thus, those estimates ignore considerable specifics relating to social, historical and institutional characters of analysed samples or sub-samples. Further, most papers that deal with the effect of currency crises on growth are devoted to either countries of East Asia or Latin America (see Milesi-Ferretti and Razin, 1998; Barro, 2001 or Edwards, 2001).

In this section we explore the relation of currency crisis and economic growth in the case of ACC. Even though the analysed sample is somewhat narrow compared to those on East Asia or Latin America, it should be of higher homogeneity. We want to support or to some extent modify the general results that have recently been attained in related literature in the light of specifics of the selected sample.

The key question in the context of analysis of currency crises' impacts on selected variable(s) is how to identify and measure these crises. Generally, two most common methods have recently been employed for this purpose.[6] The first identifies the currency crisis with a large exchange rate devaluation (see Barro[7]). The second takes into account the so-called reversals in a current account balance (see Edwards[8]).

Following Barro and Edwards, we first estimate the effect of currency crises on investment, which is one of the most important determinants of economic growth. As Edwards suggests, the most severe effect of current account reversals (currency crises) on economic performance takes place indirectly, through their impact on investment. We estimate a somewhat narrower model compared to Barro's that is similar to that of Edwards:

$$INVEST_{ti} = \beta_1 INVEST_{t-1i} + \beta_2 GOVCONS_{ti} + \beta_3 OPEN_{ti} + REV_{ti} + \xi_{ti}, \quad (5.2)$$

where *INVEST* is the investment to GDP ratio, *GOVCONS* is the ratio of government expenditure to GDP, and *OPEN* is the ratio that captures the degree of openness of the economy. This ratio is calculated as a sum of imports and exports divided by GDP. Finally, *REV* is an impulse dummy variable that takes the value of one if the particular country has experienced a current account reversal, and zero otherwise.[9] We assume that the error term of equation (5.2) takes the following form:

$$\xi_{ti} = \varepsilon_i + \mu_{ti}, \quad (5.3)$$

where ε_{ti} is a country error term and μ_{ti} is a disturbance of the standard characteristics. It may appear that the coefficient of the lagged dependent variable will be upward biased because of the country-specific element in equation (5.2). Handling this problem, we employ the basic approach of a fixed-effect model combined with cross-section weights (that is, estimating by the GLS method). Although a bias resulting from correlation of the *REV* variable with the error term may occur, we do not explicitly handle this problem due to the limited size of our panel data. Nevertheless, the possible bias is eliminated to some extent by the use of the GLS method.

5.3.1 Data description and estimation results

For the purpose of economic growth modelling we focus on rather long-run relationships among the considered variables. Regarding the properties of our data pool, we have no other choice but to use yearly data. All the data used are from the International Financial Statistics database by IMF. Since we are left with a limited sample of countries and observations that are available in many cases for a slightly different period, we employ an unbalanced panel estimation procedure so as to exploit the entire data pool for estimation.

The first dependent variable is gross fixed capital formation to GDP in current prices ratio expressed as a percentage. The dependent variable used in the subsequently estimated equation is the year-on-year growth of real GDP, again as a percentage. For the purpose of investment equation

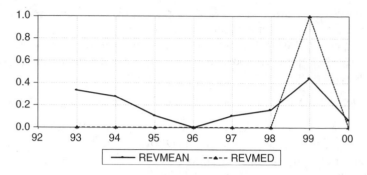

Figure 5.6   Mean and median of reversals occurrence (in each period)

estimation, we use a set of explanatory variables. This includes the government consumption to GDP ratio and an index that should measure the degree of openness; we use for this purpose the sum of imports and exports to the GDP ratio. Further, we implement a dummy variable that takes the value of one when the currency crisis probably occurred. In this respect we follow Edwards in identifying the currency crisis as a case when the particular country has experienced a positive change (reversal) in the current account deficit to GDP ratio of at least 2.5 per cent. Figure 5.6 describes currency crises occurrence during an estimated period using mean and median of those events in each period. This gives us a picture of the most exposed periods in terms of currency crises.

We can see from Figure 5.6 that the presence of currency crises is prevalent at the beginning of our sample and during the year 1999. The first period in question is most probably an outcome of substantial changes in the economic environment of countries under consideration since most of them had just initiated their transformation from centrally planned to market economies. Unlike this, the last was caused by weak economic bases of particular countries, unsustainable macroeconomic policies and also, possibly, by the contagion effect resulting from relative homogeneity of the examined region.

Estimating the growth equation, the set of explanatory variables further involves the gross fixed capital formation to GDP ratio. The list of countries included in the estimation is presented in Table 5A.1 in the Appendix. The estimation results are presented in Table 5.2.[10]

The results in Table 5.2 suggest a significant influence of all traditional variables included in the regression equation, as implied by economic growth theory. Although the coefficients were somewhat higher because

Table 5.2 First estimation of growth equation

INVEST(−1)	GOVCONS	OPEN	REV	R^2 adj.	DW-stat.
0.61	−0.33	0.03	−1.29	0.776	1.847
(10.25)***	(2.94)***	(2.87)***	(−4.03)***		
Number of countries included				19	Total
Number of observations				8	137

*, **, *** indicate 10%, 5% and 1% level of significance respectively.
t-statistics are in parentheses.

of possible incomplete specifications of the estimated equation, there was a limitation in accordance with degrees of freedom. Therefore, we can use only most significant variables that have strong support from both theory and empirical work.

In this respect, our results for the selected set of ACC propose rather an average persistence of investment ratio. Further, the size of the government sector, in terms of government expenditure *vis-à-vis* GDP, severely affects the investment ratio, since the coefficient of the GOV-CONS variable is strongly significant and of quite high elasticity. This is probably due to the well-known crowding-out effect or ineffective allocation of government funds. On the other hand, the degree of openness has only a mild effect on the investment ratio.[11] When we removed the restriction on common coefficient for the degree of openness, we found only mixed and weak evidence of significance from the less developed countries in our sample. The significance of the common coefficient stems from the estimation results for the more developed countries.[12]

Finally, the coefficient of the variable, which stands for reversals in the current account, is highly significant and may imply that currency crises are associated with a 1.3 per cent loss in the investment ratio's growth, presuming our identification of those events. It means that the occurrence of currency crises increases uncertainty in the particular economy, which adversely affects the investment decision-making process. Consequently, agents reduce the relative sum of funds that is invested. More specifically, the most important effects are probably those of interest rate and exchange rate volatility and of higher expected inflation. These variables are of essential concern for investment planning. Moreover, they probably produce significant wealth redistribution that further exacerbates the stability of the overall economic environment.

Our estimation results are generally very similar to those of Edwards and Barro; however, the estimated coefficients differ somewhat.

We have reached almost the same conclusions concerning the persistence of the investment ratio as Edwards did; however, these are somewhat lower than that of Barro's (about 0.80). Concerning the effect of the size of the government sector, our estimates suggest about three times a larger effect of this variable than in Barro's case, whereas Edwards finds that variable wholly insignificant. With respect to the degree of openness, we estimated the same effect as Edwards did, that is, significantly higher than that estimated by Barro. Finally, the effect of currency crisis is in our case lower than that of Edwards, but higher than that of Barro.

Regarding the similarity of our estimates in respect of Barro and Edwards, we could conclude that currency crises do significantly affect the investment ratio in selected ACC, as Barro and Edwards suggest. However, we could further examine the relation regarding the possible presence of a common trend, by including a slope dummy variable, which should control the relative time effect of the currency crisis on economic growth. Loayaza and Ranciere (2002) proposed the inclusion of this variable in the context of banking crises.

One way to eliminate the possible common trend in data is to subtract a cross-country average of certain variables from actual values in each period for the particular country. This would, however, result in a loss of some information, and even a bias in the data series. Thus, we prefer to control the possible presence of a common trend by simply including a joint time trend (*TREND*) as an explanatory variable. Furthermore, we have included regression equation slope dummy variables to check for subsequent effects of a currency crisis. We apply this in the period before the crisis, in the period the crisis occurred, and the period after the crisis (*REVT*).

The results are not that different from previous ones, except for the effect of the degree of openness, which is two times larger in the latter case. We found a significant but an opposite effect of slope dummy variables in the period before the crisis and the period after, whereby the slope dummy in the period of currency crisis was not significant. The lead slope dummy of currency crisis suggests a strong negative effect probably due to rising uncertainty and high interest rates just before the crisis. On the other hand, the lagged slope dummy indicates a strong positive effect that appears after the crisis and lasts, we assume, to the end of the sample. Both results could be viewed as conditional given the presence of a common time trend. The overall time effect of currency crisis appearance is then approximated by variable *REVT(1, −1)*, summarizing the influence of both slope dummies. This summarization suggests that there is probably a negative effect of currency crisis on investment, which lasts for several periods.

Figure 5.7 illustrates the consequences of a currency crisis regarding the development of the investment to GDP ratio in the case of the Czech Republic. We use for this purpose both estimations of investment equation (that is, those from Table 5.2 and 5.3). Substituting for the second estimation we obtain the results presented on the left of Figure 5.7. There, INVEST stands for actual value of investment ratio, INVEST_EST for estimated ratio, assuming the presence of currency crisis, and INVEST_EQ is the development of investment ratio had there been no currency crisis.

On the left of Figure 5.7, we have considered the effect of a currency crisis in the current period, so that there is no effect of this event lasting more than one period. On the right of Figure 5.7, INVEST_ETT is the estimated investment ratio of both the impulse and slope dummy in the regression equation and the adjustment for a common trend. In this

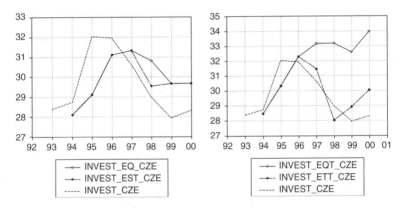

Figure 5.7   Actual, estimated and equilibrium investment ratio in the context of currency crisis

Source: Authors' calculations.

Table 5.3   Second estimation of growth equation

INVEST(−1)	GOVCONS	OPEN	REV	REVT(1,−1)	TREND	R^2 adj.	DW-stat.
0.55	−0.36	0.08	−1.38	−0.37	0.18	0.79	1.84
(8.74)***	(−2.95)***	(4.77)***	(−3.99)***	(−2.34)**	(1.40)		
Number of countries included						19	Total
Number of observations						8	137

*, **, *** indicate 10%, 5% and 1% level of significance respectively.
t-statistics are in parentheses.

example we have attempted to depict the effect of a currency crisis on the investment ratio that is allowed to last for several periods. We can see that in the case of the Czech Republic the occurrence of the currency crisis in 1998 resulted in the loss of 4 percentage points in the investment ratio in 2000. Similar graphic illustrations are presented for Estonia, Hungary, Poland and Slovenia in Figure 5A.6 in the Appendix 5.8.

In the next step, we will examine the direct effect of currency crisis on output. This will probably give us an idea whether a currency crisis affects economic growth directly or through investment. Given our concern, we estimate equation (5.3) in the following form:

$$GROWTH_{ti} = \beta_1 GOVCONS_{ti} + \beta_2 INVEST_{ti} + \beta_3 OPEN_{ti} + REV_{ti} + \xi_{ti}, \quad (5.4)$$

where the dependent variable is percentage growth of real GDP and the explanatory variables are defined as in the case of equation (5.2). Our results are presented in Table 5.4.

The results suggest that the effect of government consumption on economic growth is rather insignificant. Nevertheless, the coefficient is quite high and its removal lowers fitting ability of the model measured by R^2 adjusted. Furthermore, we can conclude that the degree of openness might be an important feature with regard to the determination of economic growth, even though it is significant only at the 10 per cent level. On the other hand, there is probably a strong significant effect of the investment ratio on economic growth. Therefore, when investment is significantly affected by the occurrence of a currency crisis, so is economic growth. This is the so-called 'indirect effect' of a currency crisis on economic growth, as stated by Edwards and Barro.

Although we found a significant negative effect of a currency crisis, the overall effect of a currency crisis on economic growth is likely to be ambiguous. This stems from the fact that when a currency crisis occurs, the home currency depreciates substantially. This enhances exporters'

Table 5.4 Third estimation of growth equation

GOVCONS	INVEST	OPEN	REV	R^2 adj.	DW-stat.
−0.24	0.19	0.04	−1.03	0.64	1.65
(−1.33)	(2.02)**	(1.66)*	(−1.93)**		
Number of countries included				8	Total
Number of observations				17	120

*, **, *** indicate 10%, 5% and 1% level of significance respectively.
t-statistics are in parentheses; without Belarus and Ukraine (eliminated as outliers).

Table 5.5 Fourth estimation of growth equation

INVEST	GOVCONS	OPEN	REV	REVT(1,−1)	TREND	R^2 adj.	DW-stat.
0.19	−0.38	0.04	−1.31	−0.76	0.58	0.65	1.70
(2.00)**	(−1.84)*	(1.61)*	(−2.24)**	(−2.95)***	(3.25)***		
Number of countries included						17	Total
Number of observations						8	113

*, **, *** indicate 10%, 5% and 1% level of significance respectively.
t-statistics are in parentheses; Cyprus was further removed from the estimation sample as an outlier concerning the effect of degree of openness (OPEN) in its case.

competitiveness in world markets, especially with economies that are of a higher degree of openness where there could be a strong positive effect of a currency crisis on economic performance in subsequent periods. On the other hand, currency crises would most probably involve strong redistributive and distortive effects. This could induce a significant negative impact on economic growth. Again, an implementation of a slope dummy and an adjustment for a possible common trend in the estimated relationship would shed light on this issue.

The estimation results in Table 5.5 are quite similar to those in the first case; but the effects of the impulse dummy (that is, the appearance of a currency crisis in the given period) and the size of the government sector have slightly increased. In the case of the growth equation, the conditional time effect of the currency crisis (that is, the slope dummy) has a similar effect on economic performance in all three cases: in other words, starting subsequently from a lead, lagged or contemporary period. Instead of summarizing these influences, we prefer to include only the current period effect of this slope dummy. The coefficient of this variable then supports the idea that there is a conditionally significant impact of a currency crisis on economic growth for several subsequent periods. We have also found a significant common trend in growth related to the selected sample of countries.

We will proceed in the same manner in Figure 5.8, illustrating the effect of a currency crisis, but in this case, on the development of economic performance from a time perspective. We begin by demonstrating the effect of a currency crisis in the present period. GROWTH is the actual value of percentage change in real GDP; GROWTH_EST is the estimated growth; and GROWTH_EQ is the prediction of economic growth if the currency crisis had not occurred. On the right-hand side of

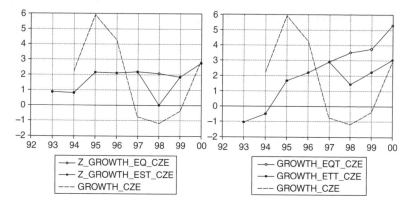

Figure 5.8   Actual, estimated and equilibrium economic growth in the Czech Republic

Source: Authors' calculations.

Figure 5.8 the possible long-lasting effect of a currency crisis on economic growth is outlined. In this instance GROWTH_ETT is estimated growth, assuming the presence of a common trend, with both an impulse and slope dummy in estimated equation.

The immediate effect of a currency crisis on growth possibly resulted in the depressed economic growth of about 2 per cent in the case of the Czech Republic in 1998. The right-hand part of Figure 5.8 depicts the potential long-lasting effect of a currency crisis on economic growth, again in the Czech Republic's case. Considering the currency crisis in 1998, the loss of economic performance at the end of the year 2000 is slightly over 2 per cent. We present a similar illustration for Estonia, Hungary, Poland and Slovenia in Figure 5A.7 in the Appendix. However, Figures 5.7 and 5.8 are not directly comparable to the data in Figures 5A.7 and 5A.8, since we did not target the period when the currency crisis occurred in each particular case. This was mainly due to the limited data identifying more than one currency crisis in these cases. Another reason is that we concentrated only on the most severe currency crises in each case according to the method of identification of such events. Nevertheless, this approach still illustrates the effect of currency crises on economic growth and investment development.

5.4   Conclusion

The objective of this chapter was to show the impact of macroeconomic and financial instabilities on the economic performance of ACC in the last ten years. To achieve that, we showed the main revisions of the transition process for selected ACC, described the activities of their fundamental indicators, and analysed the effects of their currency crises on investment and economic performance. To meet this goal we estimated an investment equation in the first stage. This equation involved a one-period lagged investment ratio, size of government sector, degree of openness and a variable that would approximate the effects of the currency crisis. We found that the investment ratio had a mild persistence of about 0.55 per cent. The size of the government sector had a significant negative result whereas the degree of openness had a positive effect on investment. The immediate effect of a currency crisis was negative by about −1.3 per cent. The long-lasting impact of this event on investment was also negative by about −0.4 per cent for each year following the crisis. In the second stage, we estimated the growth equation in the investment ratio, degree of openness, size of the government sector and variables approximating the impact of a currency crisis as explanatory variables. The insignificance of dummy variables accorded an indirect effect of currency crises on economic performance through investment. However, our findings suggested that there is a significant direct effect of currency crises on economic growth, with a slightly higher performance in the long run of about 0.4 per cent. Further, our estimates point to significant positive impacts of investment and openness on economic performance. However, when we eased the restriction on the common coefficient of the latter variable, it was evident that the impact was rather mixed. Finally, the effect of the size of the government sector was negative and significant (although only at the 10 per cent level). Even though we used only a limited set of explanatory variables and did not specifically consider the possible endogeneity of certain variables, our findings satisfactorily illustrated the effects of a currency crisis on selected variables. The overall results suggest that the negative impact of macroeconomic and financial instability may be more extensive than sometimes believed. This comprises a strong argument for policy-makers in the ACC to strengthen their efforts in order to achieve the maximum level of macroeconomic and financial stability within their region. Stop-and-go policies are simply suboptimal.

Appendix

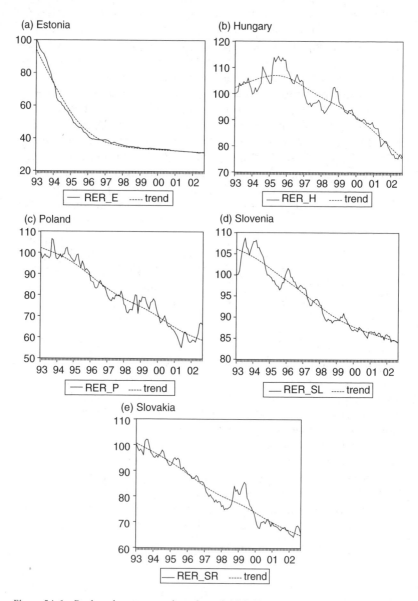

Figure 5A.1   Real exchange rates for selected ACC (January 1993 = 100)
Source: Authors' calculations based on ČNB database and IMF-IFS database.

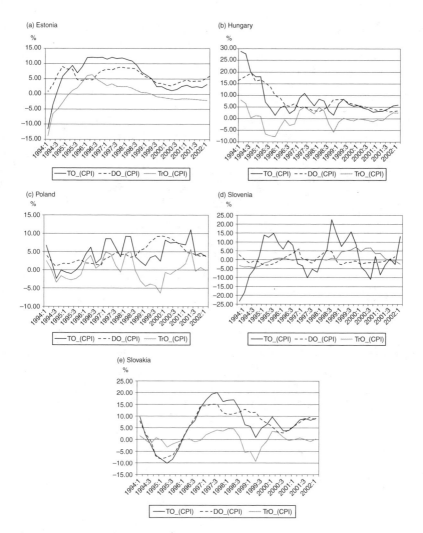

Figure 5A.2 Total, debt and trend overvaluation for selected currencies of ACC (%)

Source: Authors' calculations based on ČNB database and IMF-IFS database.

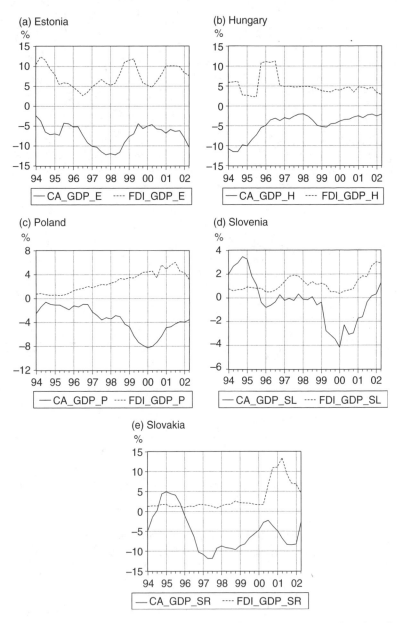

Figure 5A.3   Ratio of current account and FDI inflows relative to GDP for selected ACC (%)

Source: Authors' calculations based on ČNB database and IMF-IFS database.

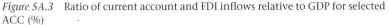

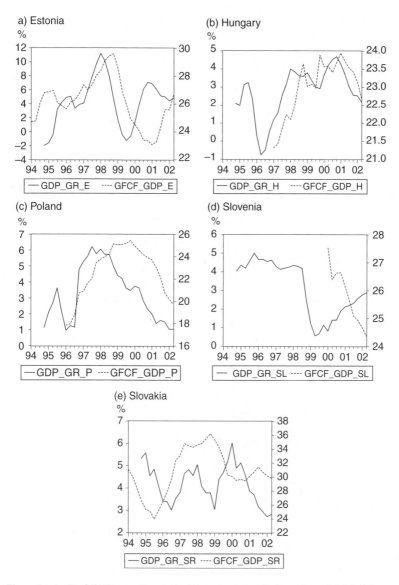

Figure 5A.4 Real GDP growth rate and investment ratio for selected ACC (%)

Source: Authors' calculations based on ČNB database and IMF-IFS database.

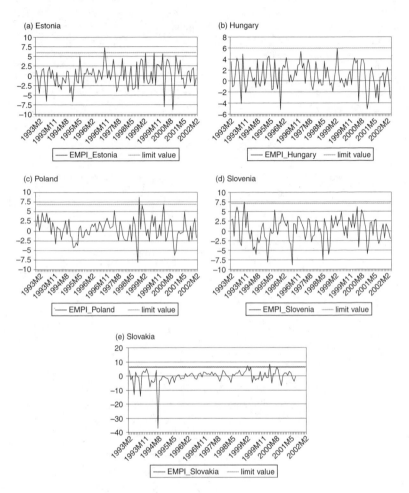

Figure 5A.5   Exchange market pressure index for selected ACC

Source: Authors' calculations based on ČNB database and IMF-IFS database.

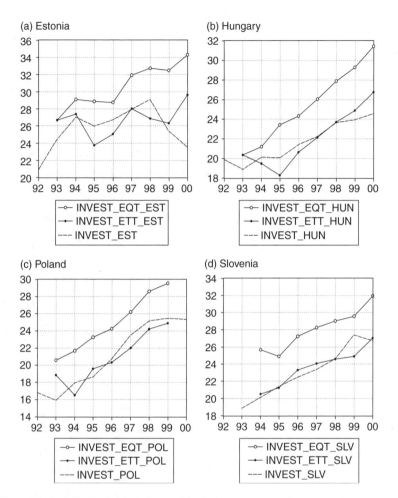

Figure 5A.6   Actual, estimated and equilibrium investment ratio in Estonia, Hungary, Poland and Slovenia

Source: Authors' calculations based on ČNB database and IMF-IFS database.

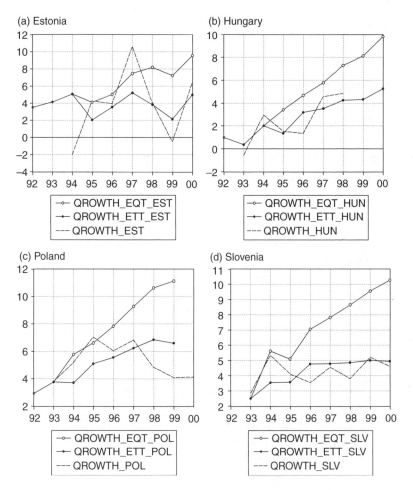

Figure 5A.7   Actual, estimated and equilibrium economic growth in Estonia, Hungary, Poland and Slovenia

Source: Authors' calculations based on ČNB database and IMF-IFS database.

DARER – construction of the model and indices of overvaluation

The difference between the 'standard' real exchange rate (R) and the DARER concept is apparent when we compare equations (A1) and (A2), where E expresses the nominal exchange rate, P^* the foreign price level, P the domestic price level and P_E the domestic equilibrium price level.

$$R = E \cdot P^*/P \qquad \qquad (A1)$$

$$DARER = E \cdot P^*/P_E \qquad \qquad (A2)$$

Estimating DARER thus involves two steps: (i) estimating the equilibrium price level (P_E), which is then used for (ii) estimating the path of the debt-adjusted real exchange rate (*DARER*). We start by defining the current account deficit as the difference between aggregate supply and aggregate demand at the current price level in the domestic economy:

$$CA = S(P) - D(P) < 0 \qquad \qquad (A3)$$

where CA is the current account, S is aggregate supply, D is aggregate demand and P is the theoretical product of the nominal exchange rate and the foreign price level [$E \cdot P^*$]. However, the build-up of the current account deficit generates present and future external liabilities which must later be repaid, that is, excess aggregate supply will have to be created at the equilibrium price level. This is formally described by the following equation:

$$DS = S(P_E) - D(P_E) > 0 \qquad \qquad (A4)$$

where DS is debt service and P_E is the price level that takes into account present and future debt service. By combining the two equations above we obtain a basic instrument for deriving the price repression (price pressures) implied by the growth in external debt ensuing from the current account deficit:

$$DS - CA = [S(PE) - S(P)] - [D(PE) - D(P)] > 0 \qquad (A5)$$

The point of this analysis is to obtain an approximation of the price repression caused by the borrowing resulting from the current account deficit. For this purpose, we can modify supply and demand as follows:

$$S(P_E) = S(P) + S_P(P)(P_E - P) \qquad \qquad (A5a)$$

$$D(P_E) = D(P) + D_P(P)(P_E - P), \qquad \qquad (A5b)$$

where $[S_P(P) = dS/dP]$ and $[D_P(P) = dD/dP]$. We can now substitute both expressions into equation (A5) and obtain:

$$DS - CA = (P_E - P) [S_P(P) - D_P(P)] \tag{A5c}$$

which rearranges to give:

$$(P_E - P) = (DS - CA)/[S_P(P) - D_P(P)] \tag{A5d}$$

This equation tells us that price repression always occurs when $[(P_E - P) > 0]$. We can make the following modifications:

$$S_P(P) = \varepsilon_s(S(P)/P) \tag{A5e}$$

$$D_P(P) = \varepsilon_D(D(P)/P). \tag{A5f}$$

where $[\varepsilon_s = S_P(P)/(P/S(P))]$ and $[\varepsilon_D = -D_P(P)/(P/D(P))]$, which are the elasticities of aggregate supply and demand respectively. Substituting these expressions into equation (A5d) we obtain:

$$(P_E - P) = \{[DS - CA)/S(P)]/(\varepsilon_s + \beta \ \varepsilon_d)\}P, \tag{A5g}$$

where $\beta = [1 + (DS - CA)/S(P)]$. By isolating P_E we obtain an equation for approximating the equilibrium price level:

$$P_E = P + \{[DS - CA)/S(P)]/(\varepsilon_s + \beta \ \varepsilon_d)\} \cdot P, \tag{A6}$$

where ε_s and ε_d are the elasticities of aggregate supply and demand and $\beta = [1 + (DS - CA)/S(P)]$. The difference between P_E and P describes the extent of adjustment of prices (exchange ratios) needed if the country is to meet its present and future liabilities.

Indices of overvaluation based on the DARER approach

Index of debt overvaluation of the exchange rate. The overvaluation attributable to the debt is expressed in concrete form by the debt over-valuation index (I_{DO}). The proposed formalized notation for the calculation of this index can be stated in the following form:

$$I_{DO} = \{100/[100 + (DARER-R)] - 1\} \cdot 100 \tag{A7}$$

The debt overvaluation index should state by what percentage the real exchange rate is overvalued owing to the build-up of external debt.

This overvaluation is expressed in per cent and captures only the part of the short- to medium-run overvaluation made possible by deferring a current account reversal.

Index of debt trend overvaluation of the exchange rate. Trend overvaluation is a rather 'imperfect' substitute for overvaluation comparing the current real exchange rate and the fundamental equilibrium exchange rate. The reason for this substitution is the continuing lack of a clear idea of the fundamental equilibrium exchange rate among economists modelling this variable in transition countries. To calculate the trend overvaluation we use as in Frait and Komárek (2001) the Hodrick–Prescott (HP) filter.

In the case under review, the value of the parameter $\lambda = 1600$ recommended for quarterly data was used. Based on knowledge of the HP filter, a trend overvaluation index is defined below. The overvaluation relative to the real exchange rate trend is expressed in concrete form by the trend overvaluation index (I_{TrO}). The proposed formalized notation for the calculation of this index can be stated as follows:

$$I_{TrO} = \{100/[100 + (HP_{TREND\_R} - R)] - 1\} \cdot 100 \tag{A8}$$

The debt overvaluation index should state by what percentage the real exchange rate is overvalued relative to its trend. This overvaluation is also expressed in per cent.

Index of debt total overvaluation of the exchange rate. The debt overvaluation only gives us an idea of the potential overvaluation of the currency due to the build-up of external debt, not of the total overvaluation. As noted above, for the latter we need to have an idea of the long-run fundamental equilibrium real exchange rate, which abstracts from the current account position. Owing to the shortness of the time series and other problems we do not have such an estimate, so to obtain the equilibrium rate we have to use the aforementioned simple econometric method: the HP filter.[13] This method has fundamental limitations, so we should emphasize that the calculated estimates must be interpreted as rough orientation indicators which need to be reconciled with the other indicators of the external position of the economy.

The total overvaluation of the real exchange rate is expressed in concrete form by the total overvaluation index (I_{TO}). The proposed formalized notation for the calculation of this index can be stated as follows:

$$I_{TO} = \{100/[100 + (DARER - HP_{TREND\_R})] - 1\} \cdot 100 \tag{A9}$$

The total overvaluation index should state by what percentage the real exchange rate trend is overvalued due to the build-up of external debt. This overvaluation is also expressed in per cent.

Alternatively, we can also obtain the value of the total overvaluation by summing the debt overvaluation and the trend overvaluation (the deviations of the actual real exchange rate from the trend). This trend is calculated with a smoothing coefficient λ that ensures near-linearity.

Table 5A.1   Countries included in the estimation of growth equation

Country	No. of observations	No. of events	Events/observ. (%)
Belarus	5	1	20.0
Croatia	7	0	0.0
Cyprus	7	2	28.6
Czech Republic	7	1	14.3
Estonia	7	3	42.9
Greece	6	0	0.0
Hungary	8	1	12.5
Ireland	6	1	16.7
Kyrgyz Republic	5	2	40.0
Latvia	8	2	25.0
Malta	8	2	25.0
Poland	8	1	12.5
Portugal	6	0	0.0
Romania	8	3	37.5
Slovak Republic	7	2	28.6
Slovenia	7	1	14.3
Spain	6	1	16.7
Turkey	8	2	25.0
Ukraine	5	1	20.0
Total	129	26	20.2

Number of observations refers to available observations for the current account to GDP ratio: 'No. of events' stands for the number of reversals in the particular country's case.

Notes

1. Estonia, the Czech Republic, Hungary, Poland, Slovakia and Slovenia.
2. For general analysis of leading indicators of currency crisis see, e.g., Kaminsky *et al.* (1997).
3. See Fabella (1996), Frait and Komárek (2002) and the Appendix.
4. The simplest method of identifying the overvaluation or undervaluation of the currency is to compare development of the exchange rate against its trend calculated by means of the Hodrick–Prescott filter.
5. Banking crises have often preceded debt crises, examples of which come from Argentina and Chile at the beginning of 1980s.
6. Nevertheless, there are other possible identifications of financial crisis, for example that applied by Hutchison (2001). His approach to indentification of banking crisis is based on large changes in the index of currency pressures. This is defined as a weighted average of monthly real exchange rate changes and monthly (percentage) reserve losses.
7. Barro (2001) recognizes the occurrence of currency crises whenever the exchange rate of a particular country experienced devaluation of at least 25 per cent in one quarter during at least one year of the five-year period used in the panel analysis.
8. Edwards (2001) employs two different measures of currency crisis. Since currency crises are consequently associated with a large positive reversal of the current account balance, the first measure Edwards applied is positive change of the current account balance to GDP ratio of at least 3 per cent in the particular year. The next measure is less restrictive and identifies currency crisis with positive change in the current account to GDP ratio of at least 3 per cent in three consecutive years.
9. As suggested by Edwards (2001), it is also possible to include initial GDP in the equation. However, in the case of the panel estimation procedure including fixed effects it is impossible.
10. For the purpose of a simple presentation we do not include the estimations of fixed-effect dummy variables.
11. This is contrary to Edwards's (2001) and Barro's (2001) results, since they found strong support for such a ratio not only in terms of significance but also of coefficient magnitude.
12. This is most likely due to data quality, since some countries have adopted the proper statistics only recently and/or there are still problems regarding which account is suitable for the particular transaction, especially for the countries of the former Soviet Union.
13. Calculation of overvaluation using the deviation of the real exchange rate from trend is routinely applied in the current empirical literature (see, e.g., Milesi-Ferreti and Razin, 1998; Kaminski *et al.*, 1997 and IMF, 1998).

References

Barro, R.J. 'Economic Growth in East Asia before and after the Financial Crisis' (*NBER Working Papers Series*, 8330, 2001).

Edison, H.J. 'Do Indicators of Work? An Evaluation of an Early Warning System' (*Board of Governors of the Federal Reserve System. International Finance Discussion Papers Series*, 2000).

Edwards, S. 'Does the Current Account Matter?' (*NBER Working Papers Series*, 8275, 2001).

Fabella, R.V. 'The Debt-Adjusted Real Exchange Rate'. *Journal of International Money and Finance*, 15, 3 (1996), 475–84.

Frait, J. and Komárek, L. 'Theoretical and Empirical Analysis of the Debt-Adjusted Real Exchange Rate in Selected Transition Economies during 1994–2001. (*The Warwick Economic Research Papers Series*, No. 646, 2002).

Goldfajn, I. and Valdés, R. 'Are Currency Crises Predictable?' (*IMF Working Paper*, 97/159, 1997).

Hutchison, M.M. 'A Cure Worse than the Disease? Currency Crises and Output Costs of IMF-Supported Stabilization Programs' (*NBER Working Papers Series*, 8305, 2001).

IMF. 'Financial Crises: Characteristics and Indicators of Vulnerability' (ch. IV), in *World Economic Outlook* (Washington, DC: International Monetary Fund, 1998).

IMF. *World Economic Outlook – Focus on Transition Economies* (Washington, DC: International Monetary Fund, 2000).

Kaminski, G., Lizondo, S. and Reinhart, C. 'Leading Indicators of Currency Crises' (*IMF Working Paper*, 97/79, 1997).

Loayaza, N. and Ranciere, R. 'Financial Development, Financial Fragility, and Growth' (*Central Bank of Chile Working Papers*, 145, 2002).

Milesi-Ferreti, G.M. and Razin, A. 'Current Account Reversals and Currency Crises: Empirical Regularities' (*IMF Working Paper*, 98/89, 1998).

Milesi-Ferreti, G.M. and Razin, A. 'Sharp Reductions in Current Account Deficits: An Empirical Analysis' (*IMF Working Papers Series*, 168, 1997).

Razin, O. and Collins, S. 'Real Exchange Eate Misalignments and Growth', in Razin, A. and Sadka, E. (eds) *International Economic Integration: Public Economics Perspectives* (Cambridge: Cambridge University Press, 1997).

6
Exchange Rate and Monetary Developments in Accession Countries

Jan Frait and Luboš Komárek

In the last two years there has been an unprecedented surge in discussions on the readiness and willingness of EU accession countries (ACC) to join EMU and introduce the euro. In 2002 most national central banks published their strategies towards the euro. They opted for rather early adoption of the euro after their countries became EU members. However, professionals in the field of economics have not reached consensus. There are also voices warning against the so-called fast-track approach. The focus of this chapter is primarily the validity of the arguments for and against early introduction of the euro in the ACC. After introducing a brief overview of discussions on the euro in Section 6.1, we will then define and compare various measures of nominal and real convergence (Section 6.2). Section 6.3 describes in detail the exchange rate developments in selected ACC with emphasis on real exchange rate trends. Section 6.4 will highlight some issues of inflation dynamics, convergence in price levels and implied challenges for monetary policy. Exchange rate regimes in the pre-accession period, the length of the period itself, as well as the relevance of the OCA theory will be discussed in Section 6.5. An overview of exchange rate strategies before the introduction of the euro will be presented in Section 6.6.

6.1 Overview of discussions on the introduction of the euro

The issue of adopting the euro has become the number one topic in macroeconomists' debates about the ACC in 2002. For central banks, strategies for monetary policy, the choice of exchange rates in various stages of the accession period, and deciding on introduction of the euro are crucial considerations. The outcomes of these discussions were strategies of central banks towards the euro, published in 2002. These strategies basically express the desire of ACC to adopt the euro very soon after joining the EU. These discussions also reflect the high level of integration of these economies with the EU, ownership of their banking sectors by international banks (see Chapter 1), and fears of potential currency instability (see Chapter 5).

The EMU accession period will probably have two main phases: up to joining the EU, and between membership and EMU. This scenario will nevertheless materialize only when the process evolves according to the current official assumptions, that is first joining the EU, then at least two years in ERM2, and finally, the introduction of the euro. Despite the fast-track strategies of central banks, opinions on introducing the euro differ significantly among the ACC. Many economists and politicians pursue the idea of adopting the euro as soon as possible. They argue that doing so will boost the convergence tendencies in their economies. Officially, this means entering the EU in 2004, spending the next two years in ERM2 and finally joining the eurozone in 2007. Some have even talked about speeding up the whole process by introducing the euro earlier. This could have been achieved by the introduction of an irrevocable currency board pegging the euro, or by a unilateral or bilateral 'euroization' of the economy. On the other hand, there were warnings against the 'as soon as possible' approach, arguing for the slowing down of the whole process and introducing the euro only after the ACC converge closely to the eurozone economy. Let us therefore evaluate these discussions by first looking at macroeconomic developments in the last ten years.

In an attempt to explain the diversity of opinions, we will highlight the development of productivity, price levels, real exchange rates and other macroeconomic variables in selected ACC. These factors are often considered to be of the highest importance in the economic debate in the ACC. We will also try to explain some specific aspects of their economies which have been often neglected. We will conclude that the strategic decision to join the eurozone, design monetary policy strategies and choose exchange rate regimes in a particular country should stem primarily from three factors: the level and dynamics of a convergence process, the mutual dependence of real and nominal convergence (Frait and Komárek, 2001), and the value assigned to the possibility of pursuing independent monetary and exchange rate policies. Since positions on convergence, structural features and time values of having a national currency in individual countries differ, we will see arguments justifying attempts of some of these countries to adopt the euro as soon as possible, as well as their potential desire to continue with national currencies for a few more years after the further expansion of the EU. As we will explain, rather a low value assigned to the possibility of having an independent monetary system seems to be more and more decisive factor underlining the efforts to substitute the euro for national currencies very soon after joining EU.

6.2   Nominal and real convergence

The process of real and nominal convergence will be crucial for central bank strategies in the next few years. Before we proceed to evaluating convergence results, let us first clarify convergence terminology. Real convergence usually means a catch-up in economic activity, which may be approximated by measuring real GDP per capita in purchasing power. Broadly speaking, it also means the ability of an economy to cope with pressures of competition from advanced industrial countries. This is what the Copenhagen criteria are all about. The dynamic component of real convergence is the degree to which the cyclical developments in economies are similar. Nominal convergence means a catch-up not only in real economic activity but also in levels and structures of prices in the economy. It may be approximated by the relative price level in a static economy and by the inflation rate in a dynamic one.

It seems natural to view convergence towards the euro primarily as a task for the central bank. The reality is rather different. When discussing convergence issues in a formal way, central bankers are usually 'forced' to talk only about nominal convergence defined as the ability of the ACC to meet the Maastricht criteria for joining EMU. The EC and the ECB take the Maastricht criteria as the key and the only measure of nominal convergence. Real convergence is often believed not to be the business of the central bank. In this manner, the real and nominal convergence processes are quite independent of each other and may be treated separately. However, this concept of nominal convergence might be a little bit misleading since both convergence aspects are jointly determined. Of course, due to their clear features the Maastricht criteria are very useful for political aspects of the accession process, but policy-makers should also pay attention to more complicated concepts that involve links between the nominal and real aspects of the issue.

That is why we find that some combined measures of convergence that bear information about levels as well as the dynamics of the process are more useful. One of the possible measures could be nominal GDP per capita in a common currency, that is in euro, in a static sense. An alternative indicator may be the relative real exchange rate or the extent of undervaluation of the exchange rate relative to purchasing power parity. In a dynamic sense, the relative growth rate in GDP per capita in euro or the speed of the real exchange rate trend may also be used as indicators of convergence. Of course, official accession is communicated via the Maastricht and Copenhagen criteria. Some have recently suggested that there were some conflicts between the two kinds of criteria. In our opinion, there is a logical sequence of priorities. The ACC must be able to cope with competition pressures and structural shocks given by direct interaction with EU economies first, and if they withstand them, they will easily be able to comply with requirements for nominal convergence. Again, there is a clear link between both types of convergence.

The economic community is now a bit sceptical about the progress of convergence in the ACC. This scepticism is usually based on real GDP-like statistics. Real economic activity is thus supposed to lag significantly behind the performance of the EU, and some countries are even believed not to have converged in the last ten years. This is mirrored by the low level of nominal convergence in the sense that local price levels and real exchange rates are rather low given the level of GDP per capita in purchasing power parity.

We find some of these comments oversimplified. First of all, it is incorrect to evaluate economic performance only by one single traditional statistical figure: real GDP in domestic currency. One has also to take into account GDP in a world currency, at best in a currency that will be relevant at the end of the accession process, that is, the euro. Both measures are important. It is surprising that this has been forgotten even by economists who have studied the decline of the socialist economies from the 1970s to the 1990s. Despite relatively high growth rates in some of these countries, the terms-of-trade deterioration was translated into a rather poor performance relative to Western Europe. We should logically expect a counter-reversal of this phenomenon thanks to the effects of technologies and knowledge imports that lead to higher quality of production and improvements in terms of trade.

Figures 6.1 and 6.2 explain the dynamics of the convergence process. Figure 6.1 compares the GDP growth trends in the ACC with that of the EU. If we use real GDP in national currencies (on the right), the ACC were not entirely successful. However, if we measure GDP in EUR (on the left), we can see more convergence, that is, poorer economies growing faster. In other words, the yearly average GDP growth in the ACC

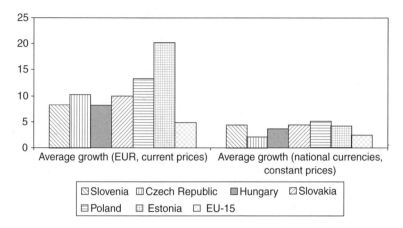

Figure 6.1 Average growth rate in EUR and national currencies (1994:1–2001:4)
Source: Authors' calculations based on the ČNB and IMF-IFS databases.

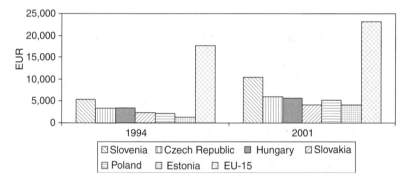

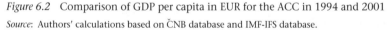

Figure 6.2 Comparison of GDP per capita in EUR for the ACC in 1994 and 2001
Source: Authors' calculations based on ČNB database and IMF-IFS database.

compared with that of the EU measured in euro was much higher than in national currencies between 1994 and 2001. Yearly average GDP growth in these years was very low in the Czech Republic measured in CZK (second column on the right-hand side). If measured in euros, however, the picture is rather different (second column on the left-hand side). It is interesting that the growth rate in the CEC is quite similar.

If we want to assess the level as well as the dynamics of convergence, we have to look at absolute values of key indicators. The picture, however, does not look too optimistic. Figure 6.2 compares GDP per capita in euro in 1994 and 2001 for the ACC and the EU. The gap is still very

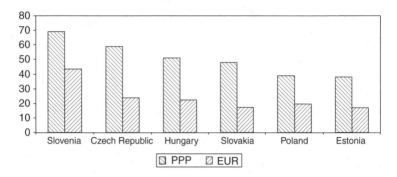

Figure 6.3   GDP per capita in the ACC in EUR and PPP in 2000 (EU-15 = 100)
Source: Authors' calculations based on IMF-IFS database.

large, though it is relatively shrinking. This gap is a result of a combination of low productivity and low price levels implied by low productivity. Convergence thus helps to close this gap. Again, it is obvious that the differences among the countries mentioned (especially among the CEC) are really minor, showing a clear sign of convergence. Slovenia is still the top leader; nevertheless the Czech economy, which traditionally has low growth rates of real GDP, keeps second position.

A standard approach for assessing the level of convergence is to use GDP per capita in PPP.[1] We also find it useful to compare values of this measure relative to EU with values of GDP per capita in euros relative to EU. These should rather be similar concepts of 'real economic performance'. However, there is not a perfect correlation between these two concepts. As Figure 6.3 shows, the differences among the countries are much lower in euros than in PPPs. Except for Slovenia, the differences in the two measures are quite large; typically the PPP measure is at least twice as high as the euro-based measure. The Czech Republic might be viewed as an extreme case since the euro-based measure is nearly three times lower compared to the PPP measure, at least up to 2001.

The problem found in the previous figure may be partially explained by differences in the timing of some steps taken at reform and in exchange rate developments. Figure 6.4 shows changes in nominal and real exchange rates. We can see first the extent of real exchange rate appreciation of ACC currencies against the euro between 1993 and 2002 (left column). Generally, the countries with lower GDP per capita and the countries that started reforms later exhibit faster real appreciation. This is in line with the basic idea of convergence. The strongest trend is confirmed in Estonia and a significant trend also applies to the Czech

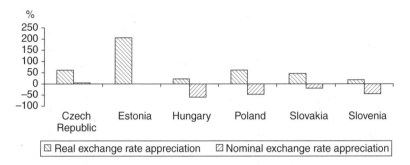

Figure 6.4 Real and nominal exchange rate appreciation (1993: 1–2002: 3, %)
Source: Authors' calculations based on ČNB database and IMF-IFS database.

Republic, Poland and Slovakia. On the other hand, Hungary and Slovenia experienced only a mild real appreciation. A relatively strong appreciation of the Czech koruna and Polish zloty may be surprising. The only explanation for the Czech Republic is that the reforms started later and the extent of initial undervaluation was enormous. The explanation for Poland cannot be so straightforward. The right column shows changes in nominal exchange rates, suggesting that the individual countries have applied differing approaches to nominal exchange rate policies. Some relied on the stability of the nominal exchange rate while others did not struggle with nominal depreciation. All this suggests that there have been significant differences in reform strategies and in certain structural features of these economies, creating rather specific paths for each individual country. This will require a closer look at exchange rate trends and policies.

6.3 Exchange rate developments in six accession countries

For several years, most of us have been active participants in the discussion on various aspects of the convergence process. We have to admit that after more than ten years of transition, the ACC can still be described as economies with three problems: relatively low productivity, relatively low price levels, and a weak currency. We know that successful transition and accession requires higher productivity, higher price levels and, as a result, a real appreciation of currency.

Given that, we often face questions that are sometimes difficult to answer. How do we achieve real appreciation? How do we model the equilibrium trajectory of the real exchange rate? Will real appreciation lead to lower external competitiveness and higher external deficit? Is real appreciation compatible with low inflation? We will not address all these questions but rather point to some specific aspects of exchange rate developments that have to be taken into account by researchers.

6.3.1   Real exchange rate as an indicator of convergence

Real exchange rate can be seen as a common denominator of a real convergence process since the external purchasing parity of ACC currencies is determined primarily by their relative productivity. Real appreciation also implies convergence of price levels of the ACC to their EU counterparts. Let us have a look at the real exchange trends in the ACC.

The initial transformation phase was characterized by sharp devaluation of the nominal and real exchange rates. The reason for this devaluation was a sharp increase in demand for foreign goods (due to the liberalization in the currency markets), an expected inflationary hike (due to price liberalization), and the tendency of policy-makers to set an initial devaluation at a sufficiently high level to create the so-called transitional pillow. In some countries, however, this caused an excessive real undervaluation of currency (see Figure 6.5, where the decline in the index means real appreciation). After the initial shock was absorbed, a period occurred during which the path of the real exchange rate moved towards the equilibrium path (left hand side of Figure 6.5). After a few years the path of the real exchange rate crossed the equilibrium path and a new phase started. As far as the Czech Republic is concerned, we believe that this happened during 1993.

In the more advanced period the developments in the individual economies might differ significantly. Generally, the success in transition should be confirmed by the appreciation trend that would lead the real exchange rate towards purchasing power parity. It seems that on this

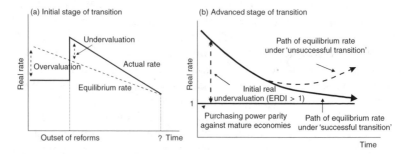

Figure 6.5   Real exchange rate paths

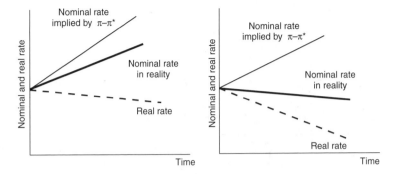

Figure 6.6 Alternative exchange rate scenarios

journey, the individual countries have an option about the way the process evolves. This applies especially to two aspects of the process: (1) the speed of real appreciation, and (2) materialization via the inflation or the nominal exchange rate.

On the theoretical level, both situations might occur (Figure 6.6). On the left, the country runs relatively high inflation and the nominal exchange rate depreciates, even though more slowly, compared to the inflation differential. This creates a real exchange rate appreciation. On the right, the country runs relatively low inflation and the nominal exchange rate appreciates. This also leads to real appreciation, presumably a faster one. This particular option may have a strong impact on some statistical features of the transition countries that are used for international comparisons to evaluate the level of success in transition – especially on GDP growth.

For an assessment of the exchange rate developments in selected CEE economies, we present monthly nominal and real (CPI-based) exchange rate indices against the ECU and euro in Figure 6.7.

Looking at the graphs in Figure 6.7, we can make the following generalizations: (i) significant nominal exchange rate depreciation prevails in countries that based their policy on exchange rate flexibility at the beginning of 1990s – Slovenia, Hungary, Poland. These countries used continually depreciating currencies against the ECU/EUR, from 1993 to 2000. However, the Polish zloty and the Hungarian forint have also begun to appreciate beginning in 2001 onwards. (ii) The countries that started with fixed exchange rates generally achieved lower inflation. The group comprises Estonia (due to its currency board), the Czech Republic (except for the relatively sharp appreciation which started in the last quarter of 2001 up to the last quarter of 2002), and Slovakia (except for the depreciation period from the second half of 1998 to the end of

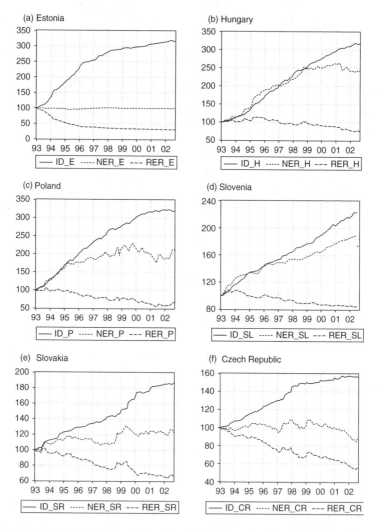

Figure 6.7   Inflation differential and exchange rates in selected ACC (January 1993 = 100)

Source: Authors' calculations based on ČNB and IMF-IFS databases.

2000). (iii) Since 1999, there is a clear switch from nominal exchange rate depreciation to the nominal exchange rate stability or even appreciation. This confirms earlier expectations that, given the political priorities, the nominal exchange rate appreciation may become a strong instrument of convergence.

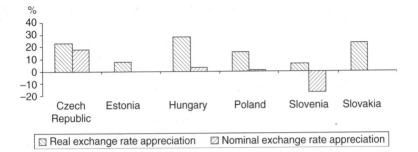

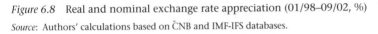

Figure 6.8   Real and nominal exchange rate appreciation (01/98–09/02, %)

Source: Authors' calculations based on ČNB and IMF-IFS databases.

Figure 6.8 repeats the calculations used for Figure 6.4, but the period chosen is 01/1998–09/2002. It shows that real exchange rate trends for individual countries during that period are rather similar. Taking other graphs into consideration, we may conclude that real exchange rates are relatively correlated in the long run. As far as the nominal exchange rate is concerned, it is clearly visible that, with the exception of Slovenia, the policy of nominal exchange rate depreciation has been terminated. All this means that convergence trends in the ACC are quite similar. Using the trial-and-error method they achieved nearly the same results. They differ mainly in the timing. We will elaborate more on this issue in Section 6.6.

6.3.2   Real exchange rate and external competitiveness

The real exchange rate is often viewed as a key indicator of external competitiveness, and real appreciation is frequently understood as a loss of external competitiveness. This is reflected in the fear that real appreciation trends needed for the achievement in convergence will conflict with the sustainability of the current accounts of transition countries.

We should take into account that the link between the real exchange rate and external competitiveness is rather complex. On one hand, real appreciation may lead to loss of external competitiveness when the actual real exchange rate becomes overvalued compared to the long-run fundamental value. On the other hand, real appreciation may reflect growing external competitiveness implied by improvements in efficiency and productivity in tradables. This means that it is necessary to study the changes in fundamentals in detail first and to discuss whether the real appreciation is a cause or consequence of external competitiveness.

The evaluation of the effects of real exchange rate changes on external competitiveness is also difficult due to the fact that production of domestic tradables is not homogeneous. This requires analysis of external competitiveness with relation to the main trading partners, various world regions and different groups of producers. In this sense, the real exchange rate relative to various countries may differ, but external competitiveness relative to these countries may remain unchanged. In other words, external competitiveness in a certain industry depends not only on the real exchange rate but also on many other factors like sophistication of production, capital intensity of production, trade pattern orientation, tariff structure or relative prices in the individual economies.

A typical problem faced by a transition economy is linked to the move towards more sophisticated product groups with tougher competition. In this process, higher productivity may not simply mean higher external competitiveness and also may not justify a stronger real exchange rate because the producers are forced to compete on a very different level than before. In other words, it is much easier to penetrate higher product leagues with a relatively undervalued currency than with a relatively strong one.

6.3.3   The real exchange rate, double-speed economy and deindustrialization

The discussion about sustainability of the real appreciation in a transition economy may be complicated by the phenomenon of the so-called double-speed economy. This term is used to describe the situation when there are two different sectors in the economy. One is the sector comprising dynamic companies usually with foreign ownership ('new' sector henceforth) and the other comprises the traditional companies owned by the local investors and government ('old' sector henceforth). The trend for the real appreciation is in line with the performance of the foreign sector and we may say that it is caused by it (through the capital inflows to the sector and its export capability). In theory, the old sector should adjust to the new sector by increasing productivity, and those that are not able to do so should leave the market. In a transition economy, with its weak institutional framework (barriers to bankruptcies, poor judicial performance, prohibitive transaction costs, week financial system, and so on), the inefficient domestic firms cannot really increase productivity and lower costs (and often they are not motivated to do so). They are not thus forced to leave the market, and through the bank system and government bailouts they burden the relatively efficient sector with extra costs.

Taking into account the links between both sectors, the excessive cost structure and low competitiveness may be transferred from the old to the new sector. In the long run the situation in both sectors may deteriorate and the economy may suffer from low growth and lack of convergence. The trend towards real appreciation may thus have rather asymmetric effects in the economy and some of these effects can motivate policy-makers to slow down the real appreciation process. However, this may turn to be rather counterproductive, especially in periods of strong FDI inflows aimed at greenfield investments. The new capacities in the new sector require not only capital and management skills, but also trained employees. If these employees are kept in the old sector by means of a structural and industrial policy, the restructuring process will be artificially delayed and its costs higher than necessary. This suggests that the real exchange rate policy in the ACC may be a razor's edge running between the risks of losing competitiveness and losing momentum in restructuring.

At this point, we should also stress the relation between the changes in the real exchange rate and deindustrialization of the economy. This is a typical feature of a transition economy given on one hand the need for reduction in size of production of the 'socialist style' industrial con-glomerates and on the other the desired development of service indus-tries. Deindustrialization itself is not a negative process and real appreciation is not usually a prime cause of it. Generally, both deindus-trialization and real appreciation are simultaneously determined by the productivity gains in industrial production (Tatom, 1992; Rowthorn and Ramaswamy, 1998). However, at a certain point of time, it is rather dif-ficult for the policy-makers in transition countries to tell whether the actual deindustrialization trends reflect the equilibrium potential growth in productivity or unsustainable disequilibrium of real apprecia-tion. This is important challenge for central bank policy.

6.4 Inflation targets and price-level convergence

One of the very lively discussions of macroeconomists in the ACC focuses on the potential inconsistency between the effort to join EMU and the low price and wage levels in the ACC.[2] The discussion is often formalized within the Balassa–Samuelson logic effect. Below we show that these considerations are often oversimplified. In reality, the discussion is rather complex and reveals tough challenges for monetary policy.

6.4.1 Price-level convergence via inflation differential

The problem of relatively very low price levels applies in all countries considered except for Slovenia. To quantify the issue, we will use the

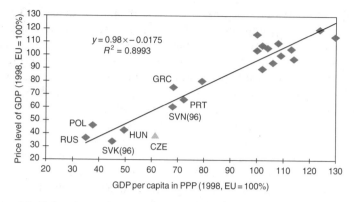

Figure 6.9   Relative price levels in selected ACC in 1998

Source: Čihák and Holub (2001).

Czech Republic as a striking example. As far as the Czech price level is concerned, it has been really low by all standards. When discussing price level, analysts usually use statistics based on results of the international comparison project completed in 1996. These statistics show that the price level in the Czech Republic reaches only 35 per cent of the German one and 39 per cent of the EU average. In addition, the Czech Republic has traditionally a much lower price level than Hungary or Poland given the level of GDP per capita (Figure 6.9). We should be rather careful when using these figures. They are several years old, and the Czech price level is now higher, especially in the last few years, when there has been major progress in the most sensitive regulated items. There are also enormous difficulties in measuring relative price levels that may lead to sharp differences in the results of various statistical projects.

The fact is that further convergence of price and wage levels (that is, real exchange rate appreciation) can be achieved only through higher price and wage inflation or through nominal appreciation of domestic currencies. It is also true that the inflation targets of ACC are generally rather ambitious. Figure 6.10 confirms that during the last two years, inflation rates in all countries considered reached levels of around 10 per cent or below.

Let us look at some simple arithmetic using the Czech Republic as an example. Currently, after the appreciation of domestic currency during 2001–02, Czech prices equalled roughly 45 per cent of the EU average. In the period before joining the EU, there is no external limitation on price-level convergence via higher inflation. The limit stems only from inflation targets of the Czech National Bank. If the inflation stays in the

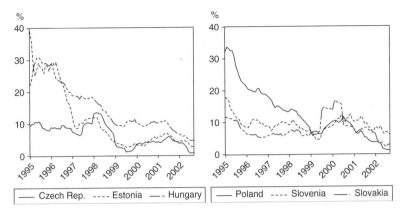

Figure 6.10 Inflation rates in selected ACC (%)

Source: Authors' calculations based on ČNB and IMF-IFS databases.

potential target corridor during 2003–05, the inflation differential might increase the relative price level by 6 per cent maximum (counting growth in administered prices). In the second period, that is, membership in ERM2, the scope for the relative price-level increase would depend on the domestic inflation target and rate of inflation rate implied by the Maastricht criterion. With current information, price-level convergence might occur in that period by only 2 per cent maximum. In the third and last period, that is, EMU membership, further price-level convergence will logically proceed only via higher inflation. The ACC as EMU members will face no formal limitation on inflation rate. The inflation target of the ECB is set for the whole eurozone and inflation rates in individual countries differ. In countries with lower price levels and faster economic growth, the inflation rate should normally be higher.

The example presented above suggests that the scope for price-level convergence via the inflation differential is really limited, especially in the decisive phase before EMU membership. Nevertheless, this does not simply mean that the inflation targets are overly ambitious. When talking about inflation targets we have to bear in mind risks implied by the potential dangers of relatively high inflation. In the environment of nearly perfect capital mobility, the small open economy with relatively high inflation faces not only major obstacles in pursuing independent monetary policy but also risks of monetary instabilities caused by external shocks.

To sum up, the scope for price-level convergence through the inflation differential is naturally limited, and before joining EMU, nominal appreciation of domestic currency might play an important role. Floating rates as well as ERM2 allow this quite comfortably. Price-level convergence via nominal exchange rate appreciation has some advantages since it effectively changes not only the absolute price level but also the structure of relative prices. Nevertheless, it is a razor-edge policy since it may slip into a position where the exchange rate is overvalued, and, therefore, domestic producers would lose competitiveness and risky current account deficits could accumulate. This is the first crucial challenge for monetary policy-makers. Exchange rate developments in the CEC have recently confirmed this fact rather abruptly. In the subsequent section, we will see some other challenges.

6.4.2   The Balassa–Samuelson effect and the real exchange rate

The kind of discussion in the previous section is usually driven within the Balassa–Samuelson hypothesis. This traditional explanation of price-level convergence is used to discuss two basic questions. The first is focused on the consistency between inflation targets implied by the Maastricht criteria and natural inflation trends in the ACC. The second is the scope for real and nominal exchange rate appreciation that would not lead to excessive appreciation. Consistency between inflation and inflation trends in the ACC is often presented as consistent in the Maastricht and Copenhagen criteria.

There is an ongoing debate whether or not low inflation requirements for adopting the euro would conflict with the need for higher inflation implied by productivity gains and structural shifts in a way that restricts the growth potential of the ACC. Low inflation in the ACC with simultaneous nominal appreciation of currencies is in this debate viewed in a similar way as deflation in advanced countries. We do not consider it to be the most crucial point where countries have very low price levels or strongly undervalued exchange rates in PPP terms. Structural and institutional changes enforced by EU requirements should allow the ACC economies to withstand pressures stemming from some increases in euro-measured labour cost. Anyway, there must be a certain degree of downward price flexibility in internationally traded goods and services. Otherwise the whole convergence process would have to be viewed as inherently slow and unsuccessful.

The 'equilibrium' nominal and real appreciation is just the second side of a coin. Given the undervaluation in PPP terms, there must be scope for nominal and real appreciation of a few percentage points per year, no matter whether or not it can be explained by the Balassa–Samuelson effect (BS effect) or by empirical investigations. Surely, if the level of asymmetric downward rigidity of prices of tradables is extremely high, ambitious inflation targets may prove to be inconsistent with growth needs of the ACC. For example, the ČNB has been following the idea that there is a trend for an equilibrium real exchange rate appreciation of around 5 per cent a year. The inflation targets create scope for an inflation differential of 2 or 3 per cent a year. Logically, there must be nominal exchange rate appreciation then that will push prices of tradables down so that the prices of non-tradables can grow sufficiently while inflation stays within target. If the nominal exchange rate appreciation were not producing any decline of prices of tradables, the whole mechanism would break up. The consequence would be such that the inflation targets would be met at the expense of medium-term movement of real income below the potential level. The experience obtained so far suggests that the rigidity is limited, though it may take some time before the appreciation of currency is translated to lower prices of internationally traded goods and commodities.

There were some attempts to estimate the level of the Balassa–Samuelson effect with the aim to give answers to the two questions posed above. It was found that the BS effect (that is, effect of the productivity differential) on inflation differential is generally rather low. These results lead some policy-makers to two conclusions. First, given the low value of the BS effect, there is no danger of conflict between the Maastricht and Copenhagen criteria. Second, the scope for currency appreciation is very low and an appreciation above two or three percentage points must be viewed as excessive.

The first problem with empirical estimations of the BS effect is the interpretation of the definition of the BS effect itself. Some view it as the impact of the productivity differential on only the real exchange rate or inflation, while others understand this effect as a trend in the real exchange rate. For example, Kovács (2002) argues that the size of the BS effect on CPI inflation in the ACC does not exceed 2 per cent per annum. He also explains that as these estimates are based on past data, when productivity differentials were higher than current figures, it is very likely that, as catch-up proceeds, the possible magnitude of the effect will be even smaller. And he concludes that that real convergence should not necessarily endanger the fulfilment of the Maastricht criteria on inflation. Mihaljek (2002) concludes with caution that despite evidence of higher productivity growth, productivity differentials in

Central Europe explain only a small proportion of inflation differentials *vis-à-vis* the eurozone. Fischer (2002) argues that the BS effect alone cannot account for the observed productivity effects, and that the results suggest instead that part of these productivity effects must be assigned to the investment demand channel. The conclusions of these empirical papers thus have a rather different logic.

The second problem, in our opinion, is that the logic in both conclusion is flawed. First, there is no natural conflict between the Maastricht and Copenhagen criteria (nominal and real convergence) *per se*. The existence of a conflict is strongly conditioned. Second, the estimates of the BS effect do not constitute a valid argument since they are not reliable due to the problematic econometric treatment of the hypothesis, and also since the effect itself is a rather poor description of the current state of affairs. There are strong arguments supporting our second point. Turek (2002), with reference to Dietz (1999), in our opinion correctly questions the validity of the Balassa–Samuelson logic based on comparative advantages, homogeneity of tradables, clear frontiers between tradables and non-tradables, dominance of non-tradables by services and other features of traditional international trade theory. He explains that the link between productivity and price level may be rather weak due to the high transaction cost of producers in transitional countries that try to sell their products in foreign mature markets dominated by well-established companies and global multinationals. On the contrary, producers from transitional countries are often forced to sell products with a low level of sophistication for low prices close to their low costs or to engage in low-income outward-processing traffic. That is translated into low wages and prices in transitional economies, no matter whether or not the producers have low or high productivity in their production leagues. On these assumptions, the growth in productivity itself does not guarantee an increase in incomes, wages and prices (and thus in the real value of domestic currencies). This can be delivered only via more sophisticated, specialized and diversified products sold for higher prices in international markets. And there is no easy way to achieve that. It is necessary to create a business-supportive environment with a modern institutional and operational framework. Of course, due to EU accession pressures, some transitional economies are adopting EU legislation and institutional standards. However, path dependency is quite strong and general acceptance with enforcement of the desired framework is still lagging behind.

All this means that changes in the equilibrium of real exchange rates and relative price levels are determined by qualitative and structural changes in the ACC, and the simple empirical application of quantitative relations of the Balassa–Samuelson kind is not very supportive. We therefore believe that the BS effect should not be used as a dominant explanation of inflation and exchange rate trends in the ACC and as a tool for explaining macroeconomic policies to the public.

6.4.3 Convergence and challenges for monetary policy

The other challenge for monetary policy of the ACC is the adequate setting of policy interest rates. It should reflect two groups of factors. The first is associated with the long-run fundamental features of the economy and the second with business-cycle fluctuations. The first group determines what we can call 'policy-neutral level' of interest rates. This is the optimal setting in a situation when there is no need to react to the deviation of inflation from the target and income from its potential level. The policy-neutral level evolves according to expected inflation and movements in equilibrium real interest rates. While expected inflation is subject to standard modelling and estimation techniques of the central banks, the movement of equilibrium real interest rates is a question of chosen theory rather than empirically based calculations.

One of the possibilities is that the decision on equilibrium real interest rates is derived from real interest rate parity. It says that expected real exchange rate depreciation equals real interest rates differential minus a risk premium on domestic assets:

$$(z_{t+1} - z_t) = (r_t - r_t^*) - \sigma_t. \tag{6.1}$$

where r_t and r_t^* are domestic and foreign equilibrium real interest rates, $(z_{t+1} - z_t)$ is expected equilibrium real exchange rate depreciation and σ_t stands for a risk premium. The equation can be used to calculate future trends in domestic equilibrium real interest rate on the basis of assumptions of trends in the equilibrium real exchange rate and the risk premium. This might be a controversial statement.

If we apply traditional growth theory, we will believe that a converging economy will have relatively high marginal returns on capital and thus relatively high real interest rates. During the convergence process, domestic real interest rates would approach the foreign ones from the upper side according to diminishing returns. However, this is a natural situation for a closed economy in the long run. In the small open economy facing arbitrage on financial markets, real interest rate parity is a more relevant framework for the real interest rate calculations. Given that, the domestic real interest rate will be higher than the foreign one only when the risk premium is higher than the rate of equilibrium of real appreciation. If we set the risk premium at a reasonably low level, domestic real interest rates may approach the foreign ones from the lower side.

To be precise, if we assume real appreciation of ACC currencies against the euro, we cannot at the same time assume a higher real interest rate compared to the eurozone without adding a relatively high risk premium to the equation. It is realistic to assume real appreciation of ACC currencies against the euro by a few percentage points a year as well as a slow decline in risk premiums. The result should be relatively low real interest rates, which may fall below the eurozone real interest rates and may even decline for a certain period of time.[3] This may be transformed to unusually low policy-neutral interest rates. One of the accompanying features of the situation might be negative real interest on deposits. In this situation, policy-makers may be pressured to push interest rates higher compared to the rates derived by way of what was presented above. However, if this way is correct, subordination of policy to these pressures will lead to the restriction of growth potential via unnecessarily restrictive monetary policy. In other words, ACC companies would pay a much higher cost for investments compared to their EU competitors.

There has indeed been a significant decline in nominal and real interest rates in the ACC during 2002. If we look at the graphs in Figure 6.11, we can see that nominal lending interest rates went down to 10 per cent or even below in 2002. Real lending interest rates are even a bit lower, given the mild inflation rates in the countries considered.[4] There is also clear evidence of convergence of both measures of interest rates. The reason behind the decline in nominal interest rates is not only the general drop of inflation but also the struggle of central banks with nominal appreciation that was often seen as excessive. The combination of fast appreciation and low real interest rates may create a conflicting environment between internal and external equilibrium. This kind of environment may be strengthened by expectation-driven appreciation episodes of a speculative kind that we saw in some economies from the end of 2001 to January 2003. This leads us to a discussion of exchange rate arrangements and policies.

6.5   Exchange rate regimes and the speed of euro adoption

The experience presented above so far suggests that floating exchange arrangements as well as the currency board can serve as adequate regimes for the period before joining the EU and also EMU. Reality is

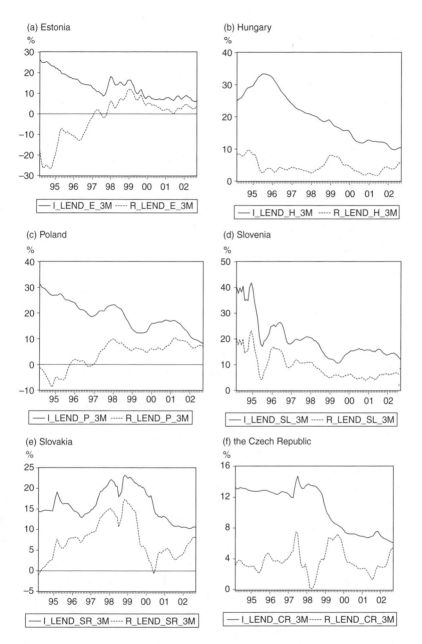

Figure 6.11 Nominal and real interest rates in selected ACC (%)

Source: Authors' calculations based on ČNB and IMF-IFS databases.

nevertheless more complicated and brings with it two sets of questions. First, what regime is optimal for the period between joining the EU and EMU? Is it really necessary to participate in ERM2? If yes, when to enter and for how long? Second, is it better to introduce the euro immediately when it is possible to wait for a few years? Will it be possible to wait even if a country meets the requirements? Is it worth changing monetary conditions radically by an 'early' adoption of the euro or 'euroization'?

6.5.1   Pros and cons of alternative exchange rate regimes

As far as the first set of questions is concerned, EU authorities insist on countries staying within ERM2 for at least two years. But many economists as well as policy-makers not only in the ACC see no reason for doing this. After the crises in the 1990s they share the opinion that 'halfway' exchange rate regimes have inherent flaws. The only viable options in the current world of free capital flows are, according to them, the two extremes or 'corner solutions': rigidly fixed exchange rate (currency union, currency board, dollarization or euroization), or nearly clean floating. ERM2 is a hybrid regime based on ideas at the beginning of the 1990s, and from today's point of view, it is rather difficult to justify the requirement for using it. From a practical perspective, the participation in ERM2 would not be a big problem, however. Thanks to the wide fluctuation band of ±15 per cent, there is large scope for nominal exchange rate appreciation.[5] However, due to the risks embodied in ERM2, it would be practical to enter at the very last minute, that is, just two years before the planned euro adoption, and for the minimum period required, that is, two years. The experience of Hungary with an ERM2-like regime obtained so far speaks clearly in favour of this approach. The countries that successfully used the currency board seem to have the best position now. They can continue with the policy up to final adoption of the euro. Countries with managed floats can also go ahead with current policies, but their situation is more complicated. Nevertheless, both groups may face difficulties if the euro accession takes longer than expected.

As far as the second set of questions is concerned, we pointed out the differing opinions of economists and countries in Section 6.1. If we omit complicated political aspects of proposals to adopt the euro earlier through unilateral euroization, the answer to the question 'when?' seemingly lies in the cost–benefit analysis. The microeconomic benefits of euroization would consist of the elimination of exchange rate risk, clarification of competitiveness and a structural state, easier comparisons of costs and yields of production, as well as lower transaction costs and uncertainty of operations. Some authors also stress the absence of a sharp exchange rate appreciation during the periods of large capital inflows.[6] These benefits would surely boost cross-border trade. The key macroeconomic benefits rest in elimination of high inflation risk and currency crisis risk. After the 1997–98 experience, very high value is attached to the latter. The costs of euroization would comprise a loss of monetary policy as a cyclical stabilizer, loss of exchange rate as a shock buffer, reduction or loss of seigniorage, and a risk of potential break-up in the case of the currency board. For the ACC, the first two aspects (derived from the optimal currency area theory) are crucial.

In the last two years, there has been a surge in the popularity of the idea of rapid switching from national currencies to the euro. This particular idea is not usually explained by the benefits of a common currency but by the disadvantages and risks linked to national currencies. This has been reflected in some ACC too. Their representatives view the value of independent interest rate and exchange rate policies as very low and the existence of a national currency is taken as a risk factor. This is quite understandable since some of these countries still have tremendous problems with pushing interest rates down even after pushing inflation to a very low level. The effects are a relatively high level of real interest rates that is not consistent with the fundamentals and risk premiums viewed by international investors that lead to losses from monetary policy due to the sterilization of monetary effects of relatively high foreign exchange reserves. The other problem is that the exchange rate channel of the stabilization policy has rarely worked. In reality, when economies needed depreciation, the opposite trend often occurred. That is why some economists and politicians argue that their economies already fit the optimal currency area definition, that is, their economies have their business cycle correlated with the EU and the probability of asymmetric shocks to their economies is seen as rather low. In addition, they argue that losses implied by the optimal currency area theory are not so important, because they must be compared to microeconomic benefits stemming from a common currency. The only problem is that we lack viable theories and empirical evidence that would support them.

This particular reasoning might be viewed as a rapid swing from an economic and political stance and therefore should be treated with caution. A few years ago, those who argued for substituting a common currency for a national currency in small economies were labelled as radicals. The benefits of national currency were valued as rather high.

Now the situation is reversed. Especially in the ACC, it is rather difficult to speak in favour of national currency without the risk of being labelled a central banker who wants to keep his power.

In our opinion, the 'as soon as possible' argument for euro adoption is rather strong, but still misses two important points. The first is the link between real and nominal convergence. It is often argued that the early adoption of the euro would have no implications for the real economy. This can hardly be true. There is at least one counter-argument. It is natural for a faster-growing converging economy in a monetary union to have a higher inflation rate compared to a mature economy. If these two economies share the same interest rate, the real interest rate in the converging one will naturally be lower. This may have some implications. Of course, the converging economy will also have a currency that appreciates in real terms. The potential for overheating given by lower real interest rates would thus be limited by current account implications of real exchange rate appreciation. The offsetting properties may be nevertheless far from perfect. Besides this one, there may be other important real aspects of the link between real and nominal convergence. One should thus be rather careful when voting for fast membership in a currency union. The second problematic aspect comes from the optimal currency area theory. The proponents of monetary unions use as a stylized fact the assumption that monetary union will lead to similarity of production structures, stronger business-cycle correlations and lower risks of adverse asymmetric shocks. However, there is also a different angle. The economy that joins an economic and monetary union may achieve a high level of production specialization. This should lead to exactly the opposite result, which partially destroys the argument against national currency. Given the complexity of the issue, some try to find the answer in the optimal currency area theory.

6.5.2   Optimal currency area and eurozone accession

The choice of the exchange rate regime and the process of its decision-making are complex situations. In the ACC this is even more intricate due to their specific economic situation. Generally, the choice of the exchange rate regime has to reflect various structural characteristics of the country, its strategic policy goals and timing. Among typically considered characteristics we can find factor mobility, size and openness of the economy, diversity of the production structure and employee skills, budget mechanisms, price and wage stickiness, financial system structure and shock symmetry. Next, it is important to take into account the broader economic, institutional and political context. This may mean credibility as drawn from the history of monetary policy, preferences about economic policy or international coordination. All these issues have direct relevance to the optimum currency area (OCA) theory that is believed to serve as an approach for thinking about monetary integration and to provide an explanation for the recent monetary integration processes in Europe. In this section, we will discuss the relevance of the OCA theory for the choice of exchange rate regimes in the ACC using again the Czech Republic's case.

We start with the paper by Horváth and Jonáš (1998) which discusses the problem of the choice of an exchange rate regime from the viewpoint of the OCA theory in the Czech Republic. They showed that the Czech Republic faced strong asymmetric shocks in relation to Germany at the beginning of the 1990s, which may suggest choice of the floating exchange rate regime. Also, there was a strong dissimilarity in inflation rates between the Czech Republic and its trading partners, thus reducing Czech competitiveness under the fixed exchange rate regime. On the other hand, low financial integration with Western European trading partners and the relatively high openness of the Czech economy was an argument to fix the currency. However, we believe it may be interesting to search not for the optimal exchange rate regime, but for the optimal variability of the exchange rate. Bayoumi and Eichengreen (1997a, 1997b, 1998) proposed an approach for modelling exchange rate variability in this respect. Their approach takes into account the multiple interdependence of the economies. This section follows this line of research. Thus, we will estimate to what degree exchange rate variability may be explained by the traditional OCA criteria, as defined in the classical OCA literature in the 1960s. Also, we will attempt to determine the so-called OCA indexes, which for given pairs of countries assess the benefit–cost ratio for adopting a common currency.[7]

Countries experiencing symmetric shocks or high trade linkages tend to have stable exchange rates. In other words, the more the OCA criteria are fulfilled among the countries, the lower the variability of their exchange rates. On this assumption we come up with the following equation:

$$SD(e_{ij}) = a + b_1 SD(\Delta y_i - \Delta y_j) + b_2 DISSIM_{ij} + b_3 TRADE_{ij} + b_4 SIZE_{ij}. \quad (6.2)$$

where $SD(e_{ij})$ measures the volatility of bilateral nominal exchange rates, $SD(\Delta y_i - \Delta y_j)$ captures the asymmetric shocks at the national level, $TRADE_{ij}$ is the proxy for intensity of trade linkages, $DISSIM_{ij}$ assesses the asymmetric shocks at the industrial level and $SIZE_{ij}$ measures the size of the economy and assesses utility from maintaining its own currency.[8]

The proxies are computed as follows: $SD(e_{ij})$ is the standard deviation of the change in the logarithm of the bilateral exchange rate between countries i and j on a monthly basis, $SD(\Delta y_i - \Delta y_j)$ is the standard deviation of the difference in the logarithm of real output between i and j, $DISSIM_{ij}$ is the sum of the absolute differences in the shares of agricultural, mineral and manufacturing trade in total merchandise trade, $TRADE_{ij}$ is the mean of the ratio of bilateral exports to domestic GDP for the given two countries, and $SIZE_{ij}$ is the mean of the logarithm of the two GDPs measured in USD.

The data sample contains 21 industrial countries for the period from 1989 to 1998. These are Australia, Austria, Belgium, Canada, Denmark, Finland, France, Germany, Great Britain, Greece, Ireland, Italy, Japan, the Netherlands, New Zealand, Norway, Portugal, Spain, Sweden, Switzerland and the USA. For convenience we label these data as representing the 1990s. When calculating variable $SD(e_{ij})$ we used the data from IFS-IMF, the data for $SD(\Delta y_i - \Delta y_j)$ were calculated from World Bank, $TRADE_{ij}$ was calculated using the data from Directions of Trade – IMF and World Bank, variable $DISSIM_{ij}$ was calculated with the use of the data from Monthly Statistics of Foreign Trade – OECD, and $SIZE_{ij}$ from World Bank data.

Since we are interested in whether exchange rate variability is explicable by traditional OCA criteria, we consider the variables with an impact across borders in all the equations. Bayoumi and Eichengreen (1997a, 1997b, 1998) find little evidence that a more open economy tends to fix its currency. But since the openness is also one of the traditional OCA criteria, we include the proxy for openness, too.[9] We therefore come up with the following equation:

$$SD(e_{ij}) = a + b_1 SD(\Delta y_i - \Delta y_j) + b_2 DISSIM_{ij} + b_3 TRADE_{ij} + b_4 OPEN_{ij}. \quad (6.3)$$

The analysis takes into account all the relationships between each of the economies. There is a pair of countries, in each row of the data matrix. Given 20 industrial countries, we obtain 190 observations.[10] The expected signs of the explanatory variables are as follows: exchange rate volatility is expected to depend positively on the business cycle, the dissimilarity in the commodity structure of export, and negatively on trade linkages. The expected sign of openness is theoretically indeterminate. We are aware that there is a possibility that the independent variable influences the dependent variable, that is, there is a potential influence of exchange rate variability on growth or volume of trade. However, taking the standard deviation of output and volume of bilateral trade considerably reduces this influence.

In this section we focus on the question of whether the adoption of the euro in the Czech Republic would not be very costly from the point of view of OCA theory. One of the concerns for adoption of a common currency is a symmetry of the shocks (variable $SD(\Delta y_i - \Delta y_j)$), as Table 6.1 depicts. If the national business cycles were fully synchronized, the value would reach zero. The shocks among some EU countries are relatively low, but here the difference between the core and other EU countries is not so striking. Symmetry of shocks in this context is measured as the standard deviation of the difference in the logarithm of real output between countries i and j.

The results for trade linkages ($TRADE_{ij}$) are straightforward. We present the results for the EU average as well as for some particular countries. The Czech Republic is closely tied to Germany by trade, as depicted in Table 6.2. However, the dissimilarity of exports ($DISSIM_{ij}$) of the countries also presented in Table 6.2 is close to the European average. The trade linkages of the Czech economy with other EU countries are not as strong as with Germany; for instance, the value for another geographical neighbour, Austria, is 0.016, slightly twice the European average.

Table 6.1 Symmetry of shocks for selected countries, 1990s

Germany	France	0.0053
Belgium	France	0.0076
Belgium	Germany	0.0113
Austria	Germany	0.0120
Germany	Czech Republic	0.0298
Austria	Czech Republic	0.1344
EU average		0.0460

Source: Authors' calculations.

Table 6.2 Trade linkages and dissimilarity of exports for selected countries

		a	*b*
Belgium	Germany	0.0687	0.129
Germany	Netherlands	0.0676	0.416
Germany	Czech Republic	0.0665	0.131
Austria	Germany	0.0529	0.052
Germany	Ireland	0.0426	0.304
EU average		0.0070	0.293

a The mean of the ratio of bilateral exports to domestic GDP for the given two countries.
b The sum of the absolute differences in the shares of agricultural, mineral and manufacturing trade in total merchandise trade.

Source: Authors' calculations.

The descriptive statistics results for the Czech Republic constitute evidence of strong linkages with Germany and one may put forward the view that its economy should not encounter big problems when adopting the euro. However, as shown by Horváth and Komárek (2002), the results can be different when the whole EU instead of just Germany is considered as the benchmark. The authors compare the structural similarity of the Czech Republic and Portugal to the German economy and find that the Czech economy is closer to the German economy. The results are reversed when the EU economy is taken into account as a benchmark country. In the following tables we therefore calculate equations (6.2) and (6.3) above. These calculations yield the results shown in Tables 6.3 and 6.4.

All variables are jointly and significantly different from zero, suggesting that the OCA criteria do explain some of the variability in the exchange rates. The assumptions for the classical linear model are confirmed.

Contrary to the estimations of Bayoumi and Eichengreen (1997a, 1997b), the variable 'openness' is significant and explains a large extent of the exchange rate variability. This suggests that the more open economies tended more to fix their currencies in the 1990s. It also seems

Table 6.3   Results of estimation of equation (6.2)

	Coefficient	t-statistic
Variability of output	0.089	0.78
Trade ratio	−0.121	−5.6
Size of economy	0.016	4.15
Dissimilarity of exports	0.016	1.9
Number of observations		190
R^2		0.2
SEE		0.04
F-statistic		11.47

Table 6.4   Results of estimation of equation (6.3)

	Coefficient	t-statistic
Variability of output	0.177	1.63
Trade ratio	−0.084	−4.13
Openness	−0.001	−6.45
Dissimilarity of exports	0.007	0.85
Number of observations		190
R^2		0.29
SEE		0.04
F-statistic		18.42

that openness is a better proxy for explaining exchange rate volatility in the 1990s by the traditional OCA criteria measured by R^2 or by the joint significance of the variables rather than by the size of the economy. All our estimates can be compared with the results of Bayoumi and Eichengreen (1997a), data gathered from the 1960s to the1980s.

From the above regression equations we calculated the OCA index, which is the predicted value of exchange rate variability. The lower the OCA index, the higher the benefit–cost ratio for monetary integration for the pair of the countries. The resulting ranking of the economies as well as joint significance and satisfactory high R^2 of all of the regressions strongly supports the idea that OCA indices have some explanatory power.

It is interesting to look at the OCA indices for the particular recent EMU members or the countries linked by common factors such as history or language in comparison to the Czech Republic. We presented OCA indices calculated using the estimated results from Table 6.4, that is from calculations of equation (6.3). The data available for the Czech Republic are only for the period 1993–98. The applicability of the OCA theory in the early stages of transition, for example in 1990–92, is rather low since there were specific transitional problems which cannot be considered within the OCA theory.[11] However, the inclusion of the Czech Republic in the data sample changed the estimates minimally. The OCA index represents the predicted value obtained from calculating equation (6.2).

The resulting OCA indices for the Czech Republic do not show substantially bigger structural differences between the Czech Republic and Germany[12] (or Austria) compared to the differences among EMU member countries (Table 6.5). We can argue that the costs of implementing a common currency for the eurozone countries and the Czech Republic

Table 6.5   OCA indices for specific relationships

Belgium	Netherlands	−0.0071
Belgium	France	0.0233
Great Britain	Ireland	0.0233
Canada	USA	0.0271
Belgium	Ireland	0.0489
Austria	Netherlands	0.0714
Germany	Czech Republic	0.0862
Austria	Czech Republic	0.0905
Germany	Great Britain	0.1084
Average of the sample		0.1039

Source: Authors' calculations.

should be relatively low from the point of view of the OCA theory. However, for decision-making purposes, it is necessary to consider all the ACC potentially adopting the euro together and not separately because of their interdependence and economic size, as our analysis suggests.

To conclude, in this section we discussed the relevance of the OCA theory to the choice of exchange rate regime in connection with the Czech Republic. There are several variables to be considered in the choice of exchange rate regime, that is, symmetry of shocks, intensity of trade linkages, degree of dissimilarity of exports, and openness of the economy. We took into account all these variables in the construction and estimation of the so-called OCA index. We followed the approach suggested by OCA criteria, which are to a large extent exogenous rather than endogenous. Then we calculated OCA indices for industrial countries in an effort to estimate the benefit–cost ratio of adopting a common currency between two countries, and ultimately discussed the results for the Czech Republic. We find no support for the view that the economy of the Czech Republic differs structurally from that of the EMU member countries. We also conclude that if the EMU is sustainable, the accession of the Czech economy should not change it.

We should also bear in mind that the OCA theory is not a complex theory of international money because it abstracts from microeconomic aspects of common currencies. Thus the propositions of the OCA theory should not be the only set of benchmarks for discussing the issue. It is necessary to take a broader view. In a sense, Europe has returned to the beginning of the twentieth century in that nearly the whole continent has the same currency – gold before, the euro now. What we still lack is a theory that would explain what will happen in the economy that decides to join a monetary union. A development of theory like this requires integration of a theory of money and a theory of international trade. These are the two theories that have evolved separately in the last few decades. International trade economists have a very limited belief in macroeconomic analysis and macroeconomists often ignore the findings of trade theorists.

6.6   Exchange rate strategies of accession countries

Aware of the fact that many of the ACC have not yet definitively finished their transition period, we now identify several basic determinants that should influence the candidates' nominal exchange rates before eurozone entry. As the main determinants of the central parity set for entry into the ERM2 (and later into the eurozone) we have identified the trajectory of the equilibrium real exchange rate and the assumed path of the nominal exchange rate in the ERM2. The ACC's exchange rate strategies will furthermore be illustrated using the strategies presented in the Pre-Accession Economic Programmes.

6.6.1   Exchange rate history: common features

Simplifying somewhat, two common principles can be identified for the choice and timing of the candidates' exchange rate strategies in the period from the start of the transformation process until accession to the EU. The first principle was the requirement for sufficient exchange rate flexibility. Each of the candidates had to initiate a society-wide (and, within that, economic) transformation with the declared aim of convergence towards the advanced European economies. This required considerable freedom as regards national economic policies and, by the same token, exchange rate regime. The second principle was the need to offer exchange rate predictability to economic agents. Given the size and openness of many transition economies, the exchange rate constitutes one of the most important factors of economic information. At first glance, though, these two principles would appear to be contradictory. Consequently, different transition countries have applied different exchange rate strategies (with different regimes, different timings of changes in central rates and so on). Since each was compelled to launch its transformation process at a different 'starting line', it had different short-term reform preferences (economic policies), and a different susceptibility to shifts in the external economic environment.

The current group of ACC is very heterogeneous, and not just with respect to exchange rate strategy. This heterogeneity stems from the aforementioned initial conditions,[13] which (leaving aside the special cases of Cyprus and Malta) led to the existence of two types of exchange rate strategies. The first consisted of the more advanced nations (the Czech Republic, Hungary, Poland and Slovakia), which after initial devaluations soon introduced internal convertibility and applied more fixed exchange rate systems. Owing to the introduction of reform measures, to the monetary policy scheme adopted and/or to economic developments at home and abroad, they were later forced to switch to more flexible arrangements. Simplifying somewhat, one can say that owing to sizeable inflows of foreign investment and positive interest rate differentials (exceeding the countries' risk premia) the fixed exchange rate regime became unsustainable. Of the more advanced candidates, the country with the highest economic level – Slovenia – had

Table 6.6   Segmentation of the ACC for the analysis of exchange rate experiences

Group A	Group B	Group C
Estonia	Czech Republic	
Lithuania	Hungary	Bulgaria
Latvia	Poland	Romania
Cyprus	Slovakia	Turkey
Malta	Slovenia	
Countries with a fixed exchange rate arrangement	*Countries with a more flexible exchange rate arrangement*	*Countries with a longer association process*

a rather different exchange rate strategy; its currency appreciated several times in the initial period (1992) but later steadily depreciated against the Deutschmark.

The start of the 1990s saw various exchange rate strategies applied in the less advanced ACC (for example Estonia, Lithuania, Latvia and Bulgaria). Owing to a shortage of foreign reserves needed in order to 'defend' a peg, coupled with the low credibility of their newly established central banks and their commercial banking systems as a whole (for example in the Baltic and Balkan states), they were forced to defer the adoption of a more fixed exchange rate system (currency board with DEM/EUR in Bulgaria, a currency board with USD and subsequently EUR in Lithuania, and a peg in Latvia – see Table 6.6 for more details).

6.6.2   Segmentation of the accession countries

Two common elements can be seen when we examine the exchange rates of the post-socialist ACC. The first is considerable uncertainty about the market levels of their nominal exchange rates at the start of the economic reform process. The second is the issue of finding the irrevocable conversion rates of their currencies against the euro. Between these two points in time, which clearly demarcate their often vague medium-run economic policy horizons, the different countries have been applying various exchange rate strategies in order to achieve nominal, real and institutional convergence towards the EU.

In this section, we focus on the ACC's exchange rate strategies. We divide them into three groups (see Table 6.6) based on exchange rate history. We define Group A as containing those ACC which currently apply a more fixed exchange rate regime; Group B as containing those which currently apply a more flexible regime; and Group C as containing the remaining three candidates, which still have a relatively long time to go before joining the EU.

The exchange rate history of the countries in Groups A, B and C is naturally reflected in the volatility of their nominal exchange rates.[14] We present these in Tables 6.7 and 6.8. The figures have been computed for two two-year periods. These can be viewed as the periods before and during participation in the ERM2, which these countries – should they decide to introduce the euro – will have to join relatively soon.

Period I denotes the period 0–24 months, and Period II the period 25–48 months before 'notional' adoption of the euro (on 1 January 2002). The previously described 'informal role of DEM/EUR', as confirmed *de jure* by the monetary arrangements in the Baltic States and Bulgaria, as well as by the exchange rate policies of the other ACC, was used as the reference currency.

Table 6.7 shows the volatility of each candidate's exchange rate (the arithmetic mean of the absolute deviations from the central parity, and the standard deviation), broken down by economic/territorial group (groups A–C) and time period (periods I and II). Table 6.8 shows the

Table 6.7 Exchange rate volatility of the ACC *vis-à-vis* the euro

Group	Country	Currency	Period I		Period II	
			Arithmetic mean (of absolute values; %)	Standard deviation	Arithmetic mean (of absolute values; %)	Standard deviation
Group A	Estonia	EEK	0.00	0.00	0.34	0.45
	Lithuania	LTL	14.73	3.81	3.88	4.38
	Latvia	LVL	10.58	2.38	3.80	3.60
	Cyprus	CYP	0.69	0.37	0.32	0.88
	Malta	MTL	5.25	1.27	1.66	1.71
Group B	Czech Rep.	CZK	5.56	2.67	2.93	3.68
	Hungary	HUF	2.80	2.33	3.17	4.14
	Poland	PLN	9.18	2.38	4.80	3.60
	Slovakia	SKK	2.63	1.40	6.29	6.22
	Slovenia	SIT	9.19	3.32	2.89	2.47
Group C	Bulgaria	BGN	0.28	0.21	0.34	0.45
	Romania	ROL	40.85	20.52	23.06	21.07
	Turkey	TRL	87.77	71.11	22.12	19.93

Notes:
(a) Calculations based on average monthly market exchange rate data.
(b) Period I = 2000–01; Period II = 1998–99.

Source: Authors' calculations based on Eurostat and IMF-IFS database.

Table 6.8   Assessment of criterion on exchange rate stability for 2001–2002

Group	Country	Currency	Maximum (%)	Minimum (%)	Central parity (c.u./DEM)
Group A	Estonia	EEK	0.00	0.00	15.65
	Lithuania	LTL	−20.05	−4.95	4.27
	Latvia	LVL	−14.95	−5.06	0.63
	Cyprus	CYP	−1.12	0.08	0.58
	Malta	MTL	−7.66	−2.57	0.43
Group B	Czech Rep.	CZK	−11.79	−0.90	36.88
	Hungary	HUF	−2.17	5.64	252.74
	Poland	PLN	−19.86	−1.27	4.23
	Slovakia	SKK	−5.75	−0.90	44.11
	Slovenia	SIT	2.77	13.27	194.42
Group C	Bulgaria	BGN	0.49	0.00	1.96
	Romania	ROL	12.79	72.59	2862.29
	Turkey	TRL	23.69	226.77	446541.08

Notes:
(a) Calculations based on monthly data.
(b) Direct quotation of exchange rates was used in the calculation, that is (−) denotes revaluation/appreciation and (+) devaluation/depreciation.
(c) Maximum = appreciation; minimum = depreciation.
(d) Reference rate.
(e) Central parity = average rate against EUR in 1999.
Source: Authors' calculations based on Eurostat and IMF-IFS database.

maximum deviations of each accession country's exchange rate from the central parity in the notional two years running up to eurozone entry. It is again therefore somewhat analogous to the assessment of the criterion on exchange rate stability to be conducted by the European authorities before eurozone entry.

Group A: Countries with a fixed exchange rate arrangement

The first group of ACC comprises the Baltic States and small European nations, that is, countries which have a currency board against DEM/EUR (Estonia since 1992 and Lithuania since February 2002) or whose exchange rate is restricted to a narrow fluctuation band against the reference currencies (Malta and Cyprus). For more details see Table 6.9. The monetary policy arrangements chosen by these countries were accompanied by low exchange rate volatility, something that is confirmed by our calculations summarized in Table 6.7. The calculations show high volatility against DEM/EUR only for Lithuania and Latvia, whose reference currencies were USD and SDR respectively (see Table 6.9).

Table 6.9 The 2002 PEPs: the exchange rate objectives of selected ACC

Country	Exchange rate regime	Euro target date	ERM2 participation	Changes to exchange rate regime
Group A				
Estonia	Currency board with euro	Not stated in PEP	Not stated in PEP	Not stated in PEP
Lithuania	Currency board with euro	Not stated in PEP	Not stated in PEP	Not stated in PEP
Latvia	Peg to SDR	Not stated in PEP	As of accession or later	ERM2 may allow a more active monetary policy
Cyprus	Peg to euro with wide band and soft inner band	As soon as possible after accession	As of accession	Not stated in PEP
Malta	Peg to trade weighted basket	Not stated in PEP (reference to ongoing dialogue between government and central bank)	As soon as possible after accession	Maintaining peg, raise weight of euro in basket
Group B				
Czech Republic	Managed float	Not stated in PEP	Standard fluctuation band	Maintenance of managed float, efforts to neutralize inflow of privatization capital

Table 6.9 (Contd.)

Country	Exchange rate regime	Euro target date	ERM2 participation	Changes to exchange rate regime
Hungary	Peg to euro with band of +/−15per cent	As soon as possible after accession	After accession to EU	Not stated in PEP
Poland	Float	Not stated in PEP (after publication of PEP: report on directing policies towards satisfying Maastricht criteria in 2005)	After accession	Finding optimum parity in ERM2 identified as challenge
Slovakia	Managed float (euro)	Not stated in PEP	After accession	Not stated in PEP
Slovenia	Managed float (euro)	As soon as possible after accession	Not stated in PEP	Unchanged
Group C				
Bulgaria	Currency board (euro)	Not stated in PEP	Participating, but keeping currency board	Maintaining currency board
Turkey	Float	Not stated in PEP	Not stated in PEP	Switch to peg being considered (EUR/USD basket; EUR after 2004)
Romania	Managed float (dollar)	Not stated in PEP	Not stated in PEP	Switch to euro as reference

On 2 February 2002 the Lithuanian central bank switched its currency board anchor from the dollar (at 4 LIT/USD) to the euro (at 3.4538 LIT/EUR).

Source: European Commission (2001, 2002) and Bloomberg.

Group B: Countries with a more flexible exchange rate arrangement

The second group of ACC is made up of the post-communist countries having a relatively higher economic level. The higher exchange rate volatility of the countries with more flexible arrangements relative to Group A is comparable to several real-convergence member states of the EU. The Czech Republic and Poland saw sizeable appreciation of their nominal exchange rates in the period under review (Period I). As regards 'notional' fulfilment of the exchange rate criterion, this means that the Czech Republic[15] and Poland – in the event of nearing the margin of the wider ERM2 band – would have had to make larger interventions to counter the appreciation. The only country with a significant depreciation trend in this period was Slovenia.

Group C: Countries with a longer association process ahead

The remaining group of ACC, which are some way off accession to the EU, consists of Bulgaria, Romania and Turkey. Bulgaria has been recording significantly better indicators since establishing a currency board in 1997 (stabilized inflation, a stable interest rate differential against Germany). In this respect, its results are comparable with those in the Group A countries, that is, a stable exchange rate against DEM/EUR and a very low interest rate differential. None the less, it has not made any further progress with its accession process. Considerably worse off are Romania and, in particular, Turkey, which was recently hit by a hyper-inflationary spiral.

6.6.3 Pre-Accession Economic Programmes

The ACC have been drawing up Pre-Accession Economic Programmes (PEPs) since 2001. Updated versions of these documents were published in October 2002. As precursors of the Convergence Programmes and Stability Programmes they focus primarily on the fiscal sector. They also contain four-year macroeconomic scenarios that include envisaged developments in the area of monetary and exchange rate policy. Although many analysts have questioned the credibility of the PEPs – especially the fiscal part – the PEP is without doubt a significant (albeit 'political') indicator of exchange rate policy orientation in the ACC's process of integration into European monetary structures.

It is clear from the PEPs that the prospect of membership in the ERM2 and the preparations for adopting the euro have a strong bearing on the candidates' exchange rate strategies. Most of the programmes envisage a continuation of the present exchange rate regimes until accession.

Similar constancy is also apparent if we look back to the past – the exchange rate regimes are practically unchanged compared with the 2001 PEPs (save for a number of technical details, for example a change in reference currency from USD to EUR in Lithuania). Table 6.9 summarizes the basic information on the candidates' current exchange rate regimes and the changes expected during the process of joining the EU and eurozone.

The specification of the post-accession exchange rate regimes is fairly vague. Most of the programmes only refer to the exchange rate policy restrictions implied by European legislation. However, explicit euro target dates have almost disappeared from the 2002 PEPs (by comparison with 2001). Table 6.9 shows that some of the PEPs indicate that the euro should be introduced as soon as possible, with Hungary being among the most ambitious in this respect. By contrast, the least ambitious are the Group C countries. The only two countries that make no mention of a euro target date are Turkey and Romania. Along with Bulgaria, these countries still have many reforms lying ahead of them.

The considerations of the ACC – as set forth in the PEPs – can be summarized as follows. Most of the countries envisage continuing with their present exchange rate regimes up until accession. The PEPs do not go into detail about exchange rate policy following accession, reckoning only on a two-year 'transition' period within the ERM2. Many countries express a preference for entering the eurozone as soon as possible after accession, but they do not identify a specific target date for adoption of the euro.

6.7   Conclusion

Candidate countries for EU accession have recently intensified their efforts to get ready for adoption of the common European currency after joining the EU. The main issue of the chapter was whether the adoption of the euro 'as soon as possible' is the best solution for the ACC, or whether some additional time spent with their national currency might be useful for further adjustments. It was argued that the decision on the strategy of joining the eurozone and designing monetary policy strategy, and choosing an exchange rate regime in a particular country, stems primarily from three factors. These are: the level and dynamics of a convergence process, mutual dependence of real and nominal convergence, and the value assigned to the possibility of pursuing independent monetary and exchange rate policies.

To answer the basic question, after briefly overviewing discussions on the introduction of the euro in the first section, we first defined and evaluated various measures of nominal and real convergence. Then we described in detail real exchange rate developments in selected ACC that had much useful information about the convergence process. We followed this with a debate on inflation dynamics, convergence in price levels and implied challenges for monetary policy. The results focused on the performance of exchange rate regimes, the experiences with independent monetary and exchange rate policies, and the usefulness of the OCA theory in the decision-making process. An overview of exchange rate strategies before introducing the euro was then presented as the outcome of debates between central banks, governments and the economics profession.

Using conventional economic reasoning, it seems that preparations for joining EMU will be justified after further progress in nominal and real convergence is achieved. However, there were also some fundamental points that argued for early adoption of the euro in most of these countries. These countries are to a large extent integrated with EU economies. They are also very open and have achieved quite a high level of nominal convergence measured by paths of inflation rates and interest rates. Some of them have kept the level of nominal exchange rates close to a certain level for many years. Locking exchange rates permanently by adopting the euro thus would not change the framework that has been in place for quite a long time. In addition, in some of the CEE the exchange rate channel of macroeconomic adjustment has not been working properly, monetary policy has been strongly dependent on external conditions, and some alternative adjustment channels have been created.

However, the value of having an independent currency is different for individual countries and may change in reaction to shocks affecting external as well as internal conditions. This may justify the attempts of some of these countries to adopt the euro as soon as possible, even before EU membership, or the intentions of others to continue with their national currencies for some time. There may be some changes of institutional or economic conditions relative to their current setting that could also cause changes to the opinions and strategies of policy-makers during the accession period. However, the possibility of a rather low value assigned to having an independent monetary system plus the fear of exchange rate instability seem to be more and more decisive factors that underline the efforts to substitute the euro for national currencies very soon after joining EU.

Notes

We are grateful to Roman Horvath for helpful comments and participation during the estimation process in Section 6.5.2.

1. In 1999, this particular figure was 71 per cent for Slovenia, 59 per cent for the Czech Republic, 51 per cent for Hungary, 49 per cent for Slovakia, 37 per cent for Poland, and 36 per cent for Estonia.
2. The need for a higher price level is not an abstract political goal. It is to a large extent a structural issue. It reflects a low level of structural convergence, not only administrative regulation of prices, income policy, taxation policy, and so on.
3. Convergence in levels of real interest rates will occur only during EMU membership through a decline in real appreciation implied by convergence in productivity.
4. Our calculation of real interest rates can surely be questioned since we used CPI inflations of the same period. The approach was motivated by general availability of data. Since we focus on lending interest rates, we could also use PPI inflation. In this case, real interest rates would be a bit higher.
5. We ignore the discussion whether the definition of exchange rate stability is ± 15 per cent or ± 2.25 as in the old days of ERM.
6. They argue that modernization of the economy requires a great deal of capital which must be imported from abroad. With national currency, the expectation of inflow will appreciate currency in a overshooting manner, with a negative effect on competitiveness. With the euro, large capital inflow would also mean real appreciation due to relatively high wage increases, but this is usually a much slower process compared to exchange rate swings.
7. Horváth (2001), Fidrmuc and Korhonen (2001) or Fidrmuc (2001) follow the other view, suggesting endogeneity of OCA criteria. Hallett and Piscittelli (2001) try to answer in their theoretical model the question of whether the OCA criteria are endogenous or exogenous.
8. The lower the size, the lower the relative utility of maintaining its own currency. $SIZE_{ij}$ can possibly capture the effect of adjustment costs, too. The bigger the countries are in economic terms, the higher the costs of transition to adopting of common currency.
9. The proxy was calculated as an arithmetic mean to the ith and jth country ratio of trade (export + import) to its GDP.
10. The relationship of the first country with the second is the same as the second with the first. That is why the number of observation equals $20!/18!2!$. Since the data for calculation of the variable DISSIM were not available for Greece except for the year 1997, we finally excluded Greece from the analysis. At first, we took the data for the year 1997 as an average measure of Greece's $DISSIM_{ij}$ for the period 1989–98, but the tests on outliers using studentized residuals showed that many observations on Greece are outliers even at p-value lower than 0.01. Whether this was caused by lack of data or for another reason is uncertain.
11. See Goldberg (1999), Horváth and Jonáš (1998), Horváth and Komárek (2002) and Schweickert (2001) for discussion of specificity of the transition processes in relation to the OCA theory.

12. We present the Czech Republic OCA index versus Germany since obviously we need a benchmark, and Germany is the most straightforward one.
13. These included the process of creating an independent history in each of the five ACC. For the Baltic States, the collapse of the Soviet empire implied – with respect to the exchange rate issue – a need to exit the Soviet monetary union and establish a new central bank and currency. Of the reviewed countries, both Slovenia and the successor states of the former Czechoslovak Federal Republic have a similar experience.
14. The countries' nominal exchange rate paths against the euro can be broken down according to the common features of their nominal exchange rate indices, into those which, between the start of 1993 and the present, have predominantly appreciated, depreciated or have been (by definition of their exchange rate regime) stable against the DEM/EUR or ECU/EUR rates.
15. The Czech Republic's maximum deviation from the average CZK/EUR rate for 1999 (19.4 per cent on the appreciation side) occurred in the first half of 2002.

References

Bayoumi, T. and Eichengreen, B. 'Optimum Currency Areas and Exchange Rate Volatility: Theory and Evidence Compared', in Cohen, B. (ed.) *International Trade and Finance, New Frontiers for Research: Essays in Honor of Peter B. Kenen* (Cambridge: Cambridge University Press, 1997a).

Bayoumi, T. and Eichengreen, B. 'Exchange Market Pressure and Exchange Rate Management: Perspectives from theory of Optimum Currency Areas', in Blejer, M.I., Frenkel, J.A., Leiderman, L. and Razin, A. (eds) *Optimum Currency Areas: New Analytical and Policy Developments* (IMF, 1997b).

Bayoumi, T. and Eichengreen, B. 'Ever Closer to Heaven? An Optimum-Currency-Area Index for European Countries', *European Economic Review*, 41 (1998), 761–70.

Čihák, M. and Holub, T. 'Price-level Convergence Towards the EU – Few Questions Not Yet Answered', *Finance a Úvěr*, 51, 6 (2001), 331–49.

Dietz, R. 'Exchange Rates and Relative Prices in Central and Eastern European Countries: Systems and Transaction Cost's Approach', *Forschungsberichte WIIW*, 254 (1999).

European Commission. *The Pre-accession Economic Programmes of Candidate Countries: Main Results*, various issues (Brussels, EC (DG ECFIN), 2001 and 2002).

Fidrmuc, J. 'The Endogeneity of the Optimum Currency Area Criteria, Intraindustry Trade and EMU Enlargement', BOFIT Discussion Papers, No. 8.

Fidrmuc, J. and Korhonen, I. 'Optimal Currency Area between the EU and Accession Countries: The Status Quo', Austrian National Bank, Mimeo.

Fischer, Ch. 'Real Currency Appreciation in Accession Countries: Balassa–Samuelson and Investment Demand', Discussion Paper, Economic Research Centre of the Deutsche Bundesbank, 19/02 (2002).

Frait, J. and Komárek, L. 'On the Way to the EU – Nominal and Real Convergence in Transition Countries', *Finance a Úvěr*, 51, 6 (2001), 314–30.

Goldberg, L. 'Is Optimum Currency Area Theory Irrelevant for Economies in Transition?' in Sweeney, R.J., Wihlborg, C. and Willett, T.D. (eds) *Exchange Rate Policies for Emerging Market Economies* Boulder, CO: Westview Press (1999).

Hallett, H. and Piscitelli, L. (2001) *The Endogenous Optimal Currency Area Hypothesis: Will a Single Currency Induce Convergence in Europe?*, papers presented at The Royal Economic Society Annual Conference, University of Durham, April 9–11.

Horváth, J. *The Optimum Currency Area Theory: A Review*, Mimeo, Central European Univeristy (2001).

Horváth, J. and Jonáš, J. 'Exchange Rate Regimes in the Transition Economies: Case Study of the Czech Republic 1990–1997', ZEI Working Paper (1998).

Horváth, R. and Komárek, L. 'Theory of Optimum Currency Areas: An Approach for Thinking About Monetary Integration', *Warwick Economic Research Papers*, 647 (2002).

Kovács, M.A. *et al.* (eds) *On the estimated size of the Balassa–Samuelson effect in CEC5 countries*, mimeo, prepared by the CEC5 National Banks for the Basle Meeting of March 2002.

Mihaljek, D. 'The Balassa–Samuelson Effect in Central Europe: A Disaggregated Analysis', in *Monetary Policy and Currency Substitution in the Emerging Markets* Dubrovník: Croatian National Bank (2002).

Rowthorn, R. and Ramaswamy, R. 'Growth, Trade, and Deindustrialization', IMF Working Paper, WP/98/60 (1998).

Schweickert, R. 'Assessing the Advantages of EMU-Enlargement for the EU and the Accession Countries: A Comparative Indicator Approach', Kiel Working Paper (2001).

Tatom, J. 'Currency Appreciation and Deindustrialization: A European Perspective', Federal Reserve Bank of St. Louis Working Paper, 92–006A (1992).

Turek, O. 'Should We Be Concerned about Appreciation of the Crown?', *Politická ekonomie*, L, 5 (2002), 520–34.

Index

Note: 'n.' after a page reference indicates the number of a note on that page.